A Bible Study on the Book of

JOHN

A Deeper Understanding of
The Way, The Truth, and The Life

Dr. Lewis A. Foster

CONTENTS

CHARTS:

MAPS:

LISTS:

PREFACE

John's Gospel is the keystone that holds together all four canonical narratives telling of Jesus. Written by a disciple who had been with Jesus from the early days of His baptism, who stayed with Him to stand before the cross at His death, and greeted Him on the shores of Galilee in His resurrection, this Gospel is filled with feeling and appeal. The author had been young when these things happened. He was impressionable and enthusiastic to share in everything His Master did. When he wrote this Gospel, however, he was near the end of his days, and he wanted to leave solid grounds for belief in the lives of all he could reach. This was not to be a placid story designed to tie together pleasant memories of long ago. This narrative had as its purpose to inspire belief and to force every reader or hearer to a point of decision concerning Jesus Christ.

John had certain themes that interested him most, and he used these like threads to tie together the episodes in Jesus' life. His interests are timeless. They speak to our generation.

The purpose of this commentary is to attempt to capture the very emphases that John gave. He had a keen grasp of the import of what he actually saw (1 John 1:1-4). But John was also aware of a reality that lay beyond the physical eyesight, and he gave attention to that spiritual realm as well. He does not convey history as a hollow, mechanical march of human events, but neither does he alter history to satisfy theology. He weaves them together realistically.

This commentary seeks to follow the interests that John introduces and to join them with the recognized subjects that absorb our attention today. We will allow our interests to flow with John's direction. The manner of treatment ties together different approaches — sometimes subjects, sometimes verse by verse, sometimes charts, but always with the same goal in mind that John has: "that you may believe that Jesus is the Christ, the Son of God, and that by believing you may have life in his name" (John 20:31).

VIEW THE EVENTS

Before you are able to appreciate the details of any section of John, an overview of the Gospel is necessary to help you in the study of an individual scene. In listing the progression of material in John, you should note different factors. Is the setting in Galilee (Capernaum) or Judea (Jerusalem)? Is the time early in Jesus' ministry or toward the close—or somewhere in between? Is the teaching in the form of a controversy, a discourse, or a miracle (sign), or private instruction to an individual or to the disciples?

John

Prologue   John 1:1ff
    The Word became flesh

Baptism
    (No record of special temptation.)

First Sign   John 2:1ff
    Water into wine
    At Cana, Galilee

First Passover   John 2:13ff
    Cleansing the temple

Second Sign   John 4:46ff
    Jesus heals the official's son
    At Capernaum, Galilee

Second Passover (?)   John 5:1

INTRODUCTION

The Focus

Some camera lenses have an extraordinary depth of field. They can take pictures focused on something close at hand, but when the film is developed, you can see objects at a distance, and they are in focus, too. Some lenses, however, with the focus set at infinity, focus only on the distant objects and leave the close objects entirely distorted and fuzzy. When a close-up is taken, the distant objects are not discernable. In this respect, the Gospel of John is a magnificent book—the depth of field is phenomenal. John tells you what was happening then, and yet he speaks of eternal life as well. He writes of historical events, but he focuses on spiritual truths at the same time. He has a focus on life that includes three dimensions: physical life, spiritual life, and life eternal.

The purpose of this work on the Gospel of John is to focus upon those subjects important to the author, John, and to emphasize the major truths he wishes to convey to his readers, both then and now. In doing this, it will help you note how John's depth of field not only bridges the physical and the spiritual, but how it reaches from the first century to each succeeding generation, including your own.

CHARACTERISTICS

The Spiritual Gospel

An early Christian scholar, Clement of Alexandria, put into one word the striking characteristic of the Gospel of John. He called it the "spiritual" gospel.[1] Some have taken this to mean that the fourth Gospel is not historical. This is not true, nor was this Clément's intended meaning. Clement was not saying that John was less historical than the other three Gospel narratives, but that they handled more the "bodily" events that could be seen. John went further to probe the significance in the spiritual realm of God's existence and the true life of man as a child of God.

When one looks into the Gospel of John, he finds that the opening of the narrative goes back before the beginning of Jesus' ministry, before His beginning in Bethlehem, even before the beginning of time. "In the beginning was [past tense] the Word. . . ." Matthew and Luke begin their narratives with the birth of Jesus and the birth of John the Baptist. Mark begins with the baptism of Jesus. But John begins with the Heavenly, eternal existence of the Word. This is spiritual in contrast with earthly.

The Gospel of John is marked by the use of key words. These words are frequently rich in contrast: light and darkness, seeing and blindness, spirit and flesh, earthly and Heavenly, life and death, love and hate, to be troubled and to trust.

John introduces these words in the opening chapter and then returns to use them time and again throughout his Gospel: for example, light and life, truth and witness. Another phrase introduced in the first chapter that appears later is "the way." John the Baptist proclaimed "the way of the Lord" or "the way for the Lord" (John 1:23). Jesus affirmed, "I am the way and the truth and the life" (John 14:6). To follow "the way" taught in John's Gospel leads a person to true life.

Double Meaning

Another characteristic of John's Gospel is the use of words that have double meaning. These are words that have a surface meaning but then penetrate to another level. Darkness is not able to overcome the light (John 1:5, RSV). But this word for "overcome"

---

[1] Eusebius, Ecclesiastical History, 6.14.

also means to apprehend or understand. So a person comes to another level of meaning when he recognizes the companion truth that darkness is unable to come to a comprehension of the light. In another passage, Nicodemus is told he must be born again (John 3:3); but the word *again* in the Greek also means *from above.* This takes a person beyond the idea of a physical reentry on earth to the thought of spiritual birth from above. So also the word *way* may refer to a highway over the land, or it may denote one's course of life and destiny.

Another characteristic of John's Gospel is its record that the disciples or other inquirers often misunderstood Jesus' use of a word and missed the deeper meaning. Then it became necessary for Jesus to pull back the curtain and reveal the spiritual significance. This is what happened concerning the way. Jesus said to His disciples, "You know the way to the place where I am going" (John 14:4). Thomas would not allow this statement to go unchallenged. He did not know where Jesus was going; so how could he know the way? Jesus would have to give him directions. But instead of pointing to the east or west, to a road through the mountains or to the sea, Jesus pointed to himself: "I am the way." Then Thomas knew *the way* had a deeper meaning. It was not just a traveled road on the surface of the earth. Thomas had to probe for the meaning just as we do.

The Way

Way was a word of many meanings in the Old Testament before Jesus used it during His earthly ministry. It could be used of a literal road or journey, but it could also have a great variety of figurative meanings. It was used for God's purpose or action. When Moses replied to God's call, he said, "Now therefore, I pray thee, if I have found grace in thy sight, show me now thy way, that I may know thee, that I may find grace in thy sight: and consider that this nation is thy people" (Exodus 33:13, KJV).

Along with numerous passages denoting God's way, there are also examples of man's way. Man's moral conduct can be described as his way of life, his lifestyle. This can be a way of goodness: "So you will walk in the way of good men, and keep to the paths of the righteous. For the upright will live in the land, and the blameless will remain in it" (Proverbs 2:20, 21, NASB). But the way of man is often evil. "Do not enter the path of the wicked, and do not proceed in the way of evil men. Avoid it, do not pass by it; turn away from it and pass on" (Proverbs 4:14, 15, NASB). These are separate ways, the ways of good and evil. The ends of these ways offer the contrast between life and death. "He is on the path of life who heeds instruction, but he who forsakes reproof goes astray" (Proverbs 10:17, NASB). Furthermore, that evil way is often a deceitful way. "There is a way that seems right to a man, but in the end it leads to death" (Proverbs 14:12).

A clear distinction is made between God's ways and man's ways. "For my thoughts are not your thoughts, neither are your ways my ways,' declares the Lord. 'As the heavens are higher than the earth, so are my ways higher than your ways and my thoughts than your thoughts" (Isaiah 55:8, 9).

In the New Testament as well as the Old, there are two ways before man. One of them leads to life, peace, and happiness; and the other to death, trouble, and misery. Jesus gave the classic expression of the two ways in His Sermon on the Mount: "Enter through the narrow gate. For wide is the gate and broad is the road that leads to destruction, and many enter through it. But small is the gate and narrow the road that leads to life, and only a few find it" (Matthew 7:13, 14). The figure of the two ways is also used in early Christian literature (e.g. *Epistle of Barnabas*, 18.1ff.; 20.1ff.; and the *Didache*, 1.1ff.; 5.1ff.).

TRACE THE THEMES

The more you study the Gospel of John, the more you realize the intricate design of the book. This is not a work carelessly thrown together, but carefully laid out with special themes running through the whole of the narrative. Introduced in the opening chapter and recurring again and again in later chapters, certain words stand out to draw your attention: believe, light, world, life, know, love, truth, witness.

The following chart indicates how many times each of these words is used in each Gospel. Note how many more times they appear in John than in the other Gospels. Underline them in your mind as you read.

Special Words in John

Word	Number of Times It Appears in Each Gospel			
	Matthew	Mark	Luke	John
Believe	11	14	9	98
Light	7	1	7	22
World	9	3	3	76
Life	7	4	5	38
Know	37	30	43	90
Love	12	5	12	46
Truth	2	4	3	43
Witness	1	3	3	22

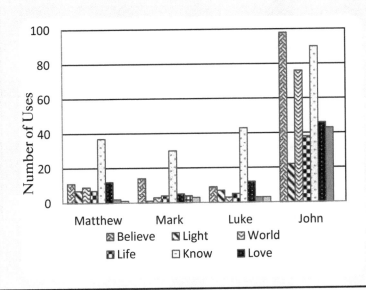

Special Words in John (Part 1):

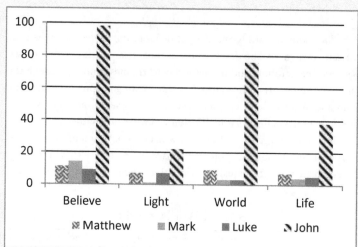

Special Words in John (Part 2):

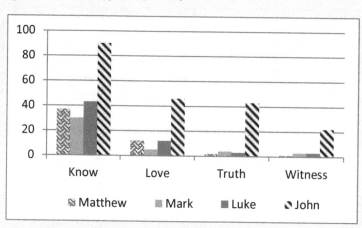

The Only Way

Another dimension is given to the way, however, in the person of Jesus Christ. He is the teacher of the way in truth (Matthew 22:16; Mark 12:14). He himself is the only way to God (John 14:4-6). Everything about Jesus is important to us: the way He lived, the way He died, the way He rose again. He is the one who has opened for us the new and living way to God (Hebrews 10:19, 20). It is no wonder that the Christians in the early church were known as followers of "the Way" (Acts 9:2; 19:9, 23; 22:4; 24:14, 22). This name may have been given to Christians because Christ had claimed to be "the way" (John 14:6), or perhaps because of the straitened way He had referred to in the Sermon on the Mount (Matthew 7:14). Or the name may have been given because in Jesus was fulfilled the prophetic saying, "Prepare ye the way of the Lord, make straight in the desert a highway for our God" (Isaiah 40:3, KJV).

When all the ways of God and man are studied, it is clear that the Scriptures teach there is only one way to real life, the true life, and this is Jesus. This is the message of Jesus himself; it is the testimony of the Gospel of John. Jesus is the only way.

PART ONE

The Way

John 1:1-8:30

CHAPTER ONE

When Heaven Came Down
John 1:1-18

As the curtain rises on the drama of life, two are already on stage. God and the Word are there. But it is difficult to determine whether they are two or one. The Word (*Logos*) is with God, facing toward God; and yet the Word is also God. They are not identical, but they are one. The setting is not on earth, for there is no earth. And this is not a play. This is real.

THE BEGINNING (1:1-13)

The Eternal Word (1, 2)

The opening verses of the Gospel of John are a formal prologue to the whole narrative that follows. They are like an explanation given by a narrator before a play. They give the setting and introduce the main character. In the description, key words are carefully chosen, words that will be important later on (like *life, light, witness,* and *believe*).

Who is the leading figure in this account? He is introduced as the Word (the Greek is *Logos*). After this prologue, the term is not used for Christ in the rest of the Gospel of John, nor in the rest of the New Testament except for Revelation 19:13, where "the Word of God" appears to be Christ, and 1 John 1:1, where "the Word of life" can be identified with the Son, Jesus Christ.

Logos was a term familiar to the Greek philosophers. They used it to mean "reason," frequently a reason above the reason of men, an independent force that gave order to the universe and generative power to nature. Besides "reason" or "thought,"[2] it also meant "word" or "speech." John did not borrow his meaning of the word from the philosophers. He simply chose a term that people had been debating about for centuries and declared who He was and what He did. This was new to the world; it was the good news, the gospel.

In the beginning can include all beginnings, whether of creation, or time, or the world, or man. The verb *was* emphasizes that the Word was already in existence before the beginning. The word translated "with God" shows the existence of both the Word and God, the distinction between them, and the close association between them.

The translation "the Word was God" is best at the end of verse 1, though other translations have been suggested. John is not saying the Word was divine (this would be another Greek word, *theios*, instead of *theos*), nor that He was like God or had God's attributes, but simply the Word was God. "God" is the name ordinarily reserved for God the Father, but it is applied, though infrequently, to the Son. It is so used in this very chapter (John 1:18), also in John 20:28. Paul uses it thus in Titus 2:13 and possibly Romans 9:5 and Colossians 2:2. Hebrews 1:8 is an example; 2 Peter 1:1 and 1 John 5:20 are other examples.

These opening words of John's Gospel have the ring of the opening of Genesis, "In the beginning God created the heavens and the earth." John, however, starts with a scene before the beginning of the earth. He uses the past tense, continued action, "was," to depict the existence of the Word. Even in the beginning, the Word

---

[2] C. H. Dodd, *The Interpretation of the Fourth Gospel*, (1953), pp. 3, 4.

was eternally preexistent, was distinguishable from God but had a relationship with God, and, in fact, the Word was God. How all this can be true at the same time is beyond the comprehension of man. If one did indeed comprehend it fully, he must be God.

Among the first of God's creative acts was to bring forth light. This was spoken into existence: "Let there be light" (Genesis 1:3). Since the *Logos* is noted as the agent through whom God made all things, it is appropriate that Logos be translated "Word" rather than "reason." Speech goes forth, whereas reason is confined within.

Real Life (3, 4)

With the presence of the Word comes life, for "in Him was life." But what is life? One can examine objects that have life, but no one has isolated life itself and put it under the microscope. One can take a synthetic grain of wheat containing all the physical ingredients of a true grain of wheat, plant it and nothing grows. No life is implanted there. Yet some grains of wheat, retrieved from the tombs of the pharaohs in Egypt, have been planted after thousands of years and have grown because life was still present. Life cannot be seen, but it is real.

There are different kinds of life. The vegetable has life, but the beast of the field has a different kind of life. Plato said, "A pig eats, sleeps, and breathes, and still remains a pig." His point was that if all a man does is eat, sleep, and breathe, then he is living the life of a pig and not of a man. Life to an intelligent being should be more than the life of a beast. The message of the Gospel of John concerns life, but the life he presents is still more than existence at the highest reaches of the mind of man. He points to the true life as a child of God.

Life is an important theme in the Gospel of John. The word is used thirty-six times in the book, more than a quarter of all the New Testament references. The kind of life offered by Jesus is the gift of God, eternal life (John 3:16). He came that men might have more abundant life (John 10:10). This new life is to know God and Jesus

Christ whom He sent (John 17:3). This is what the message of the Gospel of John is about. He introduces the Word, not simply as the one who brings life, but the one in whom life itself resides. Jesus said, "I am the way and the truth and the life" (John 14:6). To explain what this life is, another figure is introduced. "That life was the light of men" (John 1:4).

The Light in the Darkness (3-5)

John lays down words like stepping-stones, leading a person from the creation to light and down the course of man's existence. The Word is essential to each of these stepping-stones. With *darkness*, the conflict is introduced, but darkness is not victorious.

Light has long been associated with understanding, and/or enlightenment. Darkness is its opposite, representing ignorance and uncertainty. Light is likewise an indicator of goodness and purity, whereas evil prefers the cloak of darkness. Light is the setting for the joy and blessings of Heaven, but outer darkness describes the fate of the lost. The Word was a light-bearer ready to dispel the darkness from the lives of men. The whole of the Gospel of John tells of Christ as "the light of the world" (John 8:12). The one who follows Him will not walk in darkness, but will have the light of life. Men are urged to believe in the light (John 12:36). Just as He brought sight to the blind, He brought light to a world in darkness (John 9:5).

In mentioning the conflict between light and darkness, John uses the phrase, "*but the darkness has not understood it*," or as the New International Version has in a footnote, "*the darkness has not overcome it*" (John 1:5). The one Greek word can have either of these meanings, "understand" or "overcome," and it is difficult to determine which fits the context better. Perhaps John had both meanings in mind. An English word that has a similar dual meaning is *grasp*. The darkness could not "grasp" the light—neither understand nor take hold of it. This is an assuring quality of light. Wherever there is light, it drives back the darkness. Darkness can never win out as long as light is there. Only when light is removed can the darkness advance. As long as Jesus dwells in the heart of an individual, light prevails.

Near the first of God's creation was, "Let there be light."

The Dependable Witness (6-9)

Now the scene changes. We leap ahead in time from the beginning to the century of the Gospel writer, and the point of view changes from Heaven's perspective to earth's. It seems that John the Baptist is introduced at this point for two reasons. First, the occasion of the Word's entrance into the society of people was so momentous that it required a forerunner to announce His coming, both in the happening and in John's telling of it. But a second reason is that the Gospel writer is eager to introduce another word important to the unfolding of his account. The word is *witness* (John 1:7). John the Baptist was sent from God to give his testimony concerning Christ. (See John 1:15, also.) John the apostle uses this word *witness* fourteen times in the Gospel, and the verb form thirty-three times. The other Gospel writers use both the noun and the verb only six times altogether. Besides John the Baptist, God bears witness to Jesus (John 5:37), the Holy Spirit testifies (John 15:26), Christ testifies of himself (John 8:14), His works give testimony (John 5:36; 10:25; 14:11), and the Scripture gives sufficient witness (John 5:39). Human witnesses also lend their voices: the disciples (John 15:27), the Samaritan woman (John 4:39), and the multitude (John 12:17).

The witness is valuable in establishing the truth. This gives strength to John's Gospel. In addition, the word for witness is *marturia*, which provides the basis for the English word *martyr*. As a matter of fact, John the Baptist did give his life in carrying out his task as a witness. Many died in those early centuries for their testimony of faith in Christ. The continuing witness today is an important part of the Christian's life. May all of us have the vigor and courage to repeat the testimony of the ancient martyrs and to be faithful even to death.

John the Baptist is introduced as a man sent from God. It may be that later, some of the Baptist's followers held to him rather than Christ (John 3:26). In any event, John's Gospel clearly presents John the Baptist as sent from God, but also makes clear his subordinate role: he himself was not the light: he came only as a witness to the light. The Word was the true light (real, genuine, authentic), and He was coming into the world (John 1:8, 9).

Some translations relate "coming into the world" (John 1:9) with every man. The King James Version, for example, reads, "the true Light, which lighteth every man that cometh into the world." It seems better to join the phrase to the true light, as the New International Version does. However, in a sense, Jesus does give light to every person in the world. Every man has some indication of God and is responsible for the degree of opportunity he has been given (Romans 1:20). Jesus said, "But I, when I am lifted up from the earth, will draw all men to myself" (John 12:32). This does not say that all will respond to His drawing power, but His death on the cross provides Christ's offer. Even so, He lights every man, whether every man follows the light or not. Some flee from the light, loving the darkness and their evil deeds (John 3:19-21).

The True Light (10-13)

In the Greek, John 1:11 has *his own* first in the neuter gender, meaning His own things. The second *his own* is in the masculine, meaning His own people. The universe had been made through the Word; but when He came into His own things (neuter), they who were His own people (masculine) did not receive Him. This is one of the most tragic verses in the Scripture. All of God's creation accepted His Son except the very ones who were made in the image of God. His own people rejected Him.

To receive Jesus is to believe in His name (John 1:12), to accept Him as the incarnate Word, the Christ, the Son of God. This implies not only intellectual assent, but also personal trust and an action in response that gives evidence of full acceptance. John 3:3-6 tells more fully how one is reborn a child of God.

The new birth is not of bloods, to translate the Greek literally (John 1:13). This means it is not dependent on one's physical lineage, his blood line, his natural descent from Abraham or any other. Neither is the new birth a natural result of some desire of the flesh or planning of the husband or wife. Birth as a child of God is dependent upon the power of God and the believer's acceptance of His Son.

The Incarnation (1:14-18)

"The Word became flesh and made his dwelling among us" (John 1:14). This places a great gap between what John says and the musings of the philosophers and the teachings of such Jewish instructors as Philo. They had not suggested that the *Logos* became a man and lived as a human being. They had not suggested that the eternal Word was God's one and only Son and that the one true living God, who was a Spirit and could not be seen, became incarnate and lived among men. The law had been delivered through Moses, but grace and truth came through Jesus Christ (John 1:17).

The Word Became Flesh (14)

John does not tell of the virgin birth, but notice his careful language describing the arrival of God's Son: "The Word became flesh." He took on a physical, human body. Jesus became man in order to bear man's sin on the cross.

In the next phrase, the translation reads, "made his dwelling among us." However, the Greek does not denote a permanent residence. Up until 1984, the New International Version rendered it, "lived for a while among us." Literally it means, "lived in a tent among us."

Full of grace and truth. The Greek word for "grace" has various meanings, but among Christians, it most often means favor, especially favor that is not deserved. Into a world of sinners came the Savior, full of favor, kindness, and mercy. But He is equally full of truth. He will not give up truth in order to favor those who persist in preferring falsehood.

Israel saw God's glory at Mount Sinai by hearing His voice from the midst of the fire (Deuteronomy 5:24-26). Now, however, man has seen the fullness of God's glory in His one and only Son ... full of grace and truth.

The greatest tragedy of all is that the world did not recognize Him. His own people would not receive Him. This is the same tragedy present in the world today. But there are some who do receive Him, and everyone who believes in His name has the right to be born again as a child of God.

The Pre-eminence of the Word (15-18)

Although John's ministry began before Jesus' did, Jesus' work was of higher importance. But He was before John in more than importance. He existed before John even though He was born later. His authority was also higher than John's.

"Grace for grace" in the King James Version (John 1:16) may be literally translated "grace instead of grace." It pictures one gift of grace merging into another. The New International Version gives the thought well: "one blessing after another." God's grace is continuous and does not run out. It is centered in the gift and presence of Jesus Christ.

The law was given through Moses; grace and truth came through Jesus Christ. Although no man can look upon God and live, God has been made known by the life and teaching of His Son. This is one of the instances where the Son (Word) is called God: "God the only Son" (John 1:18, NIV, 1973, 1978). Some manuscripts differ at this point, leaving out the word "God" and reading "only begotten Son." The King James Version follows that reading, but the most recently discovered early manuscripts (P66 and P75) have added enough weight to the former witness to give the preference to the former New International reading, "God the only Son."

This is the prologue of John's Gospel. He is going to tell us of the true life made possible through God's one and only Son, the eternal Word.

THE ONE AND ONLY SON (1:14, 18)

The Gospel of John is noted for its emphasis on the deity of Christ. Its language is unmistakable. John identifies the Word with God (John 1:1) and then identifies the Word with the person of Jesus (John 1:14ff.). Thomas calls Him God (John 20:28), and Jesus claims to be one with God (John 10:30). Equally clear is Jesus' claim to the Sonship role with God. In the fifth chapter of John, Jesus makes explicit to his Jewish audience: "... whatever the Father does the Son also does" (John 5:19). He is the "only begotten son" whom God has sent into the world (John 3:16, KJV). This claim was particularly infuriating to the Jews who denied the truth of Jesus' claim. "For this reason the Jews tried all the harder to kill him; not only was he breaking the Sabbath, but he was even calling God his own Father, making himself equal with God" (John 5:18). Without an understanding of what Jesus was claiming and what the Jewish leaders were denying, it is impossible to follow what transpired in the ministry of Jesus and in His death, burial, and resurrection.

The word μονογενής (*monogenēs*) has long been translated "only begotten" Son. Some deny this is the best rendering of the word and insist that the Greek root is more closely related to γενής (*genēs*: one of its kind, tribe, clan) rather than γεννάω (*gennao:* to beget). Thus they translate μονογενής with the single word *only* saying that both μόνος (*monos*) and γενής (*genēs*) reiterate the "one" aspect. Using the single word *only*, however, is insufficient. Since μόνος alone means "only one," this leaves γενής untranslated. The English word *unique* is a good English word denoting "only one of its kind"; but many readers do not appreciate the meaning of this rather rare word. Many of those who object to the use of the word *begotten* in the description of the Son are the very ones who deny the virgin birth and insist that Jesus was not different in kind from other human beings but only in the degree of His closeness to God. For this reason, it is all the more objectionable that they render μονογενής as simply "only" and then water down the meaning of "only" to "the best" by comparison. On the other hand, the rendering of the NIV translation is commendable. It translates μονογενής as "the one and only," thus giving the emphasis needed by the Greek. This brings out the uniqueness of Jesus and at the same time retains a certain warm association of the Son, the one and only. Only John uses the term μονογενής in the New Testament. Its emphasis is not on the begetting but on the uniqueness of Jesus. Others may be called "sons of God" (Galatians 3:26), but not in the same way Jesus is. He is the one, the only one divine Son of the divine Father.

Despite John's emphasis on the deity of Christ, he does not relate the virgin birth of Jesus. This is John's usual procedure of omitting much material already given in the Synoptics, just as the instituting of the Lord's Supper is missing. He does, however, give an introduction to this important ordinance in the preliminary teaching of Jesus concerning "the Bread of Life" (John 6:25-59). In the same way, then, John does not tell of the earthly birth of Jesus but introduces Him in His preexistent state of the eternal Word. Still, he guards the miraculous birth of Jesus in choosing his words carefully to describe how Heaven came to earth: "The Word became flesh and made his dwelling among us. We have seen his glory, the glory of the One and Only, who came from the Father, full of grace and truth" (John 1:14).

CHAPTER TWO

How Jesus Began
John 1:19-2:25

When Jesus began His ministry, He needed identification. But if He identified himself as the Messiah immediately, without giving instruction about what the Messiah was really like and about His kingdom, people would not find the true life. So John the Baptist acted as the announcer to identify Jesus. Then Jesus gathered His disciples to give them instruction. He worked miracles as signs to authenticate His message. In this way, Jesus began His ministry among His people: announcement, followers, and signs.

INTRODUCING JESUS (1:19-34)

John the Baptist was the link that joined the old and the new, the prediction and its fulfillment. He himself had been predicted; Isaiah had foretold the coming of one who would prepare the way of the Lord. And John identified himself as this voice crying in the wilderness (Isaiah 40:3).

John came to call sinners to repentance. The prophets of old had done that, too, and Jesus also made it a basic note in His preaching. John was a link between the two. With the spirit and power of Elijah from the past, John preached a baptism of repentance. This baptism was a link with the future and the coming baptism in the church.

The Gospel of John does not emphasize the reforming preaching of John the Baptist as do the Synoptics. (See, for example, Matthew 3:7-12; Luke 3:10-18.) But only the fourth Gospel tells of John the Baptist's role in identifying Jesus. John does not even tell about the baptism of Jesus, but he tells of a later time when John the Baptist spoke of the descent of the Spirit at Jesus' baptism as positive proof that Jesus was the Son of God (John 1:29-34.)

At that time, John pointed Jesus out as "the Lamb of God, who takes away the sin of the world" (John 1:29). This figure of the lamb was in itself a link between the past and the future. The lamb was significant in the sin sacrifices of the Old Covenant (Exodus 29:38-42). Especially important was the Passover lamb, both in the actual time of the exodus and in the subsequent annual remembrance of the occasion. But Jesus is our Passover lamb (1 Corinthians 5:7). Isaiah describes the suffering servant as one "led like a lamb to the slaughter" (Isaiah 53:7). Again, in the book of Revelation, the figure of the lamb is applied to Jesus (e.g. Revelation 5:6-8, 13; 7:9, 10). John links the figure in the Old Covenant to the person and sacrifice of Christ and His eternal role in Heaven.

The Lamb provides a particularly appropriate figure. Innocence and gentleness were associated with it. But John designated Jesus "the Lamb of God." Other lambs had been offered by men, but now God had provided the Lamb, the one belonging to God. He was to provide a sacrifice for the whole world.

Who John Was Not (19-21)

One kind of definition of anything is to tell what the object is not. This is the way John started to describe himself. He was not the Messiah, the long awaited Savior (John 4:25). He was not Elijah, the prophet expected to precede the day of the Lord (Malachi 4:5). These Jews who questioned John were looking for the very body of Elijah that had been taken to Heaven (2 Kings 2:11), and John was not that. On the other hand, the angel had announced before John's birth that John was coming in the spirit and power of Elijah (Luke 1:17). In that sense, John did fulfill the prophecy of Elijah's coming

(Matthew 11:14). But the Jews were asking about a literal return of Elijah's body. To their question John could say, "No, I am not Elijah."

"Are you the Prophet?" (John 1:21). With this question, the Jews probably had reference to the prophet Moses had promised, a prophet like Moses himself (Deuteronomy 18:15). But his prophecy referred to the Messiah, and John the Baptist did not fulfill it.

Who John Was (22-28)

Then who was John? He was the voice prophesied in Isaiah 40:3. He was like the servants who prepared a roadway when the king was soon to travel that way. In this case, the King was already there. He was among them, John said, but the people did not know Him. He would begin His work when John had made the way ready for Him.

John baptized with water, but the King would be much greater than John; He would baptize with the Holy Spirit (John 1:33).[3]

John gave his testimony in Bethany, not the Bethany on the Mount of Olives, near Jerusalem, but another one on the other side of Jordan. Some manuscripts read Bethabara instead of Bethany. This reading may have been the result of Origen's attempt to identify the place in the third century. Bethany is the preferred reading, although the location is uncertain today.

Who Jesus Was (29-34)

The day following John's questioning by the Jews, he saw Jesus and pointed Him out to others who were present. Jesus was the Lamb of God, the one greater than John. John was preparing the way for Him, and in His earthly ministry, He was coming after John. Still, He had lived in Heaven before John existed, and even before the world was made.

John the Baptist had baptized Jesus some time before (Matthew 3:13-17). The Gospel of John does not describe the baptism of Jesus

---

[3]See also Acts 1:5; 2:1-4.

as the Synoptic Gospels do, but it refers to the Spirit's coming at that time. This was the positive identification of Jesus as the Christ. John knew who Jesus was before that, but did not know He was the Son of God until the Holy Spirit descended upon Him as a dove. This does not mean He became the Son of God at that time, but that His identity was made clear to John.

John gave further testimony. Following his description of the descent of the Spirit upon Jesus, John stated, "I have seen and I testify that this is the Son of God" (John 1:34). Although some manuscripts carry the reading, "This is God's chosen One," it is more likely that "the Son of God" was in the original.

JESUS' FIRST DISCIPLES (1:35-51)

On the next day, Jesus again passed by. This time John pointed Him out to two of his disciples, who then followed Jesus and spent the rest of the day with Him. John's Gospel probably uses the Roman designation of time, so the tenth hour means ten o'clock in the morning.

The day after He talked with the two disciples and Simon, Jesus prepared to leave the area where John the Baptist was ministering and go back to Galilee and invited them to follow Him. Nathanael was a true Israelite, not having any deceit, such as Jacob at times had exercised in his earlier days (Genesis 27:35). We are not told what Jesus had seen Nathanael doing under a fig tree, but it was a surprise to Nathanael that Jesus could know about it. Jesus made further reference to Jacob when He associated himself with Jacob's vision of the angels ascending and descending (Genesis 28:10-12).

Jesus Talks With His First Disciples

What would Jesus have talked about the first day He spent with two of John's disciples? One of these was Andrew (John 1:40). The other is unnamed, but he may have been John, who always avoids the use of his own name and that of his brother in his narrative. Whatever they talked about, Andrew then went to his brother,

Simon, and declared, "We have found the Messiah" (John 1:41). And after Jesus was with Philip for a time, that disciple went to Nathanael and declared they had found "the one Moses wrote about in the Law, and about whom the prophets also wrote" (John 1:45). This no doubt refers to the whole of the Old Testament Scriptures, the law and the prophets. Philip learned as did the two on the way to Emmaus when the resurrected Jesus "explained to them what was said in all the Scriptures concerning himself" (Luke 24:27). This is what Jesus and His first disciples talked about in those opening days also: who the Messiah was, what He was like. And their conclusion? Jesus is the Messiah! Nathanael further concluded, "You are the Son of God; you are the King of Israel" (John 1:49).

Jesus added His own witness: "You shall see heaven open, and the angels of God ascending and descending on the Son of Man" (John 1:51). In other words, Jesus was providing the bridge for communication between God and man, Heaven and earth, the spiritual and the fleshly.

SIGNS CONFIRM JESUS' IDENTITY (2:1-25)

The three days after Jesus talked with Philip and Nathanael allowed time for Jesus to go with His disciples from the Jordan to His home in Nazareth, and then to the wedding in nearby Cana.

Jesus Works His First Miracle (1-11)

How would one begin if he had power to work miracles? He would be tempted to set up headquarters in Jerusalem or establish regular hours at an important center. But note that Jesus was attending an important social function where other people had the place of prominence: the bride and groom, the parents, and the "master of the banquet" (John 2:8), the individual employed to make all the arrangements and serve as manager of the banquet. But this type of festival lasted about a week, and they had run out of wine. This was a little town and an unnamed family, but a need arose. This was the occasion for Jesus' first sign.

It seems an unlikely time, but there was a need. Jesus' mother made the suggestion that Jesus could do something to replenish the exhausted supply of wine. His reply to her was a rebuke. He let her know that she could not run His life nor plan His schedule. Even then, she alerted the servants to do anything that Jesus might require of them. Did she sense that the time had come?

Now Jesus added a miracle to the testimony of John the Baptist and to the convictions of the disciples He had talked to. He told the servants to fill six large jars with water. These were not wine jugs, but large receptacles used for water. Each held between twenty and thirty gallons. Then He turned the water into wine. It is useless to debate about what kind of wine this was. The making of it was a miracle; therefore, the product was unique. The taste was better than any they had had before. This is always true of the way God does things.

Jesus Indicates His Authority (12-25)

After His first miracle, Jesus spent more time in the big cities. Capernaum on the Sea of Galilee was important in the northern section; and Jerusalem, in the south, was the center of activity for the Jews. Jesus moved from the little town of Nazareth to the important center, Capernaum. (See Matthew 4:13.) At this time, however, His stay was a brief one before He went up to Jerusalem for the Passover, one of the three great feasts commanded for the annual observance of the Jews (Deuteronomy 16:1-6).

What He found there was cause for disappointment and anger. It was not the worship of God and the observance of His law that met the eye. There was much commercial activity accompanied by the lowing of cattle, the bleating of sheep, and the wrangling of the money changers. The temple area had become a marketplace, and not a very honest one at that. Edersheim estimated that the Sadducees were clearing about three hundred thousand dollars a year in their temple monopoly.

Not in the inner sanctuary, but in the large outer court of the temple, animals were being sold for sacrifice. Worshipers, therefore, did not have to drive them from a distance, but exorbitant prices were charged for the convenience. Also, money had to be changed for the temple contributions because coins with forbidden images were not acceptable. The Roman denarius, for example, was stamped with the head of Caesar (Matthew 22:18-21). This was held to be a violation of the commandment against graven images (Exodus 20:4). Such coins could be changed for Jewish money, but the exchange was made costly. Thus, the temple became not only a market (John 2:16), but even a den of robbers (Mark 11:17).

Jesus would not tolerate it. Righteous indignation flashed as He drove out the oxen and sheep, freed the pigeons, and overturned the tables of the money changers. Psalm 69:9 is quoted to describe Jesus' burning indignation over the misuse of the temple: "Zeal for your house will consume me." The disciples were reminded of this passage as they witnessed the mood and actions of Jesus. It is significant that this action aroused the first of the opposition that brought about Christ's crucifixion. Thus Jesus' zeal literally led to His being consumed.

The Synoptic Gospels do not record a cleansing of the temple this early. They describe a similar incident in the final week of Jesus' life. Some maintain that there was only one cleansing and that John has disregarded chronological order at this point. It is more likely, however, that there were two cleansings: one early and one late in His ministry. It is understandable that the Synoptics do not mention this first occasion, for they tell nothing about Judean activity during His early ministry. On the other hand, if Jesus did cleanse the temple in the first year of His ministry, this explains the early and intense hostility of the religious leaders. Not only had Jesus defied their authority, but He had interfered with their money-making!

Jesus added another stone to the foundation of His claims. When He was challenged for His authority to halt the temple procedures, He boldly declared: "Destroy this temple, and I will raise it again in three days" (John 2:19). This led to further exasperation on the part of the Jewish leaders. These words of Jesus were brought up as an accusation in His trial three years later (Mark 14:57, 58). Note, however, that Jesus did not say He was going to destroy the temple. In fact, John adds the explanation: Jesus was figuratively giving a prophecy that they would destroy His temple, that is, His physical body, and three days later He would rise from the dead.

At the outset of Jesus' ministry He built upon John's testimony, instruction to His disciples, miraculous works, and declarations of authority. Our reaction today should be the same as that of the disciples: "Then they believed the Scripture and the words that Jesus had spoken" (John 2:22).

Historical Note (18-25)

The Jews said this temple had been under construction for forty-six years. This helps in determining the date of this occasion. Herod had begun the temple in 19 B.C. Although the essential part had been completed in eighteen months, work continued until A.D. 64, just six years before the temple was destroyed in A.D. 70. The forty-sixth year in construction, and the year that Jesus first cleansed the temple, was A.D. 27.

CHAPTER THREE

What Jesus Taught
John 3:1-4:42

Nicodemus came to ask a question, but he never really stated the question. Instead, Jesus began to answer what was in Nicodemus' heart without waiting to hear it expressed. This relates to the closing verse of the second chapter of John, where we read that Jesus "knew what was in a man." Nicodemus came by night, and there was darkness over his understanding as well. When he departed, one does not feel that he had reached the light of noonday, but one can see the morning star rising in his heart (2 Peter 1:19).

Nicodemus must wait for the unfolding of events in the three years ahead to understand the meaning of Jesus' teaching. He must hear the full gospel proclaimed and see the church established. But already, the new day was dawning. His darkened understanding was exposed to the true light that enlightens every man (John 1:9).

What could he learn? Nicodemus learned about the entrance to the kingdom of God. He learned about the love of God and the importance of belief. He was on the threshold of true life. It is not recorded that he entered later, but we like to think he did.

QUESTIONS AND ANSWERS (3:1-10)

What Was the Question?

Nicodemus was a Pharisee. The Pharisees were one of the sects of the Jews that had their origins in the period between the Old and New Testaments. The name denotes "separatists." They considered themselves separated from people who were less careful about keeping the law. They were noted as interpreters and teachers of Scripture, but they honored their own traditions as much as the Word of God. They claimed that these traditions went back to Moses himself. Unfortunately, they assumed a self-satisfaction that nullified their worthy points and brought a common hypocrisy to their lives. (See Jesus' warning to them in Matthew 23.) It seems plain that Nicodemus was more sincere and open than most of his fellow Pharisees.

One can recall some of the questions the Pharisees asked on other occasions. "Is it lawful to heal on the Sabbath?" (Matthew 12:10). "Is it lawful for a man to divorce his wife . . . ?" (Matthew 19:3). "By what authority are you [Jesus] doing these things?" (Matthew 21:23). "Why do you eat and drink with tax collectors and 'sinners'?" (Luke 5:30). "When will the kingdom of God come?" (Luke 17:20).

Nicodemus, however, was not just an average Pharisee. He was a ruler of the Jews. Each synagogue had its rulers. But this was Jerusalem, and Nicodemus seems to have been involved with the Sanhedrin, the highest council of the Jews, numbering from seventy to one hundred members. In this case, *ruler* probably means a member of this august body, the Sanhedrin; so the New International Version translates it "member of the Jewish ruling council" (John 3:1). His question may not have been the question of any ordinary Pharisee.

Moreover, Nicodemus came to Jesus by night. At least he was not trying to impress a crowd with his question. He was not trying to trap Jesus in order to belittle Him before an audience. But why did he come by night? Was he ashamed of being seen with Jesus? Or was it because he wanted to have some privacy after the rush and turmoil of the day was over? After all, the Jews were noted for using the night for the deepest of Scripture studies. Whatever the reason for it, Nicodemus was not afraid on later occasions to stand up for Jesus, first to raise questions about action to arrest Jesus (John 7:50-52), and then, finally, to assist Joseph of Arimathea in burying the body of Jesus (John 19:38-42). It took real courage to do that.

But what question was on his heart in this encounter with Jesus? All one has to go on is the answer that Jesus gave. From this, one must conclude that Nicodemus' unasked question had something to do with the kingdom of God. In the mind of a first-century Pharisee, this phrase probably was limited by his understanding of the coming messianic age. If he had a misconception of the Messiah, his view of the kingdom would also be off the mark. In fact, Nicodemus' intended question probably had to do with both the Messiah and the kingdom, and Jesus' relationship to both.

Jesus' reply began, "I tell you the truth." In other versions, this is translated "verily, verily" or "truly, truly." The Greek "amen, amen" comes from the Hebrew. It means "so let it be" or "of a truth." The phrase is used to introduce words of particularly solemn import.

The Kingdom of God

It may be helpful to use the phrase "kingship of God." In a sense, this kingship is eternal since God's rule and authority are from everlasting to everlasting. But when Jesus came, He preached, "The kingdom of God is near" (Mark 1:15).

In one way, a person could say the kingdom was already here when Jesus was here, because He is the king. Jesus told the Pharisees, "The kingdom of God does not come with your careful observation, nor will people say, 'Here it is,' or 'There it is,' because the kingdom of God is among you" (Luke 17:20, 21, NIV footnote).

But the kingdom was yet to come in another sense, and Peter was to have its keys (Matthew 16:18, 19).

The second chapter of Acts tells how Peter used the keys to open the entrance of the kingdom. Even though the church in its militant state today is the kingdom, another phase of the kingdom remains for the people of God triumphant. We still can pray, "Your kingdom come, your will be done on earth as it is in heaven" (Matthew 6:10).

This is another aspect of the kingdom—its eternal state—equivalent to Heaven and eternal life. *Kingdom of heaven* is a phrase used only in Matthew, but it is concluded that the two phrases (*kingdom of God* and *kingdom of heaven*) are used interchangeably.

Jesus swept all this aside with a warning that Nicodemus would not see the kingdom of God unless he himself was ready to enter it. He must be born—*anothen.* This Greek word means either "again" or "from above." Perhaps it has both meanings here. It is obvious that Nicodemus took it to mean "again," and in a literal sense. Jesus explained further. One must be born of the water and the Spirit. If nothing more than this was said, it is doubtful that Nicodemus would have associated this new birth with Christian baptism. Nicodemus could not have understood this as Christian baptism at this time, but the teaching of Jesus often has two levels of significance, one on the surface and one in the depths. Nicodemus could understand that he must humble himself and that he must not look for a kingdom on an earthly level, something that could be seen. Birth into the kingdom is not a physical birth, but a spiritual one. To describe the Spirit, Jesus mentions the wind. In the Greek, as well as the Hebrew, the same word means either "wind" or" spirit." Only by the context can one determine which meaning is intended. One can hear the sound of the wind, he can see the results of its power, but he cannot tell where it comes from or where it is going.

Besides being a birth of the Spirit, the new birth is a birth of the water. Not until Christian baptism and the establishment of the church could Nicodemus see the full significance of these coordinates, water and Spirit, in the rebirth by which one enters the kingdom of God. The apostle John has already written of John the Baptist's baptism with water and Jesus' baptism with the Spirit (John 1:32, 33); and from the Day of Pentecost on, baptism was linked not only with the outward presence of water, but also with the indwelling gift of the Spirit (Acts 2:38).

In Titus 3:5, the "washing" is joined to rebirth and the Spirit. One should not wonder at Jesus' giving teaching that could not be completely understood at the time it was given. The Gospel of John presents the early teaching of Jesus anticipating the Lord's Supper (John 6:53, 54), and the people could not understand it. Here it seems that the teaching anticipated the baptism, though it would not be understood till a later time. Some deny that the passage refers to baptism. The water is interpreted as meaning physical birth. It is significant, however, that the Greek has only one preposition for both the water and the Spirit. It does not say "of the water" (one birth) and "of the spirit" (second birth), but it says, "of the water and the Spirit" (one rebirth).

What could Nicodemus understand of this? He had started out affirming, "We know you are a teacher who has come from God"; but he ended up saying, "How can this be?" In other words, he now confessed, "I don't know." The profound truth that Jesus taught was beyond his understanding. Then Jesus gave a gentle rebuke: "You are Israel's teacher, and you do not understand these things [concerning the Spirit]?" (John 3:10). After all, the Old Testament tells of the last days. It records that God said, "I will put my Spirit in you" (Ezekiel 36:27). Shouldn't a teacher of Israel be ready for additional truth about the Spirit?

"We know," said Jesus, using the same expression Nicodemus had used. "We know" what we are talking about, but you don't believe the earthly, let alone the Heavenly. (See John 3:12.)

In the simple statement, "Christ died for our sins" (1 Corinthians 15:3), one sees the earthly and the Heavenly. Christ died a physical death on the cross. This was the earthly. But "for our sins" transcends the physical and enters another realm. It has spiritual, Heavenly consequences of an eternal nature. Even so, Nicodemus was told of a rebirth of water and the Spirit. In Christian baptism, the water is earthly, but the Spirit is Heavenly. When Ananias told Paul, "Get up, be baptized and wash your sins away" (Acts 22:16), he spoke of the earthly (water baptism) and the Heavenly (eternal spiritual consequences).

WHAT DID NICODEMUS LEARN? (3:11-21)

Nicodemus Learned About the Entrance

Nicodemus began with a polite recognition that Jesus was worthy of being addressed as "Rabbi," a duly respected teacher of the Jews. He went further than this. He recognized that Jesus was a teacher come from God and could work miraculous signs. Perhaps this is what Nicodemus wanted to talk about, these signs and the coming kingdom.

He had come with a view about the kingdom of God, but it was too materialistic, too earthly. In effect, Jesus told him, "You must get turned around before you can even see the kingdom or enter it." The things of the Spirit are essential to the true life.

The phrases *earthly things* and *Heavenly things* are keys to an understanding of John's Gospel. The earthly things are material. They can be seen, or heard, or felt. Examples are water, wind, and flesh. The Heavenly things are truths that cannot be perceived with the physical senses. They are spiritual rather than material. If Nicodemus, and all related beings, have trouble with the earthly, how much more difficult it is to comprehend the Heavenly.

Nicodemus Learned About the Love of God

From this point on (John 3:12), Nicodemus fades from the account. The Greek manuscripts have no standard way of indicating where a quotation ends. Thus, it is uncertain whether the verses 13-21 were spoken to Nicodemus, or to a wider audience on another occasion, or whether John is adding this as an editorial comment. Some students end Jesus' quotation at verse 12, some at 13, some at 15, others at 21. Since the language and thought are so well knit together, it seems best to consider the whole as delivered to Nicodemus. The same thoughts may have been repeated at other times. As He moved about the country and spoke to different audiences, Jesus doubtless repeated many things over and over.

God loved and He gave. This is the Heavenly. *One and only* (John 3:16) is from the Greek word *"monogenes,"* which is translated in different ways. The King James Version has "only begotten," apparently taking the latter part of *monogenes* from *gennao*, to beget. However, in Hebrews 11:17, monogenes is used of Isaac, who was not Abraham's only begotten son, but he was Abraham's only son of his kind, born of Abraham's wife, Sarah. Another Greek word, related to *gennao*, means a race or kind, so *monogenes* can mean the only one of a kind. Jesus is God's Son in a unique way. He is divine, He existed from eternity, yet He became flesh on earth. People who accept Him may also become children of God, but no one else is God's Son begotten in the same way Jesus is.

The Greek word *krino* can mean either "judge" or "condemn." "Condemn" is to be preferred in John 3:17, 18. Those who are Christ's will be approved, and those who reject Him will be condemned.

"Enter the kingdom of God" (John 3:5) is another way of saying "have eternal life" (John 3:15, 16). This is why Jesus continued His instruction by speaking of necessary conditions to eternal life for the saved. First the Son of Man descends from Heaven (John 3:13). Jesus had earlier identified himself as the communicating channel between Heaven and earth (John 1:5 1). Then the Son of Man must be "lifted up" (John 3:14). Later, Jesus used this language again, and the meaning of it is indicated: "He said this to show the kind of death he was going to die" (John 12:32, 33). As the children of Israel were spared in the wilderness by turning to look upon the bronze serpent (Numbers 21:8, 9), so the sinner must look to Jesus, who died on the cross for our sins. This is another condition. The sinner must look in belief to Jesus and His atoning gift.

Why has God done this? The answer is simple. God loves you so. This is one of those instances where the intellect of man is not adequate. Man cannot reason his way to establishing the love of God and the gift of His Son. Only through God's revealing himself can we be assured of this love. Accepting this in belief adds another dimension to the life of man when he finds true life as a child of God. John Calvin maintained that man can reason his way to God the Creator, but we are dependent upon revelation to know of God the Redeemer. His way of salvation is not to be searched out by the mind of man unassisted.

Nicodemus, as a Pharisee, was concerned about the minutia of the law's requirements. He wanted to know the signs of the kingdom. He wanted to know how Jesus related to all this. Jesus pointed to another of the Heavenly things that Nicodemus was missing. In all the detail, one of the main points had been forgotten. God loves you. This is a message from the spiritual and is unlike the earthly. Then too, Nicodemus learned that Jesus is God's one and only Son, given to save the believers.

Nicodemus Learned About the Importance of Belief

Perhaps Nicodemus was like the rich young ruler, who wanted to know what he could do to inherit eternal life.[4] Jesus' answer to the man of wealth was to sell all he had, give the proceeds to the poor, and then come and follow Jesus. To man, the biggest obstacle is getting rid of what separates him from God. In the rich young ruler's case, it was his material wealth. But the second part is all-important: follow Jesus.

---

[4] Luke 18:18-25

In the case of Nicodemus, it was not mere wealth that was his obstacle. Perhaps it was his knowledge as a Pharisee, his ties to the material world, his hopes for a material messianic kingdom, a resistance against receiving Jesus, a reluctance to come out into the open and follow the Master. To him was given the challenge to turn to the matters of the Spirit, to know that God loved him, and to accept God's Son. "Whoever believes in him is not condemned, but whoever does not believe stands condemned already because he has not believed in the name of God's one and only Son" (John 3:18).

Jesus and Nicodemus were talking together at night. Jesus warned that "men loved darkness instead of light because their deeds were evil" and that one who does evil "will not come into the light for fear that his deeds will be exposed" (John 3:19, 20). Jesus challenged Nicodemus to accept the Light that God had sent into the world, even God's one and only Son.

This chapter ends with another testimony from John the Baptist, but the words form a fitting summary of what Nicodemus learned: "Whoever believes in the Son has eternal life, but whoever rejects the Son will not see life, for God's wrath remains on him" (John 3:36).

THE HEAVENLY SUPERIOR TO THE EARTHLY (3:22-4:42)

The Christ Superior to John (3:22-36)

More testimony is given about Jesus in John 3:22-36. He left the Jerusalem area and went into the countryside of Judea. While He and His disciples were carrying on a ministry there, John and his disciples were ministering and baptizing about thirty miles north of Jerusalem at Aenon near Salim. John continued his wholehearted support of Jesus. The friend of the bridegroom works to see that everything is prepared for the wedding, all the arrangements are made, the bride is protected, and the details are accounted for; but at the sound of the bridegroom's voice, the friend steps aside and puts everything in the hands of the one for whom all this was done. Even so, John recognized that Jesus must become the center of attention, and he rejoiced to see His coming. John was only a man among men, but the Christ brought His witness from Heaven. To accept Him is to gain the true life.

John identified himself with the earthly and Jesus with the Heavenly (John 3:31).

When Jesus testifies about the Heavenly, He tells of what he has actually experienced and observed. God has given the Holy Spirit to others in some degree, and such a gift may enable them to prophesy in part[5] or to work other limited miracles. But to Jesus, God gives the Spirit without limit (John 3:34). His wisdom and power are complete.

Living Water Superior to Well Water (4:1-38)

John 4:1-3 forms a transition paragraph explaining Jesus' departure from Judea and His return to Galilee. The Pharisees are associated with His leaving. As Jesus' popularity grew, the resistance of the Jewish religious leaders also increased. Jesus did not wish to antagonize His opponents so much that they would murder Him before He had time to prepare His disciples to continue His work. He withdrew from Judea, where the opposition was strongest. About this time, John was put in prison (Mark 1:14). He had many Galilean disciples, and probably some of them now were ready to follow Jesus.

Jacob's well (John 4:6) is one of those rare Biblical sites that can be positively identified today. Genesis 33:18, 19 tells that Jacob came to Shechem and bought some land. No mention of a well is made in Genesis, but Jacob naturally would dig one where he expected to live for some time. The town of Sychar (John 4:5) is not so easily identified. Some think it is Shechem, about a mile west of the well. Others think it is the modern Askar, which is north of the well and closer than Shechem.

---

[5]1 Corinthians 13:9.

The sixth hour (John 3:6) would be twelve noon by Jewish time, but six in the morning or six in the evening by the Roman way of counting time. If this Gospel narrative was written at Ephesus toward the close of the first century, the author may well have used the Roman method that was familiar to his readers. Probably, Jesus and His disciples traveled by day, and then meals and rest came at the end of the day. Thus, six in the evening is indicated. That would be about sunset.

John's note that "Jews do not associate with Samaritans" requires a history lesson to understand. When the Assyrians conquered the Northern tribes of Israel (of which Samaria was the capital), many of the Jews were deported, and people of other nations were moved to Israel. The native Israelites and these foreigners intermarried, producing a nation of mixed races and mixed religions (2 Kings 17:22-33). When pure-blooded Jews returned from the Babylonian captivity to rebuild Jerusalem, there was mutual animosity between them and the Samaritans, and it continued until the time of Jesus.

The woman Jesus met at Jacob's well asked for the water· Jesus offered (John 4:10-15), but she was thinking on the earthly level. She wanted water to slake her physical thirst and make her daily trips to the well unnecessary. But again Jesus was speaking of the Heavenly. He would give her water that would supply eternal life.

"Our fathers worshiped on this mountain" (John 4:20). The woman referred to Mount Gerizim, plainly seen nearby. The Samaritans once had built a temple there. Their temple had been destroyed before the time of Jesus on earth, but they continued to worship on the mountain. The woman implied that a prophet should be able to tell which was the proper place to worship.

Jesus' answer would have surprised orthodox Jews as much as it did this Samaritan woman. "God is spirit" (John 4:24), just as God is light (1 John 1:5) and God is love (1 John 4:8).

He is definitely Heavenly and not earthly. God is not bound by places and things. This would be earthly. We are earthly, at least in part; but our worship or service to Him must be spiritual. At the same time, Jesus does not wish us to cut loose from the moorings of truth. Being spiritual does not mean that man is left to wander at will through his subjective feelings for his guide in spiritual worship. Jesus spoke to one who was entangled in the false notions of Samaritan worship. These could not be made true just by putting the label of "spiritual" on them. There must be spirit and truth. Jesus came to lead men to both, and His Word is now our guide in worship.

"'I know that Messiah' (called Christ) 'is coming'"(John 4:25). The Samaritans were looking for a Messiah, but they accepted only the first five books of the Old Testament, those written by Moses. This limited their view of the Messiah. They did not expect an anointed King, the son of David. Rather, they looked for a prophet like Moses. He would be a teacher of the law, one who would understand all things and explain them correctly.

"Could this be the Christ?" (John 4:29). When the woman went to the townspeople, she announced Jesus as the one who had told her everything she ever did. This certainly was an exaggeration, but Jesus had told her enough to convince her that He was aware of all things. But the question is framed in the Greek as though it is a remote possibility. Could this possibly be the Christ? The woman gave this cautious question rather than a positive statement, but she had enough conviction to bring the whole town to see Jesus. Many believed because of her testimony, even before they heard Jesus himself.

"Four months more and then the harvest" (John 4:35). Wheat and barley probably grew around the well where Jesus was sitting. Perhaps the disciples had been estimating how long it would be before the very crops in sight would be ripe. If this is so, one should be able to calculate the time of year. Harvest in this area is in May and early June. Four months before this would be January or early February. This would be a cold, wet time to be traveling. Jesus' concern was not with the earthly crops, however, but the harvest of souls ready right now for the gathering. The people of Sychar were thronging out to see Jesus. These were the fields ripe for harvest.

"Many of the Samaritans . . . believed" (John 4:39). This is an instance where a most unlikely prospect brought unexpected results. The Samaritans had great obstacles to overcome before they could listen to a Jew, let alone accept Him as the Messiah. Here we see the power of testimony given by a lone woman, a Samaritan, and about a Jew. Then Jesus gave His own testimony. No miracles were given as signs, but when the people heard Jesus for themselves, they were convinced. For two days, He stayed with them. They hailed Him as the "Savior of the world" (John 4:42). The expression occurs again in 1 John 4:14. *Savior* was a word applied particularly to God in the Old Testament. In New Testament writings, it is applied to Jesus as well. Here, the Samaritans used it to mean the Messiah. They were elated. They had gained a glimpse of the Heavenly. Jesus is not only the Savior of the Jews. He is the Savior of the World!

A PACKAGE OF SURPRISES (4:1-42)

Jesus was a package preacher. He enjoyed giving people unopened packages of truth and allowing them to discover the significance of the contents for themselves. Time after time, Jesus sent an individual on his way with an armful of packages he would be struggling to open for the rest of his life. One such person was the Pharisee, Nicodemus. Another was the Samaritan woman.

The First Surprise: He Spoke to Her

Jesus and His disciples were returning to Galilee from Judea. They could go by any of several routes. The ordinary way for a Jew was to cross the Jordan near Jericho, proceed north on the eastern side of the river, and then cross back into Galilee just south of the Sea of Galilee. This was done to avoid going through the territory of the Samaritans. The deep-seated hatred between the Jews and Samaritans made it advisable to stay out of one another's reach. But in times of emergency, the Jew might feel it necessary to use the short, quick route through Samaria. It would still be a three-day trip.

The Scripture says, "Now he had to go through Samaria" (John 4:4). The reason is not given. It was not a geographical necessity. There were alternate routes. Perhaps the pressure of enemies made it necessary to leave suddenly and in an unusual direction. This was probably about the time John the Baptist was put in prison (Matthew 4:12), and this may have added to the necessity. Or it simply may have been the will of God for Him to go that way.

While the disciples went into the town of Sychar to buy food, Jesus sat down at Jacob's well, tired at the close of a day's journey. If this is six o'clock in the evening, the way Romans indicated time, it would fit the arrival of a woman to draw her evening water.

Jesus asked this woman for a drink. This was the first surprise. A strange man did not speak to a strange woman. This was not the custom. But more than this, He was a Jew, and she was a Samaritan. This erected a barrier that could not be ignored. Furthermore, if she drew water for Him in her jar, He would be drinking from a Samaritan receptacle, a most unusual thing for a Jew to do.

The Second Surprise: He Had Living Water

When the woman expressed her surprise that He made the request, Jesus gave her a package to puzzle over. He told her if she only realized who this was asking for water, she would be asking Him for living water.

Now what is living water? It was ordinary to refer to water of a flowing stream or spring as living water. This was in the physical realm, however, and Jesus was not speaking of that. As water is to earthly life, so this living water is to eternal life, the true life. So what is this living water? Jesus did not mean himself as the living water. He was the one who had it and could supply it. Jesus was saying that His teaching, God's revelation, was the living water that could nourish and keep the soul alive. The figure was used in the

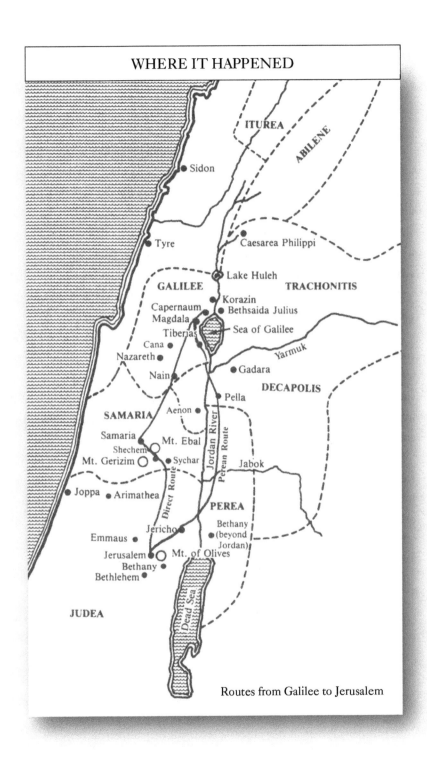

WHERE IT HAPPENED

Routes from Galilee to Jerusalem

Old Testament: "Come, all you who are thirsty, come to the waters" (Isaiah 55:1); "They have forsaken me the fountain of living waters" (Jeremiah 2:13, KJV); "As the rain and the snow come down from heaven . . . so is my word that goes out from my mouth," [declares the Lord] (Isaiah 55:10, 11).

Some would press the figure farther and feel that Jesus had reference to the Holy Spirit in His words *living water*. In fact, later in the Gospel of John, these words of Jesus are recorded: "If anyone is thirsty, let him come to me and drink. Whoever believes in me, as the Scripture has said, streams of living water will flow from within him." John adds the explanation: "By this he meant the Spirit, whom those who believed in him were later to receive. Up to that time the Spirit had not been given, since Jesus had not yet been glorified" (John 7:37-39; see also 1 Corinthians 12:13).

There is no reason Jesus could not have referred to both the truth of His teaching and the gift of the Spirit by His figure "living water." But how much of this would the Samaritan woman understand? When she started opening the package, she looked at it in a materialistic way. She asked Jesus, "Where do you get it? How can you carry it to someone else? Are you greater than Jacob?"

Jesus helped her unwrap the package. He explained that the living water would become "a spring of water welling up to eternal life." She decided to accept it, but still was earthbound in her concern. She would never be thirsty again; she would not have to come to this well (John 4:15).

The Third Surprise: He Knew Her Past

Jesus handed her another package. "Go, call your husband and come back" (John 4:16). The woman decided this package was better left wrapped up. She tried to hand it back to Jesus. "I have no husband," she replied. Jesus then proceeded to unwrap the package for her. "You have had five husbands, and the man you now have is not your husband" (John 4:17, 18).

When this was brought to light, the woman thought she had better offer a package of her own to divert attention from the subject of her husbands and her non-husband. So she introduced a subject long debated between Jews and Samaritans. Was Jerusalem or Mount Gerizim the proper place to worship God?

The Fourth Surprise: Neither Here nor There

Now it was Jesus' turn to open a package. He did not hesitate to do so, but His conclusions gave the woman another surprise. To carry out the commands of the Scriptures, the Jews maintained, a person must worship in the one true temple in Jerusalem. The Samaritans, however, maintained that Mount Gerizim, here within the sight of the Samaritan woman and Jesus, was the holy mountain. They had erected a rival temple there. It had been destroyed years before (by John Hyrcanus in 129 B.C.), but worship continued on the mountain, as it does even to this day by a people clinging to their Samaritan lineage. The Samaritan woman naturally thought that Jesus would defend the beliefs of His Jewish heritage; but He said no word for or against either Jerusalem or Gerizim, no word to settle the ancient quarrel. Instead, Jesus introduced the important point that the time was just then coming when the worship of God would not be bound either to Jerusalem or Gerizim. The sacrifice and regulations of the old covenant were of the letter, and earthly worship was to be of the spirit, that part of man that most readily responds and relates to the Spirit of God. After all, God is spirit and not flesh. On the other hand, though Jerusalem would cease to have a monopoly on worship, Jesus was not saying the Samaritans were right. They had introduced false claims and false practice. This new worship Jesus spoke of must be both in spirit and in truth.

The Fifth Surprise: Jesus Is the Messiah

The woman was not prepared to carry the subject further in this direction. She had heard the question discussed before, but not by a prophet. Still she had to try to get ahead of Jesus some way. Previously she had tried to slow Him down by asking if He was claiming to be greater than Jacob. Now it had become evident that He was some kind of prophet. So she gave Jesus one final package. The ultimate prophet would be the Messiah. Would Jesus at least admit the superiority of the Messiah? When they began opening this package, Jesus gave the Samaritan woman the greatest surprise of all. Jesus declared, in effect, "I am the Messiah" (John 4:26).

The Disciples' Surprise

Just then, Jesus' disciples returned with the provisions they had bought. Now it was the disciples' turn to be surprised. What was Jesus doing talking to this strange woman? She was a Samaritan woman at that. And one might wonder just what kind of woman she was. Yet none of the disciples dared question Jesus about her.

The disciples had another surprise. Jesus did not eat. He must have kept to himself, deep in His own thoughts. When urged to eat, He assured them He had food they did not know about. Once again the spiritual was transcending the physical. To do the will of God was His food. Could this be related to the beginning of the passage, "Now he had to go through Samaria" (John 4:4)? It was the will of God that this Samaritan woman receive the seed of the gospel, a sip of living water, a glimpse of the true life. She in turn stirred up the whole town to come to see and hear this one who claimed to be the Messiah.

Then the disciples were surprised to see the townspeople coming out to meet Jesus. Here was a harvest that could not wait. The seed had been so recently sown, but this spiritual field was already overdue. Once more, the spiritual transcended the physical. Their crops might not be ready for four more months, but their souls were ready for harvesting that day.

Many Samaritans Believed

When the Samaritan woman left Jesus at the well the first time and went back into the town, she did not take her water jar with her. Did she forget it? Or did she leave it as a pledge to come back?

In either case, the forsaken jar was a sign that she had found something more important.

John's Gospel is a report of testimonies, and the Samaritan woman gave her testimony. it was so strong that some believed because of what she told. Others came to see and hear more. Many became believers "because of his words" (John 4:41).

This was an exceptional occasion. Jesus gave His disciples instruction in this period to go only to the people of Israel (Matthew 10:5, 6). But it was the will of God that the seed be sown among the Samaritans; and for two days, Jesus gave instruction in the heart of Samaritan land, at the foot of their holy place of worship. When Philip the evangelist came preaching in Samaria over three years later (Acts 8:5), how many of his converts were people who had heard Jesus preach at this time? When He was there in person, many declared, "We know that this man really is the Savior of the world" (John 4:42).

MEET THE PEOPLE

John has written a "spiritual" Gospel, which tells of truths beyond the world we can see with our physical eyes. But he also has an interest in historical events, real places, and living people. He has his share of the individuals named in the other Gospels, but he is second only to Luke in designating individuals he alone tells about. His characters have an individuality that gives them personality. John the Baptist is a voice crying the wilderness. Nathanael is without guile. Nicodemus is the inquiring scholar, and Judas, the treacherous thief. One cannot help but admire Peter for his daring devotion, and the Samaritan woman for her zeal to spread the good news. These are not fictional characters, but real people in the company of Jesus. We can discern the spiritual blindness of Caiaphas, the weakness of Pilate, and the joy of Mary Magdalene at the resurrection of Jesus.

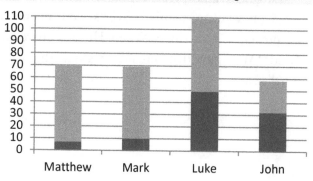

Individuals Noted in the Gospels

Gospel	Total Number Named	Named in One Only	Named in More Than One
Matthew	70	7	63
Mark	69	10	59
Luke	109	49	60
John	58	32	26

CHAPTER FOUR

The Call to Believe
John 4:43-6:71

How can Jesus prove to a lost and dying world that He himself is the only way to true life? By affirmation, He can simply declare the truth. He has the authority. But will the people listen? Will they recognize Him as God's Son? What of reason then? Can He use cold logic to lead them to the truth? Not if their feelings are strong in another direction. Can He use the testimony of others about himself and have the truth established by supporting witnesses? Not if the people refuse to believe the witnesses. Surely, then, by demonstration people can be convinced, can't they? If He can show His power by miracles, they will have to accept His message, won't they? Even so, it is possible to acknowledge the miracle on the surface, but miss the spiritual truth established in the depth. How can Jesus win people to himself, as He must do to bring new life? People come to Him by their own commitment. If a person puts his trust in Jesus, then all these proofs have their proper place and all of life begins to fall into place. Jesus is the only way to true life, but the only way to Jesus is by faith.

THE WAY TO CONVINCE (4:43-5:15)

Unless You People See Miraculous Signs (4:43-54)

Jesus' arrival in Galilee is introduced in John's Gospel by a curious combination of statements. First, notice is given that Jesus had used the saying "a prophet has no honor in his own country" (John 4:44), but in the next verse, John tells that the Galileans welcomed Jesus. How are these both true, and why put them alongside one another? The key to this seeming contradiction lies in the two levels John is writing about, the earthly and the Heavenly. On the surface of things, Jesus was welcomed in Galilee. The people were proud and excited about the miracles He had performed in Jerusalem. How He had challenged the authorities in the temple! How He had taught the people! It was great to have a Galilean so captivating in the nation's center in Jerusalem, and Jesus received a hero's welcome as He came into Galilee. This was all on the earthly level, however. When Jesus taught of His Father, of the spiritual truths, of repentance, of love and commitment to himself, this was another matter. When it came to His deeper teaching, Jesus was rejected and without honor.

As an example of a healing miracle, the story of a nobleman is given (John 4:46-53). This was a royal official, or a "nobleman," as the King James Version translates the word. The Greek word means literally "one pertaining to the king." Herod Antipas was king of Galilee, and this official probably was attached to his court or his army. (Some later followers of Jesus may have been influenced by this man: Joanna, whose husband was the manager of Herod's household,[6] and Manaen, foster brother of Herod the tetrarch.[7]) His home was Capernaum, but Jesus was in Cana, about twenty miles away. The official had a son who was close to death. When the father heard that Jesus was at Cana, he came to beg Him to come and heal his son.

It is significant, however, that in Jesus' response to the nobleman's plea, the verbs are plural. Jesus was not speaking directly to the man; He was addressing the people: "Unless you people see. . . ." These excited, curious crowds who were

---

[6] Luke 8:3.
[7] Acts 13:1.

welcoming Him to Galilee were looking for more miraculous signs. This is one basis for faith, but it is not the best. There are deeper levels to faith; there are deeper levels to life.

"Signs and wonders" (John 4:48-54). Both of these words indicate miracles, but *signs* indicates that the miracles have a meaning to help establish some truth, whereas *wonders* indicates that they are sensational, defying natural explanation and causing people to marvel. We also marvel, but let us not miss the meaning of the signs.

The nobleman would not allow himself to be discouraged or delayed. Again he insisted; "Sir (or Lord), come down before my child dies" (John 4:49). Jesus answered with the simple statement, "You may go. Your son will live" (John 4:50). The man had faith based on Jesus' simple affirmation. It was not until the next day that he had confirmation of the miracle when he met his servants coming to tell him that his son's fever was gone. It had ceased at the very hour when Jesus had given His assurance to the father.

"The seventh hour" (John 4:52). By Jewish time, this would be one in the afternoon. By Roman time, it would be seven in the evening (or morning, but evening is more likely). Here again, the Roman time fits well. If the father arrived in the evening, after a trip of over twenty miles, uphill most of the way, and Jesus' statement was made at 7:00 P.M., then it is easily understood why the man did not begin his return until the next day. He met his servants as he traveled the road back in daylight.

"So he and all his household believed" (John 4:53). This was a deeper faith than that which had originally brought the nobleman to Jesus.

Jesus had done miracles in Jerusalem, causing many people to believe in Him (John 2:23). This healing of the official's son was not the second of His miracles, but the second one done in Galilee (John 4:54). The first is recorded in John 2:1-11.

Another Man Believed (5:1-15)

The next episode takes place in Jerusalem. Some scholars complain that the Gospel of John gives evidence of having some of the material moved around from the original order of the author. They point out that Jesus is in Galilee at the close of chapter 4 and at the beginning of chapter 6, but He is in Jerusalem in chapter 5. The proposal is made that chapter 7 should be put before chapter 5. This would make for fewer trips and a smoother narrative. Such revisions are not supported by the manuscripts, however, nor by necessities in chronology or geography. The record as we have it simply reflects the trips Jesus was making back and forth between Galilee and Jerusalem. Furthermore, there is a way that chapter 4 relates to chapter 5. One healing resulted in the faith of a family in Galilee and another resulted in both faith and persecution in Jerusalem.

John 5 records action that took place at the time of a feast of the Jews (probably the Passover) and at the pool of Bethesda in Jerusalem. Alongside the pool lay a man who had been ill for thirty-eight years. He was suffering from a type of paralysis. About him was a crowd of invalids, physically handicapped in different ways. Their belief sounds strangely like a superstition. The water of the pool was disturbed periodically, and the first one to enter the pool after this disturbance was supposed to be healed. This is what the paralytic man believed, as we see in John 5:7, but he had never been able to jump in before someone else could get there before him. Notice that the Scripture does not affirm any magic healing by the pool: that is, if verse 4 is not a part of the original text. This verse explains that an angel stirred the water at times, and the first to enter the pool after this was healed of whatever ailments he had. The oldest and most trustworthy manuscripts do not include these lines, however. It is likely that some scribe wrote them in the margin to explain why the invalids were waiting by the pool. Most newer translations place it in a note rather than the text. Besides its being textually unlikely and intrinsically doubtful, a natural explanation is possible. The present-day Virgin's Pool at Jerusalem is fed by underground springs that are intermittent. They flow for a time, stop when a siphoning effect is exhausted, and then start again when enough water is built up in the sources. Such action probably accounted for the occasional stirring of the water and led to an unfounded belief in an angel and healing. Naturally, one who was not very sick would be able to get into the pool first, and might easily imagine he was healed.

By counting the Passovers recorded in John (John 2:23; 5:1; 6:4; 11:55), one concludes that the length of Jesus' ministry was three years and a little more. This is counting the feast mentioned in John 5:1 as a Passover, though the text does not specify what feast is indicated. Some students think it may have been Pentecost in June or the feast of Purim in February or March; but it was probably the Passover feast in March or April.

The pool was most likely called Bethesda, though some manuscripts have Bethzatha and others Bethsaida. It was located near the Sheep Gate, according to the New International Version. The word *gate* is supplied by the translators. The Greek word simply means something pertaining to sheep. Some students think a sheep market or a sheep pool may be meant. In any case, the gate or market or pool probably was associated with sheep to be sacrificed in the temple, and therefore was close to the temple area.

The paralytic was alongside the pool; he had desperate hopes but no results. Jesus confronted him and gave a question not hard to answer. "Do you want to get well?" (John 5:6). The implied answer was, "Yes, but I'm not having any success." Having called attention to this, Jesus was ready to give him another solution. He said, "Get up! Pick up your mat and walk" (John 5:8). By that command, the man was challenged to put his trust in Jesus. He did so, and he was healed. In fact, Jesus issued a whole series of challenges when He told the man to pick up his mat and walk. There was a challenge to the faith of the man, both in Jesus and in His healing. There was a challenge against the oral law of the Jews, because this was the

Sabbath and the oral law forbade carrying things on that holy day.[8] There was a challenge to the religious leaders, particularly the Pharisees, who were anxious to see that the oral law was enforced. There was a challenge to the man for obedience in response to the authority of the one in whom he had placed his trust.

This was another step beyond his initial trust in Jesus. When he was halted by the Jewish authorities (John says the "Jews") for carrying his mat on the Sabbath, he explained that he had been told to do so by the one who healed him; but the former paralytic did not know his benefactor.

When John says the "Jews," he means the hostile religious leaders of the Jews. The lame man himself was a Jew. So was John, and so was Jesus. But the ones who stopped the healed man were the Jewish authorities.

Later, Jesus looked him up and found him in the temple. How much later one cannot tell. The man had told the Jewish inquirers that he did not know the man who had healed him. Now Jesus identified himself and gave a further challenge, one that moved beyond concern for the physical to regard for the condition of the soul. "Stop sinning" (John 5:14), which means, "Sin no longer," or, "Give up sin." This is good advice for anyone; we need not suppose that this man had been an exceptionally great sinner. Neither need we suppose "something worse" must refer to still greater physical suffering. It may refer to the eternal consequences of sin.

This man then went to the authorities and told them he could now identify his healer. This need not be interpreted as betraying Jesus, as some maintain. It took courage to face the Jewish authorities again and identify the individual he had been unable to name at the first questioning. Perhaps his wish was not to betray Jesus, but rather to confess Jesus. He may have hoped the miracle would lead the authorities also to believe in the miracle worker.

---

[8] This was set down later in the Mishnaic tractate, I Sabbath 7.2, with implicit reference to empty beds in 10.5.

DOING THE FATHER'S WORK (5:16-47)

One of the most frequent charges against Jesus concerned His activity on the Sabbath. In this case (John 5:16-30), He answered that He was only doing as His Father in Heaven did.

One is not told specifically how the Jews "persecuted" Him (John 5:16). Excluding Him from Jerusalem synagogues, warning the people not to associate with Him or to listen to Him, threatening Him with death if He continued to stay in this area or to teach the people—all of these may have been included in the persecution.

"Not only was he breaking the Sabbath, but he was even calling God his own Father, making himself equal with God" (John 5:18). Some theologians of today seem to have difficulty deciding about Jesus' claims. Did He really claim to be divine? The Jewish religious leaders of Jesus' time had no trouble seeing the implications of what He was doing and saying. They charged that He was making himself equal with God, and Jesus did not deny that charge. He claimed to be divine, the very Son of God. This would indeed have been blasphemy if it had not been true. Jesus, rather than deny it, set out to prove it. In doing so, however, He wanted to make clear His own dependence upon the Father. He did nothing by himself, but sought to please the one who sent Him.

The Role of the Son (16-30)

The healing of the lame man at the pool of Bethesda was a link to the next episode that John records. After working this miracle on the Sabbath, Jesus was forced to defend His action. In His reply, He referred to God as His Father (John 5:17), and the Jewish leaders became still more incensed, accusing Jesus of blasphemy. This presented occasion for the longest discourse of Jesus recorded up to this point in John. Earlier chapters have recorded Jesus' words on the new birth and then on the water of life, but now we see how Jesus presented the role of the Son.

The Son does what God, His Father, does. Although the Sabbath was a special day, God went right on sustaining the world that day as well as other days. And the Son went on healing and doing good on the Sabbath as well as other days: "He can do only what he sees his Father doing" (John 5:19).

Jesus spoke of the love between the Father and Son (John 5:20). Because of this love and harmony, there is understanding and unity in the work that is done by both. As the Father gives life to the physically dead in a bodily resurrection, so the Son can give true life in a spiritual resurrection to those who honor Him. This true life is eternal life, and the person who believes on the Son will not be condemned. In fact, when the spiritually dead hear the voice of the Son and heed His call to believe, they immediately cross over from death to life. Eternity has already begun for the dead who have been brought to the true life. And Jesus has the authority to judge. He is the Son of Man.

After this spiritual resurrection, this rebirth as one who honors the Son of Man, there will also be the resurrection from the physical graves. The good will rise to perfect life and the evil will rise to condemnation (John 5:29).

The Call for Witnesses (31-47)

Beginning in John 5:31, Jesus cites the testimony of a list of witnesses. If He makes His claims without corroboration, He says, this is not sufficient. "There is another who testifies in my favor" (John 5:32). The identification of this other one is made in John 5:37: "And the Father who sent me has himself testified concerning me." The honor given by men meant little to Jesus (John 5:41). He looked beneath the surface and found that "the Jews" lacked the love of God, and therefore they rejected Him who was sent of God. Jesus saw them accepting one another and honoring one another (John 5:44), but everything was done on an earthly level. They failed to penetrate the Heavenly places and recognize the honor and praise that came from God.

John the Baptist is the next witness. He was a human witness, like a lamp compared to God's sunlight (John 5:33-35).

The work that Jesus did is another witness to the truth of His message and the divinity of His person. The Father assigns that work to Him, and this is one way the Father bears witness for His Son. The Son in turn reveals the Father to His children (John 5:36-38).

The Scriptures are called to the witness stand. "You diligently study the Scriptures because you think that by them you possess eternal life. These are the Scriptures that testify about me, yet you refuse to come to me to have life" (John 5:39, 40).

Finally, Moses is called as a witness to accuse those who reject Jesus. Moses wrote of Him; and if they will not believe Moses, how will they believe what Jesus says? (John 5:45-47).

What kind of proof does it take to convince the world that God indeed became flesh and lived among us for a while in the person of His Son, Jesus Christ? The testimony is there. It included statements of authority, appeals to reason, supporting witnesses, demonstration through miracle, and revelation of spiritual truths. Jesus provided ample basis for His plea for man's faith. Man can believe in Jesus with full assurance.

JUST A LITTLE BOY AND JESUS (6:1-24)

"Some time after this," John says (John 6:1). The Greek is an expression often used in this Gospel to denote an indefinite passage of time. The close of chapter 5 told of Jesus while He was in Jerusalem, but the verses following have the Sea of Galilee as their setting. The words *some time after* are suitable for providing such a transition. John is not so much interested in geographical location or even time sequence, but he is showing the buildup of testimonies and miraculous signs along with Jesus' claims and the oppositions He faced.

John alone in the New Testament uses the name "Sea of Tiberias" for the Sea of Galilee.[9] Herod Antipas built the city of Tiberias about the time Jesus began His ministry. The Jews were not pleased with the new town named for a Roman emperor, and it was probably considerably later in the century that the city became important enough to gives its name to the lake.

This was a day to be remembered. It was filled with good news and bad news. First the good news. The disciples had just returned from an evangelistic campaign, and the successes were great. They had preached repentance, healed the sick, and driven out many demons (Mark 6:12, 13). But now the bad news. John the Baptist had been beheaded, and his disciples had buried his remains. Then they came to tell of his death, and the news reached Jesus and His disciples on this very day. They were heartbroken (Matthew 14:12, 13).

In the middle of all this, Jesus said to His disciples, "Come with me by yourselves to a quiet place and get some rest" (Mark 6:31). This was a welcome invitation. The press of the crowds, exhaustion from their trip, and the weight of the tragic news of John the Baptist were taking a toll on their strength. They set out by boat across the Sea of Galilee.

The next development cannot be counted all bad; when they reached the opposite shore, they found a crowd of people already waiting for them (Mark 6:33, 34). This was unfortunate in that they could not continue their solitude, but it was good in that Jesus had compassion on the people and preached the good news of the kingdom to them. But the day wore on—and there was more bad news. Mealtime had long since gone by, and there was nothing to eat. This was a remote spot, and no stores were near. But then, great news! Just a little boy and Jesus were able to feed this whole multitude of five thousand men, besides the women and children

---

[9] Luke 5:1 uses "Lake of Gennesaret."

(Matthew 14:21). The little boy gave all he had—five loaves and two fish—and Jesus did the rest.

Good news again. Jesus' popularity reached a climax on that day. People were so excited and drawn to the words of Jesus and so satisfied with their food that they looked to Jesus as their hero. But bad news, also. The people were so engrossed in their earthly, material desires that they failed to grasp those spiritual insights of Jesus, those challenges to live the true life as children of God. Instead, they wanted to take Jesus by force and make Him a worldly king, a military conqueror.

Then good news. In the evening, Jesus thwarted the worldly plans. He went into a mountain to pray, and sent the disciples away in a boat. But the day was not over, even when darkness came. More bad news. A storm arose that threatened to swamp the disciples' boat. Then it all ended with good news. Jesus came walking on the water and took them to the opposite shore. What a day to remember!

Where and When It Happened (1-4)

It was a beautiful time of the year. Wild flowers in great variety abounded on the hillsides. The rainy season was over, and the crops were ripening. People were on their way to Jerusalem for the Passover—those who were going this year. If Jesus went to Jerusalem for this Passover, there is no record of it. A year before, and two years before, He had attended. Each time, great controversy had resulted, and John tells us about it. The cleansing of the temple, the challenge to Sabbath tradition, the claim that God was His Father, and a teaching that stirred hearts to repentance—these left memories one could not overlook. The law commanded that every male Jew go to Jerusalem three times each year for the main observances, and the Passover was one of them. The Jews, however, had become so scattered that it was impossible for all of them to get to Jerusalem even once each year, let alone three times. Many of those living in far parts of the world counted themselves fortunate if they could return for one visit in a lifetime. Even from Galilee, not everyone went each year.

But what of Jesus? Was He breaking the law if He did not go? One must remember that Jesus was God's Son. He fulfilled the law, but He was not subject to the law in the same way as those who were not the Son. This year, He was at Capernaum when the Passover feast was about to begin. If any place could be called His home at this time, it was Capernaum.

The Sea of Galilee is about six and a half miles wide at its northern end. Jesus decided to set out with His disciples from the vicinity of Capernaum and cross eastward to the other side. But the crowds of people could see the departure and the course of the boat. The excitement was so great that they began running along the shore to keep the boat in view.

Why were the people so excited? Their main interest was in the miracles of healing, the signs that He was performing. Three good results were gained. First, individuals who were healed received relief from their physical suffering. Second, this drew attention to every word Jesus spoke, to every move He made. Third, this was His opportunity to preach and to teach repentance and the coming kingdom, to present a challenge for all to put their faith in Him.

There was another reason for mounting feelings at this time. News of the death of John the Baptist fanned the smoldering coals into flame. There must have been great indignation against Herod and the Roman government that backed him. The people of Galilee always resented the foreign interlopers from Rome and hoped to see them driven out. Now, without John, their hopes for leadership focused all the more on Jesus. They were like sheep without a shepherd. They wanted Jesus to lead them.

What Was the Problem?

This was one of their problems—they needed a leader. When Jesus and His disciples landed on the opposite shore, a crowd had already gathered. They were waiting for Him. More were pouring in by the minute. The hurrying people could be seen along the shore for a long distance. And Jesus had compassion on them. He could have turned the boat southward and avoided the crowd, but He wanted to help them.

Their need went deeper than they realized. They were in their sins. They needed more than a leader; they needed a Redeemer. Jesus healed the sick, but without doubt, His teaching went beyond their physical needs and penetrated to the needs of the spirit.

Several things are remarkable about this episode in the Gospel narrative. For one thing, one does not learn what Jesus taught on this occasion, but only what He did. Another interesting note is that, except for the resurrection of Jesus, this is the only miracle that has been recorded in all four Gospels. Is this because of its importance? It would seem from the description of Jesus' ministry in Galilee that His popularity reached a climax at this point.

A new problem emerged, however. The people had been spontaneous in leaving everything behind to gather about Jesus. He had chosen to land the boat in a remote spot with no sources of food supply. The people had been so engrossed in what was said and done that they had not noticed the passage of the day. The time had come when food was needed for physical strength to return home at the close of an eventful day. Their souls had been fed with spiritual food, but Jesus was practical and knew they were in need of physical food as well.

An Easy Answer (5-13)

Jesus was not ready to provide the answer without having both His disciples and the people struggle with the problem. In putting together the information gained from all four Gospel narratives, it becomes clear that Jesus himself first asked the question about who was going to feed all these people. Why did Jesus ask Philip, "Where shall we buy bread for these people to eat?" He probably wanted to arouse the awareness of the need. When the time came and the disciples realized that they could not provide the needed food, then their faith in Him would be tested. Could He cope with the situation? The other disciples would be asking this along with Philip.

Then the disciples became disturbed and returned to put their own question to Jesus. Yes, how were these people going to get any food? In the meantime, they had been searching throughout the crowd to see how much food was available. This increased the problem because the minute a person was asked if he had any food with him, his immediate reaction would be to realize his hunger all the more.

It is evident that Jesus knew what He was doing from the beginning. He had deliberately steered the boat toward a remote place. He was aware of the passage of time during the day. He knew it would take hours for people to return home. He increased the apprehension by directing their attention to the need. The people, no doubt, were looking for some miraculous sign. After all, had He not changed the water into wine? Had not Moses seen to it that the people were provided manna and quail in the desert? What was going to happen here?

In desperation, Philip said it would take at least two hundred denarii to pay the bill for feeding all these people, even if they could find a place to buy the food. It is impossible to estimate adequately the value of a sum of money in antiquity. One good way to have an impression of the value is to consider what the money would buy. Matthew 20:2 indicates that one denarius would buy a day's work from a laboring man, so two hundred denarii would be about eight months' wages, as the New International Version translates.

Mark 6:38 records that Jesus sent the disciples to see how much bread could be found. They probably searched frantically through the crowd before Andrew reported that one boy had five small barley loaves and two small fish. An ordinary loaf was like a flat bun, and small fish were probably about the size of sardines. Barley seems to have been less expensive than wheat loaves, so this was probably a poor boy's lunch.

The answer seemed to be easy when it came. All that worry was for nothing. A little boy was found with his lunch, five barley loaves and two fish. It is inconceivable that the lunch was taken from him against his will; rather, he must have willingly given it to Jesus.

To serve a meal to over five thousand people is no small task, even with the best of facilities. How could they manage it? A bread line five thousand long would be impossible. Or if someone put out a call, "Come and get your food," there would be a stampede for the spot. Jesus had it planned. Have them seated in groups of fifties and hundreds (Mark 6:39, 40) on the spring grass. Then they could be served in an orderly way, no one would be left out, and confusion would be avoided. The disciples could see to it that each received as much as he wanted.

Where had the little boy planned to spend that day? Had he been going fishing? Had he been going to see a friend in a neighboring town? Had he been on his way to his father's field? In any event, he had decided instead to follow the crowd to see and hear Jesus. After hearing, he was willing to give what he had. It does not take a great person to follow Jesus, but a follower must be willing to give all.

Jesus blessed the loaves and fish, and they were distributed to the people seated by groups on the hillside. As this was done, the supply was multiplied until all were fed.

Afterward, "they gathered them [the pieces left over] and filled twelve baskets" (John 6:13). The Greek has different words for *basket*, but the same word is used here in all four Gospel narratives. It denotes the type of knapsack carried by a Jew when going on a considerable journey, such as a trip to Jerusalem for the Passover. It is likely that each of the disciples had such a basket. It may be that they supplied the ones for this occasion. If not, certainly in such a crowd there would be a number of baskets brought along by people who interrupted their travel in order to join the crowd with Jesus.

The fact that twelve baskets of fragments were taken up serves several purposes. It shows that although the supply was inexhaustible, nevertheless it was wrong to waste God's creation. Then, too, it showed that everyone had enough.

Just a little boy and Jesus were able to feed the multitude. God frequently uses a seemingly small beginning to fulfill His purpose so man cannot mistake the presence of His power.

Gideon started out with thirty-two thousand men, but he won the battle with only three hundred. This was "in order that Israel may not boast ... that her own strength has saved her" (Judges 7:2).

False Answers (14, 15)

Some of the people looked beneath the surface for added meaning from this miracle and came up with false answers. Their first impression was that Jesus was the prophet who was to come into the world.

The prophet is another designation used for the Messiah. Jewish people were looking for the prophet like Moses who was promised in Deuteronomy 18:15. John the Baptist had declared he was not the prophet (John 1:21), but now the people were sure that Jesus was that prophet. Moses was associated with the manna supplied in the wilderness, and now Jesus had supplied food in another place where there were no stores to provide it.

This was on the right track, but they wanted to make Jesus their king. How good it would be to have a king who could provide their food every day in such an easy way, a king who could heal the sick and make whole the wounded soldiers, a king who could lead them against the legions of Rome and be victorious! They had false notions of a militant king and a materialistic kingdom.

Jesus knew some of the people were plotting to acclaim Him as their king against His will. The conquering Romans had installed Herod Antipas as king of Galilee, and Roman troops were there to support him. To acclaim another king would be to start a bloody war. But many of the Galileans thought the time for that had come.

Jesus had shown that He could feed an army by a miracle. If He would provide weapons in the same way, and heal any who might be wounded, how could they lose? But Jesus would not be that kind of a king. He was there to save lives, not destroy them.

That age had no monopoly on false answers. They are still being given today. Men still bring preconceived notions to a study of the account. Some consider it impossible that a miracle of this type could have taken place; so they try to explain away the power of Jesus. They say maybe half the people brought their own lunches, and all they did was share with one another under the influence of Jesus' preaching. Such a suggestion is far more incredible than the miracle as described. If it were true, the disciples' report would be false. They said there was no food there other than the lad's (Mark 6:38). Besides, John would be deceitful in not reporting that the people brought out their lunches later and ate them, if this is what happened. Furthermore, the reaction of the people shows they recognized that a great miracle had taken place. No sharing of lunches would have led them to such a pitch of enthusiasm. Then there were the fragments. If the people had shared their lunches, nothing would have been left over. Thus, the gathering of the fragments is useful in another way—to show that the miracle really happened. Either the miracle was real, or deceit and fabrication have lined the account. We cannot believe that this story is a deceitful invention. Too many people were involved, and the accounts came from too close to the happening.

Jesus Always Makes a Way (16-24)

When the people threatened to take Jesus by force and make Him king after their own notion, Jesus left the crowds and went into the mountain to pray.

The disciples set off across the lake for Capernaum, using the boat in which they had come earlier in the day. Other records make it clear that this is what Jesus had told them to do. (See Matthew 14:22; Mark 6:45.)

They were crossing near the northern shore, where perhaps the width was a little less than the full six and a half miles. They had been in a country place belonging to a city called Bethsaida.[10]

Now Jesus sent them toward another Bethsaida, a suburb north of Capernaum (Mark 6:45). The name *Bethsaida* means a fishing place. It was not surprising that the same name was given to two villages beside the Sea of Galilee. Any place on its shore might have been a fishing place.

It was dark before the disciples got very far. The storm came from the west, and they had to row hard to make any progress against it. They had covered three or four miles, not much more than half their journey, when they saw Jesus approaching on the water. This was not a calm, placid surface. There were high, white-capped waves with deep troughs between them. They would intermittently bring the figure of Jesus in and out of view. No wonder the disciples thought they were seeing a ghost in the night (Matthew 14:26).

Once in the boat, Jesus along with His disciples came immediately to the other side. One cannot be sure whether the storm was miraculously stopped or whether the boat completed its crossing in a miraculous way. After the miraculous signs of the day, the disciples would hardly have been surprised at one more.

BREAD FOR ETERNAL LIFE (6:25-71)

The people found Jesus "on the other side of the lake" (John 6:25). The location is Capernaum (John 6:59). The people had last seen Jesus on the east side of the Sea of Galilee, where He had fed the five thousand the day before. In the night, Jesus had walked on the water to join His disciples in a boat, and now the people found Him again on the west side of the lake.

---

[10] Luke 9:10, KJV. The New International Version of that verse seems to indicate that they were at the town itself, but Luke 9:12 shows that they were not.

"When did you get here?" they asked (John 6:25). Jesus had been on the eastern shore at nightfall. His disciples had left in a boat without Him, and He had gone into the hills alone to pray. Many of the people had spent the night in the open, waiting for Him to return. Failing to find Him in the morning, they had gone to Capernaum, and there He was. The people wondered when and how He had come to Capernaum ahead of them. Jesus ignored the question and went on with more significant thoughts.

"You are looking for me, not because you saw the miraculous signs [that is, you did not see the real meaning of the feeding of the five thousand and the other miracles] but because you ate the loaves and had your fill" (John 6:26). They were more interested in a free meal than in free salvation. Do some of us have the same problem?

"Do not work for food that spoils" (John 6:27), but spend your labor and attention to gain the food that is eternal. With all your work, you cannot earn salvation; it is a gift from the Son of Man. On Him, God the Father has placed His seal of approval. The miraculous ability of Jesus was God's seal of approval on Him. The feeding of the five thousand was a part of that seal.

"Work . . . for food that endures to eternal life," said Jesus (John 6:27). What did that mean? The people wanted Him to be specific: "What must we do?" they asked (John 6:28). Jesus replied, "The work of God is this: to believe in the one he has sent" (John 6:29). The word for *believe* in the Greek is in the present tense; so it expresses a continuing life of faith. To believe in is to have an obedient faith leading to true life.

The crowds asked to see another miracle to prove that Jesus was the one whom God had sent. They spoke of the manna in the wilderness. It had fed their ancestors for forty years, and Jesus had given them only one meal. What else could He do? But Jesus refused their demand for another miracle at that time. He wanted them to see that He himself was the true bread from Heaven (John 6:30-33).

SPREAD THE GOSPEL

Explanation

To formulate this chart, each Gospel was studied to determine how many verses were devoted to report (a) the preaching of Jesus, (b) His conversations, (c) the transition from one scene to another and the setting or action of an episode, along with the editorial comments of the author, and (d) the description of a miracle.

The numbers to the left of the chart indicate the percentage of verses found in each Gospel devoted to each of the four categories listed above. Added together, the number of the four categories for each Gospel will total 100%.

Observation

As a "spiritual" Gospel, John might be expected to contain little about the setting involved in the narrative. Instead, one might expect preaching to dominate, as it does in the Synoptics, or miracles.

Just the opposite is true, however. John contains more on setting (32%) than any of the Synoptics. (The Synoptics average only 20% in this category.) Miracle is the smallest group (8%, compared with a 14% Synoptic average). John stands in sharp contrast with the Synoptics in the area of preaching, also, devoting only 20% of his Gospel to this category. The Synoptics, on the average, spend 44% on preaching.

The largest category in John is private conversations, with 40% of his material falling in this group. This is nearly double the Synoptic average of 22%.

This comparison makes it apparent that the spiritual nature of John's Gospel does not contradict reality. John wrote of real events that happened to real people in a real time in real places, and he carefully documents the setting. If he were inventing the events to make merely a "spiritual" point, he could not have been so specific on settings and he would surely have made more of the miracles.

It also seems apparent that John made a deliberate effort to avoid what was already well known from the Synoptics. This explains the little time spent on preaching and the greater amount spent on the private conversations.

Questions

1. Why did John show more interest in recording the teaching of Jesus through conversations than through preaching (in fact, the word for preaching is not even used in the Gospel of John)?

2. How does the setting of a block of material relate to the instruction that Jesus has to give?

3. How does one explain the importance of miraculous signs in John and still the fact that Mark and Luke give more space to describing the miracles?

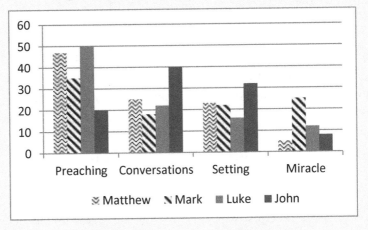

	Percentage of Material Devoted				
Material	Matthew	Mark	Luke	Synoptic Average	John
Preaching	47	35	50	44	20
Conversations	25	18	22	22	40
Setting	23	22	16	20	32
Miracle	5	25	12	14	8

Bread and Water

These are basic requirements for man's physical body. They are enough to keep a man alive. Jesus told the Samaritan woman He could provide living water (John 4:14), and now we see Him telling the crowds at Capernaum that He himself is the true bread for eternal life. His message sounds so simple. It deals with the basics of life, but it is difficult to understand the full meaning. In fact, the people around Jesus misunderstood Him. As Jesus answered one misunderstanding after another, He unfolded His teaching. Must we work for this bread? How do we know where to find it? How much does it cost? How can we believe this Jesus? What will happen if He is not accepted? These questions have been asked anew in each generation since that day in Capernaum.

Work for the Bread of Life (25-29)

Many of the people who surrounded Jesus at this time had been present at the feeding of the five thousand. These were the men who wanted to make Him king—their own kind of king. After the others had long since departed, they had watched for Jesus to come back down from the mountain. They thought He could not cross the sea because there was only one boat available, and He had not used that (John 6:22).

All through the night, they had kept their vigil. What they did not know was that Jesus had walked on the water in the midst of the storm, rejoined His disciples, and arrived at the opposite shore. In the morning, some boats from Tiberias were found in the same area. Perhaps they had been forced ashore by the storm the night before. After the remnant of the crowd was satisfied that Jesus was no longer in the vicinity, they jammed the boats and went over to Capernaum. That was the most likely place to find Jesus, since it had become His headquarters. Where they located Him is uncertain. The discourse that followed ended in the synagogue, but perhaps it included several confrontations before it was completed there.

The people's first question was, "When did you get here?" One might expect them to ask, "How did you get here?" Perhaps they were disturbed at the thought of their waiting through the night for nothing if He had already made the crossing ahead of them.

At any rate, Jesus did not even answer their question, but came right to the point, just as He had done with Nicodemus. This was a situation where they should be answering to Him. The pertinent question was, "Why are you following me?" Jesus did not even stop to ask that question, but gave the answer directly. They may have thought they were following Him to witness some miraculous sign that would indicate to them God's will and show them God's anointed one. But really, they were seeking their own materialistic, selfish gain. They had received a free meal and were interested in enjoying many more. But this was food that would spoil. It was not what they had eaten physically the day before that was most worthwhile. It was the food having to do with the spirit and eternity. This was what the Son of Man was giving to them.

Jesus used some profoundly meaningful words to get their attention aimed in the right direction: *signs, eternal life, Son of Man, God the Father, seal of approval* (John 6:26, 27). Still, they passed over all these, but latched on to the word work. Indeed, Jesus had told them to work for the food that endures to eternal life. Now the men asked, "What must we do to do the works God requires?" (John 6:28).

The answer was simple—"The work of God is this: to believe in the one whom he has sent" (John 6:29).

No More Hunger (30-40)

This appeal to believe prompted another question. "If you are the one sent of God," they said in essence, "then what miraculous signs can you perform for us?" (John 6:30). What audacity and blindness! They had just seen the feeding of the multitudes the day before. They had been seeing the healing of the sick for weeks. Still they asked, "What sign will you perform?" Jesus did not stoop to tell them of the walking on the water.

They indicated what sign they wanted to see. After all, Moses had been responsible for bringing down manna from Heaven. Now could Jesus do that? The implication was that this was a miracle greater than multiplication of loaves and fish. Jesus' reply tried to lead them a step further in their understanding. Moses had not done that, but God had provided the manna. Then Jesus associated himself with God in a way that Moses never did. God was Jesus' Father, and Jesus himself was the true bread that God had sent down from Heaven. At this time He left His identification with the bread in the third person, but the meaning was clear. Jesus also emphasized differences between the physical manna and the true bread of God.

The people followed what He was saying up to this point. They asked that they might have this bread. In reply, Jesus changed from the third person to the first person: "I am the bread of life" (John 6:35). This is the first of the great "I am's" that Jesus spoke and John recorded in this Gospel. Six more are to come: "I am the light of the world" (John 8:12), "1 am the gate [or door]" (John 10:7, 9), "I am the good shepherd" (John 10:11, 14), "I am the resurrection and the life" (John 11:25), "I am the way and the truth and the life" (John 14:6), and "I am the true vine" (John 15:1, 5). Each in a different figure presents the same truth. The divine "I am" of Heaven came to earth to join earthly life to the true life— the Heavenly, eternal life. If a man would feed on this bread, he would never hunger again. This is the will of the Father, that through the Son and a man's belief in Him, a man will not be lost but be raised up "at the last day" (John 6:40).

The bread of life is Jesus Christ himself. He satisfies the hunger of the soul; He brings true life to a spirit left lifeless by sin and separation from God; He makes righteous and sustains the relationship with God as bread nourishes the physical body. As long as Jesus holds His place in a person's life, there will be no hunger nor thirst. "But. . . you have seen me and still you do not believe" (John 6:36). Those asking for more miracles had seen not only the feeding of the five thousand; most of them had seen many other miracles in Capernaum (Matthew 11:20-24).

They had ample reason to think that Jesus was all He claimed to be; but they did not commit their lives to Him, they did not put their trust in Him, they did not believe. Some of them wanted to capture Jesus and use Him for their purposes (John 6:15), but they did not give themselves to be used for His purposes.

"All that the Father gives me will come to me" (John 6:37). God knows in advance who will accept Christ and be true to Him. On this basis, God gives the faithful to Christ. This does not exclude anyone who chooses to come to Him. God does not want any to perish (2 Peter 3:9); He wants all men to know the truth (1 Timothy 2:4).

The Price of True Bread (41-51)

The Jews objected to Christ's claim that He had come down from Heaven. They knew Joseph and Jesus' mother. They thought that Jesus had been born just like anyone else. How could He say He had come down from Heaven? Jesus did not choose to tell about His miraculous birth, but He repeated and strengthened His claim. He came from God; He had seen the Father; He told the truth; He was the living bread that could give eternal life.

The crowd was beginning to feel the pressure. They had wanted to put Jesus on the spot, to make Him demonstrate His power. But they did not want to commit themselves, especially when it came to this matter of admitting that Jesus was from Heaven while all of them were from earth. After all, they had known His father and mother. At least they thought Joseph and Mary to be His parents. This does not suggest that John did not know or did not accept the account of Jesus' virgin birth as found in Matthew and Luke. All John has done here is to report faithfully the words of a murmuring crowd, and the doubt he has expressed is theirs, not his. This record indicates that the events surrounding Jesus' birth were not common knowledge at this time and helps to confirm the note that changing the water into wine was His first miraculous sign (John 2:11).

In other words, He had grown up without any aura of the supernatural. Certainly, He had been outstanding even in His childhood, but He had not been using divine powers obvious to all. Now, however, He was asking them to accept Him as descended from God, the very bread of life.

Jesus warned them to leave their doubts and stop speaking against Him. To accept Jesus is to hear the very call of God. God draws men; His Scriptures teach men (Isaiah 54:13).

If an individual is standing within listening distance of God, then He will accept Jesus. And the one who believes has already begun his possession of eternal life (John 6:47). After all, those who ate the manna in the wilderness ended up in death anyway. But the one who eats of the bread of life will not die. The price of this bread is that the flesh of Jesus must be given to bring true life to the world, and the price to the individual is that he believes on Jesus. To put one's faith in Jesus included a commitment that this crowd was growing more and more reluctant to make. This commitment is marked by the eating of the bread of life.

How is this to be understood? There were religions that included in their practice the eating of raw flesh. This was extremely repulsive to think about. Furthermore, the thought of human sacrifice was horrible to the Jews and the Romans alike. In all the Roman Empire, every attempt was made to stamp out any practice of human sacrifice. The Druids were the last in the first-century Roman world to be stopped. Was this the type of thing Jesus was suggesting? Surely not. More than all of this was the question of eating human flesh—this would be cannibalism. The possibility that Jesus was suggesting something along this line was revolting to the Jewish mind. If His saying could not be taken literally, was it spiritual, with no literal association at all? How could it be altogether spiritual, when He spoke of body and blood? These are certainly physical. Then was it figurative, with some kind of symbolic physical action that left the true significance in the spiritual realm? One step further, could it be sacramental in character? Augustine defined a sacrament as a "visible sign of an invisible reality." Was Jesus referring to a true channel for receiving God's saving grace?

Can You Believe? (52-59)

What was the meaning? The Jews asked, "How can this man give us his flesh to eat?" (John 6:52). To the Christian who looks back on this scope from the other side of the cross, it is apparent that Jesus was giving preliminary teaching in anticipation of instituting the Lord's Supper. At the Last Supper, He told His disciples, "Take and eat; this is my body" (Matthew 26:26), but it was the bread He passed to them. Then He took the cup and told them, "Drink from it, all of you. This is my blood of the covenant, which is poured out for many for the forgiveness of sins" (Matthew 26:27, 28), but it was the fruit of the vine that they drank.

Objections are raised that Jesus could not expect these people to understand a connection between this teaching and a sacrament that was to be established later. This is true, but Jesus was not asking them to understand. He was asking them to believe on Him. A degree of understanding must serve as a basis of belief, but greater understanding also follows belief. In the middle ages, a great debate arose as to whether understanding preceded faith or vice versa. Actually it is not a question of either/ or, but both/and. From a little understanding comes faith, and when one looks at things through the eyes of belief in Christ, a far greater understanding results. But this in turn leads to a greater faith, and thus the growth continues. The people in the audience at Capernaum who looked back upon these words of Jesus from a later day of faith would see more in these truths than they saw in the hour they were delivered.

Other skeptics maintain that Jesus did not have that much planned as to what He was teaching. Such teaching ahead of time would require foreknowledge of doctrine and practice still to come in the church. These modern critics say this teaching about eating Jesus' flesh was written by a later believer who simply put words into Jesus' mouth. These critics are the modern counterparts of those who left Jesus that day in Galilee. If God sent Jesus, and He taught the truths of God, He could transcend the boundaries limiting earth-bound men. This, too, is a matter of faith.

But what would these Galileans see in these teachings if they lived before Christ's death and resurrection? One must remember that these people themselves were asking for a sign. They had introduced the example of Moses and the manna from Heaven. Jesus' sermon on the bread of life recorded here in John lies midway between the manna in the wilderness and the loaf of the Communion table. It is the connecting link. These people could have seen the connection with the past if they had believed on Jesus, even though they could not have comprehended the connection with the future until a later time. God had provided the physical manna, and He sent the person Jesus. But Jesus was more than the manna; He was the Son of God. The manna had sustained life for a time, but then the individual had died. The Son of Man was the spiritual food that brought life everlasting. Jesus was not actual bread any more than He was an actual gate (John 10:7). Figuratively, He was bread, and they would partake of His flesh and blood. He must give himself in death, and they must give themselves in belief. Only then could this true bread bring true life.

"Whoever eats my flesh and drinks my blood has eternal life, and I will raise him up at the last day," Jesus said (John 6:54). The believer who has accepted Christ has already entered eternal life and has the promise of the resurrection in the end of time. These words of Jesus naturally call to mind the Lord's Supper, but of course, they mean much more than partaking of the loaf and cup. A spiritual reality is presented both in these words and in the Lord's Supper. Just as Christ was dependent upon the   living Father for sustenance, so the believer feeds spiritually upon the living Son and will live forever.

Those Who Disbelieve (60-71)

"Many of his disciples said, 'This is a hard teaching. Who can accept it?'" (John 6:60). These disciples were not the Twelve, but some of the larger group who had been following Jesus, curious to know more about what He was doing and teaching. They said this teaching was hard to grasp. The difficulty was not only in what Jesus said about eating His flesh and drinking His blood, but also in His claim that God was His Father, that He came down from Heaven, that He was bread greater than the manna of Moses, and that they would have life because of Him.

Jesus asked, "Does this offend you?" (John 6:61). The American Standard Version reads, "Doth this cause you to stumble?" The puzzled disciples were complaining that this difficult teaching was a stumbling block in the way of their understanding and accepting. But there was more to come: "What if you see the Son of Man ascend to where he was before!" (John 6:62). Later, a few disciples would actually see Jesus ascend (Acts 1:9). What if these puzzled ones could see that? Would they then understand and accept, or would they only be puzzled the more?

"The Spirit gives life; the flesh counts for nothing" (John 6:63). Jesus' teaching was indeed difficult, but that was only half the problem. The other half lay in the hearers. They were interested in physical things like bread and fish (John 6:26). These are worthless in comparison with the eternal life Jesus was telling about. The spiritual man is led by the Spirit of God into the true life, while the man with only physical interests stumbles on in the unbelieving descent of death. Many left Jesus to take that barren way. But Peter affirmed that Jesus had the words of eternal life. He was and is the Holy One of God.

John uses different expressions to describe those who were listening to Jesus. At first it was the "crowds" (John 6:24) who followed Him; then it was the "Jews" who began to murmur against Him (John 6:41, 52); and finally, many of His "disciples" turned back and no longer followed Him (John 6:66). "The Twelve," however, remained with Him. A contrast is given between Peter and Judas. One confessed Him, the other was later to betray Him. Peter's good confession at Caesarea Philippi is not recorded in John; but at this time Peter made a similar statement: "We believe and know that you are the Holy One of God" (John 6:69).

Jesus used this moment to point out the fact that He had chosen the Twelve, but that one of them was a devil. The Gospel writer adds the note that this was Judas, who was to betray Him later.

Why this note of tragic betrayal? Why this general desertion by the crowd and many of His disciples? What the disciples said was, "This is a hard teaching" (John 6:60). There are different ways a teaching can be hard. It may be hard to understand, or it may be difficult to accept even when understood. That these people did not fully understand Jesus is evident. There was more to it, however. They were reluctant to go in the direction He was leading. He said the flesh counts for nothing, but the Spirit gives life. That day in Capernaum, many were too much concerned with fleshly, worldly things, and they turned away from Jesus. Today we face the same choice. The offer of Jesus is not to be modified. With Peter we can only say, "To whom shall we go? You have the words of eternal life" (John 6:68).

CHAPTER FIVE

The Way of Light
John 7:1-8:30

One of the hardest tasks in life is to say the right thing at the right time. Each one of us must continually make decisions about when to talk and when not to talk. How much should one say in order to win a person? How much is just enough and not too much? How should one speak against wrong? Is it cowardly to remain silent in the presence of falsehood? Is it foolish to condemn the enemies of truth when there is little hope of converting them? What should one do when to speak will mean the loss of his physical life? Still more appalling, by remaining silent a person may put the souls of many into jeopardy for eternity. How hard it is to know just what to say! Jesus faced such decisions daily during His earthly ministry.

BRINGING THE LIGHT (7:1-52)

Jesus had suffered rejection on many occasions, especially in Jerusalem. He had fed the five thousand near Passover time (John 6:4), and now, six months later, the feast of Tabernacles was approaching. During that six-month period of time, Jesus went around in Galilee, purposely staying away from Judea because the Jews there were waiting to take His life. Jesus intended to give His life at Jerusalem, but not until the time He and His Father had chosen. He needed more time to give instruction both to the Twelve and to the larger audiences.

"The Jewish Feast of Tabernacles was near" (John 7:2). This was one of the annual feasts of the Jews. It lasted for a week, beginning on the fifteenth of Tishri (about September). During the week, the people lived in huts made of tree branches in memory of the time when their ancestors lived in tents as they wandered in the wilderness after leaving Egypt.[11] Coming in the fall after the fruits had been gathered in, it was a time of gratitude for the harvest. Thus, it may be compared with Thanksgiving Day in the United States, though it was a week instead of a day.

Ministry in Spite of Opposition (1-13)

Jesus had been teaching for about two and a half years. Only half a year remained before His crucifixion. His brothers did not believe on Him at this time. It must have been a great disappointment to God's Son to be rejected by members of His own family. How could they resist His love and truth? This does not indicate any weakness of Jesus' testimony; it shows the nearsightedness, the jealousy, and the stubbornness of man's usual way. In fact, these brothers were not satisfied with refusing to accept Jesus' message and His life; they wanted to tell Him what to do. Jesus' brothers told Him He ought to go to Judea to do miracles and show himself to the world. These brothers were not among Jesus' followers, but were His own brothers referred to in John 2:12 and Mark 6:3. They did not believe in Him, and this makes us suspect that their advice was not the best.

"The right time for me has not yet come," Jesus said (John 7:6). That was Jesus' way of saying that the right moment had not arrived for Him to make the step they were demanding. For them to go up to Jerusalem did not involve the hate and rejection that would accompany Jesus' arrival there.

A little later, Jesus did go to Jerusalem. He did not go publicly, however, but in secret (John 7:10). The crowds at Jerusalem had

---

[11] "See Leviticus 23:33-43; Deuteronomy 16:13-15.

been wondering whether He would come to the feast in the face of threats made by the Jewish leaders. They were debating whether He was a good man to be believed or whether He was a deceiver.

If He was truly the Messiah, why would He stay in Galilee? "Go up to Jerusalem," His brothers advised; "assert Your messiahship openly at the very center of Jewish activity." If Jesus would do this along with miracles to prove His claims, then perhaps His own brothers would accept His message. But Jesus chose not to make such an open declaration at this time. His brothers did not know all that was involved. If He went with them now, He would be accepting their direction. He would also be accepting publicity and fanfare as He arrived in Jerusalem with the large numbers of pilgrims going to the feast of Tabernacles. The people were watching to see whether He would meet the challenge that had been issued to Him. The Jewish leaders in Jerusalem had said they would kill Him if He came within their reach. Jesus had much left to accomplish in His work. He was not ready to precipitate the final confrontation; so He said, "I am not yet going up to [Jerusalem]." This meant He was not going up with His brothers at that time in the usual manner.

What did He accomplish by refusing the invitation of His brothers? He was free to make His own plans. When He did go to Jerusalem, His appearance was unexpected. His enemies had been unable to lay plans to apprehend Him. His coming was not a spectacular entry, but a quiet appearance that enabled teaching sessions with great crowds of people. Months later, when the fullness of time had come, He did make His triumphal entry; but in that same week came His death. He was not ready for this end to come as yet; so He planned to go unobtrusively after the feast had begun.

Teaching in Spite of Disputes (14-24)

Jesus arrived in Jerusalem halfway through the feast, when the week of celebration was at its height. He began teaching in the temple in the midst of those who were opposing Him, but also among many who had not heard Him before this time. They were amazed at the way He taught. "Such learning without having studied" (John 7:15) was a way of describing a person who did not have formal schooling under the rabbis but had a knowledge expected only of those who had spent long years in training. It may have been Jesus' use of the Scripture that caused the amazement. He did not come as a follower of some outstanding rabbi; He had no degree from their formal educational centers. How could He speak with such authority, clarity, and challenge? Jesus answered that His teacher and authority was the one who had sent Him.

To the amazed hearers, Jesus explained that His teaching came from God. In contrast with Jewish teachers, who vied with each other for honor, Jesus gave the honor to His Father. He was not seeking His own glory, and He quickly pointed out that the truth He taught was not only His, but God's. He then accused the Jewish leaders of being faithless to the law they taught. If they were sincerely keeping the law, they would not be trying to kill Him. The threatened attacks upon Jesus were evidence that the very ones who were loudly acclaiming their loyalty to God and His law were actually rejecting God's leading, as they were seeking to kill the one who was sent by God.

At this, some said a demon must have driven Him out of His mind. Some in Jerusalem knew Jesus was telling the truth (John 7:25), but the crowd at the feast included Jews from foreign countries as well as those from Judea and Galilee. Many of them knew nothing of the threats against Jesus. They were not acquainted with the intense hatred of the Jewish leaders. They thought He must be insane to imagine such things. (The later developments that led to Jesus' death make clear how right Jesus was.)

In answer to their charges, Jesus referred to a miracle He had worked in Jerusalem at a former feast. (See John 5:1-15.) A lame man had been healed; but it was on the Sabbath, and bitter condemnation had followed the deed. Jesus now called attention to the fact that a baby was circumcised on the Sabbath despite the law, or rather because of the law.

The law ordered circumcision on the eighth day (Leviticus 12:3), and this was considered more important than the regulations concerning work on the Sabbath. Jesus reasoned that to make a man's whole body well on the Sabbath was certainly more important also.

Jesus added the admonition to look beyond the surface appearances and exercise proper judgment. Judgment must also take into account the whole man, the whole spirit of the law and its author. True judgment would take into account the depth of meaning in this miraculous sign. Not only were the limbs of a man healed, but he was made whole in spirit: a life was introduced to true life.

Claims in Spite of Denials (25-30)

Now some of the people of Jerusalem had their say. It seems that three kinds of people were in Jesus' audiences on these days in the temple area. First, there were "the Jews," the hostile religious leaders of the Jewish people (John 7:1, 11, 13, 15). Then there were the "multitudes" of Jewish pilgrims who had come from various places to commemorate the festival. Some of these had firm opinions about Jesus; others were now hearing Him for the first time (John 7:12, 20). Finally, there were the people of Jerusalem (John 7:25). These were the local crowds. They knew of the threats to stop Jesus by taking His life, but now they began to question the sincerity of such threats. Here was Jesus teaching openly in the temple area, and no apparent steps were being taken to stop Him.

"Have the authorities really concluded that he is the Christ?" they asked (John 7:26). The people were puzzled. Could it be that the authorities had said they wanted to arrest Jesus, even to kill Him, and now were doing nothing? Did the Jewish leaders secretly feel that He really was the Messiah? Was this why they had not touched Him?

Some of the people argued that Jesus could not be the Messiah, because they knew He came from Nazareth. They thought they knew all about His family and boyhood. But the Messiah—they knew He was to come from Bethlehem, of the lineage of David. They knew nothing more about His home and origin.

As Jesus taught in the temple court, He took up this question about His origin. To make His point to the crowd of people talking among themselves, Jesus raised His voice to a shout. He agreed with the people that they knew who He was and where He was from. But once again, Jesus carried His hearers below the surface facts to the more significant truths. Jesus' origin went back to the one who had sent Him. The people knew He meant God. Furthermore, He affirmed, "You do not know him, but I know him" (John 7:28, 29).

This remark angered some within the crowd. "They tried to seize him, but no one laid a hand on him, because his time had not yet come" (John 7:30). This refers to the time of His death. (Compare Luke 4:29, 30.) Since the final hour had not yet been reached, all attempts to arrest Him were failures. It is fruitless to question whether this was a miraculous deliverance or not. Whether by natural or supernatural means, the will of God was accomplished.

Jesus was never cowardly. He was willing to face the world and tell its people what they needed to hear. There were easier ways, but this was the best way. This made them think. It made them consider their own relationship with God. And if they refused to recognize Jesus for what He truly was, then this was evidence that they did not know the Father who had sent Him.

Freedom in Spite of Pursuit (31-44)

Some of the people believed on Jesus. They were impressed by the miraculous signs that He could perform. They felt the Messiah could not be expected to perform any more miraculous signs than

Jesus had already shown. These signs indicated that Jesus was what He claimed to be. Nicodemus had recognized this earlier when he had said, "Rabbi, we know you are a teacher who has come from God. For no one could perform the miraculous signs you are doing if God were not with him" (John 3:2).

Others resented being told that they did not know God. They muttered darkly about laying hands on Him, perhaps to turn Him over to the authorities seeking His life, or possibly to give Him a beating themselves. When the Pharisees heard what the crowd was whispering, they decided it was time for them to make their move. They sent the temple soldiers to arrest Jesus.

Even as the soldiers came to lead him away, Jesus declared to the people that He was going back to the one who had sent Him. Again, this clearly meant God. But then Jesus went on to say that they would look for Him but would not be able to find Him. This does not mean they would still be trying to arrest Him, but after His glorification, they would be looking for Him that He might save them.

Jesus also warned that when He went away, they would not be able to follow. Jesus was free to go and come, to leave the world and return, but the people were confined to the world they lived in. His hearers did not want to accept this meaning. Some asked if He might be going to the Hellenistic Jews who lived in many cities around the Mediterranean.

It was the last day of the feast when Jesus stood and shouted in His deepest, loudest voice, "If you are thirsty, come to me for living water." This was the day for a priest to conduct the pouring of the water. A golden pitcher was filled with water at the pool of Siloam. The words of Isaiah 12:3 were repeated: "With joy you will draw water from the wells of salvation." Then the procession of people accompanied the priest to the temple area, where he poured the water into a vessel at the altar of burnt offering. This was done seven times on the final day of the feast. In the midst of this scene, Jesus was preaching in the temple area with bold affirmations that

He could give living water, meaning the Holy Spirit. The Gospel writer explains that believers would receive this gift at a later time, after Jesus had been glorified.

Perhaps the Scripture Jesus referred to was Joel 3:18: "A fountain will flow out of the Lord's house."

Jesus is the source of living water (John 4:10), but His followers become channels through which it flows to others. They receive the Holy Spirit (John 7:39; Acts 2:38), and from them the blessings of the Spirit flow abundantly to others.

The chief priests and the Pharisees had sent the temple guards to arrest Jesus (John 7:32). What were the soldiers doing all this time? They certainly made no move to arrest Jesus. It seems that they were enthralled along with the people. Some were saying that He was "the Prophet." Others were calling Him "the Messiah (Christ)." Still others were objecting that the Messiah would not come from Galilee. Some wanted to arrest Him, but no one dared lay a hand on Him, not even the soldiers.

Recognition in Spite of Confusion (45-52)

The soldiers went back to the chief priests and Pharisees empty-handed. Jesus had not been stopped.

The chief priests were Sadducees (Acts 5:17), and the Pharisees were their rivals for power among the religious leaders; but they united forces against the common enemy, Jesus. Together they were the ruling force in the Sanhedrin, the highest governing body among the Jews. And they were most disturbed when the soldiers returned without Jesus.

The angry Jewish authorities demanded an explanation from the officers of the temple guard. All they could report was, "No man ever spoke like this man!" Despite the hostility and confusion, they could not help adding their testimony to the mounting recognition given to Jesus.

The Pharisees felt obligated to discredit the soldiers' reaction; so they accused them of being led astray by Jesus. Those religious leaders were wealthy. They had ample time for their religious pursuits, and many of them were born to the high status they occupied. The multitude, the common people, were a different lot. They struggled for everything they had in life. They were not supposed to know and understand the law, but only to do what they were told was expected of them. The Pharisees claimed that only the lowest of the land were impressed by Jesus.

Nicodemus, one of their own number, reminded this important body that they themselves were violating the law if they condemned Jesus without a hearing.

Did these leaders in the Sanhedrin know that Nicodemus had visited Jesus? One does not know. But Nicodemus heard the statement of his fellow Pharisees and could not let it pass in silence. The Pharisees said the people knew nothing of the law because they accepted Jesus as a prophet. Now Nicodemus said that they were the ones who were violating the law.

"Are you from Galilee, too?" they asked (John 7:52). Their only response was to accuse Nicodemus of being sympathetic toward Jesus. People from Galilee were likely to stand together. The chief priests and Pharisees could not defend themselves against the charge that in their own minds they had condemned Jesus without a hearing; so they ignored the charge and attacked the one who made it. They went on to insist that no prophet was to rise from Galilee. In the past, the prophet Jonah had come from that region (2 Kings 14:25). Perhaps the Pharisees meant that no prophecy in Scripture predicted a prophet from Galilee in the future.

The irony of the Pharisaic insistence about the origin of Jesus lay in the fact that He did not really come from Galilee. Ultimately, He did not come from Bethlehem of Judea, but from the side of God. Jesus proclaimed this in all boldness, and Nicodemus was bold enough to break his silence and at least ask a question.

Each generation sees people of the same kind that were present that day in Jerusalem. There were those who curiously looked for the truth but never reached a conclusion; there were those who put their faith in Jesus; there were those who rejected Him; and there were those who tried to crush Him because He did not fit their plans. Jesus faced them all and spoke the truth.

THE WOMAN CAUGHT IN ADULTERY (7:53-8:11)

These verses are not found in most of the early Greek manuscripts. In some manuscripts, they appear at different places in John or in Luke. Many able scholars think they present a true record, though they doubt they were originally written by John at this point. It is possible that the subject matter may have led to omission in public reading at an early time and resulted in some manuscript differences. Thus, the passage may be both a genuine episode in the life of Christ and a genuine part of John's Gospel.

The teachers of the law and the Pharisees brought in a woman caught in adultery. This whole episode has the earmarks of a deliberate plot. How could anyone be caught in the act of adultery unless witnesses were planted? Why was the man not arrested also? Was he immune from prosecution because he was part of the plot?

They were using this question as a trap in order to have a basis for accusing him. The trap was carefully designed to get Jesus in trouble with the Roman authorities or else to ruin His reputation with the people. If He excused the woman, many people would condemn Him for contradicting the law of Moses (Leviticus 20:10; Deuteronomy 22:23, 24). But the Jews were not allowed to inflict capital punishment without Roman approval (John 18:31). If Jesus said the woman should be put to death, the Roman authorities might arrest Him for inciting rebellion. But if He advised taking the case to Roman authorities, this would lead patriotic people to condemn Him as a sympathizer with the hated foreign oppressor.

But Jesus bent down and started to write on the ground. What did He write on the ground? Some have suggested that He began writing the sins that these men were guilty of. As each one saw his own sin written, he departed quickly lest more be said about it. Others suggest He began to write down Old Testament laws that turned attention upon their sins. Perhaps He wrote down just what He turned to them and declared: "If any one of you is without sin, let him be the first to throw a stone at her" (John 8:7). After saying that aloud, He again ignored the accusers and continued to write in the dust with His finger.

Another possibility is that this whole incident had been staged. Perhaps a man had been paid to commit adultery and the time and place agreed upon. The reason that the woman was brought to Jesus and not the man was not an example of double standards, of condemning the woman and not the man, but a case of the man's going free because it was a part of the bargain to let the man escape. What if Jesus began writing down some of the details of such arrangements and the names of those involved? Certainly it would not take the guilty parties long to be leaving the premises in great haste. It seems there was no more to be said. The men decided to drop the case.

When the accusers had slipped away one by one, Jesus turned to the woman, who was left standing alone. She could have fled, too, but now she recognized in Jesus her protection and Savior. He did not condemn her; but neither did He condone her sinful life. He charged her, "Go now and leave your life of sin."

Follow the Light (8:12-30)

Given the choice between light and darkness, which would you choose? No one in his right mind would choose darkness. In the darkness of Mammoth Cave, the very fish that swim in the deep, dark waters of its caverns have lost their eyesight. They are blind because there is no light.

One wants light so he can find his way. One wants light so he can see the beautiful. One needs light in order to have life.

When one looks for a figure to depict comprehension, he speaks of the light of understanding, but the darkness of ignorance. When one symbolizes goodness and purity, it is with light. When Heaven is described, it is filled with light; but eternal punishment is associated with outer darkness.

The evil person desires darkness to hide his evil deeds (John 3:19). Most would like the gray at times—not light enough to show the imperfections and not dark enough to lose the way. The choice for eternity is not somewhere in between, however; it is either light or darkness, saved or lost.

From the opening paragraphs of the Gospel of John, Jesus was presented as the light shining in the darkness (John 1:4, 5). He was the light to every man; He was the true light coming into the world (John 1:9). In the last week of His ministry, Jesus warned the Jerusalem crowd, "You are going to have the light just a little longer. Walk while you have the light, before darkness overtakes you. The man who walks in the dark does not know where he is going. Put your trust in the light while you have it, so that you may become sons of light" (John 12:35, 36).

Just as Jesus offered the Samaritan woman living water (John 4:10, 14), and just as He introduced the multitude along the shore of Galilee to the bread of life (John 6:5 1), even so He declared to the crowds in Jerusalem, "I am the light of the world. Whoever follows me will never walk in darkness, but will have the light of life" (John 8:12).

The Old Testament prophets had predicted this light. "The people walking in darkness have seen a great light; on those living in the land of the shadow of death a light has dawned" (Isaiah 9:2; see also Isaiah 10:17). These predictions penetrated still further into the future: "The sun will no more be your light by day, nor will the brightness of the moon shine on you, for the Lord will be your everlasting light, and your God will be your glory" (Isaiah 60:19).

This light is identified with God: "The Lord is my light and my salvation—whom shall I fear?" (Psalm 27:1). When Jesus claimed to be the light of the world, it was another assertion of His deity. He was the light that brings the right way into view. He was showing the way to salvation. He was driving back the darkness of sin, despair, and destruction. Life for man was a matter of following the light.

The Light Is Identified (12)

The feast of Tabernacles was coming to its end when Jesus preached His sermon on the light of the world. Two great ceremonies associated with the feast of Tabernacles through the centuries were "the pouring out of the water" and the "temple illumination." The first of these probably furnished the occasion for Jesus to call out, "If anyone is thirsty, let him come to me and drink" (John 7:37). "The temple illumination" gave a similar opportunity for Him to say, "I am the light of the world" (John 8:12). In the court of women were four huge golden lampstands, each with four large lamps. They were lit with great ceremony in the evening, and Edersheim says, "There was not a court in Jerusalem that was not lit up by the light."[12]

This was symbolic of the Shekinah, the radiance and glory of God's presence that once had filled His holy temple (2 Chronicles 5:14). Another light from God was recalled at the feast of Tabernacles and was associated with Israel's long stay in the desert on the way to the promised land. In that period, Israel had been led by a cloud in the day but a pillar of fire by night. In the midst of the pageantry that called all this to remembrance, Jesus stood in the temple area and calmly but boldly announced to the throng, "I am the light of the world." Jesus did not restrict His light to the temple, or even to Israel. He affirmed that He is the light of the whole world.

"Whoever follows me ... will have the light of life" (John 8:12). The invitation is offered to all, "whoever." The invitation is for action; light comes when one follows Jesus. The light is the true life, and the true life is Jesus himself (John 1:4).

---

[12] Alfred Edersheim, *The Temple, Its Ministry and Services* (Grand Rapids: Eerdmans, 1950), p. 246.

The Light Is Challenged (13-18)

Though this talk of Jesus is usually called His sermon on the light of the world, the only reference to light is in the opening verse (John 8:12). In the next chapter, John records that Jesus again said, "I am the light of the world" (John 9:5), as He gave light to a blind man. But here in chapter 8, John records the sharp challenge that interrupted what Jesus was saying.

It was quite ordinary for a preacher to be interrupted by elders in the front row. They did not hesitate to question or contradict the speaker if they wished. Jesus made a simple, forthright claim, "I am the light." The Pharisees made a blunt denial, "Your testimony is not valid" (John 8:13). It is a well-known principle that truth is established by two or more witnesses (Deuteronomy 19:15; Matthew 18:16; 2 Corinthians 13:1).

Jesus had acknowledged this in an earlier controversy. He had pointed out that He was not alone in His testimony. He had named four other witnesses: John the Baptist, the miracles, the Father in Heaven, the Scriptures—all these testified for Jesus (John 5:31-40).

So here in John 8:17, 18, He made a good rabbinic reply by appealing to the law. A person needed two witnesses, and He had two witnesses. He was His own witness and God was His witness. But before saying this, Jesus made another point. His testimony was true whether anyone else supported it or not, because He knew all about himself (John 8:14).

The questioners were demanding more testimony because they were in darkness. They did not know Jesus' origin nor His destiny. But Jesus did. He knew where He came from and where He was going. He could give reliable information about himself. But the Pharisees who challenged Him were unable to perceive the truth. Their way of judgment was distorted by selfish desires and ambitions of the flesh. Jesus did not judge anyone in the way they were judging Him. After saying all this, Jesus came again to the answer He had given before. He did not stand alone, a solitary witness about himself. God, the one who sent Him, verified all that He did and said.

"You people judge according to the flesh," Jesus said. This is the New American Standard translation in John 8:15. The New International Version has, "You judge by human standards," but the term *flesh* emphasizes the weaknesses and limitation of man. (See Matthew 26:41, "The flesh is weak," NASB.) Jesus' enemies saw Him in the flesh, but failed to perceive that He was the Son of God. They had their selfish ambitions and determined plans that prevented them from accepting Jesus as the Christ. When Jesus went on to say, I judge no man, He meant that He did not judge the way the Pharisees did. He had not come in His earthly ministry to condemn as a judge, but at His second coming the role of judge will be filled. His judgment will be true, however, because it will coincide with God's judgment: "I stand with the Father, who sent me" (John 8:16).

A Bright Light Throws Dark Shadows (19-24)

Citing the law about two witnesses, Jesus specified His Father and himself as two witnesses who spoke for Him. Then the Pharisees objected again. They said, "Where is your Father?" (John 8:19). In effect, they were saying, "Produce your other witness. Let us hear him." But sad to say, they would not listen to God any more than to God's Son.

The questioning by these Jewish leaders shows not only that they did not accept Jesus, but also that they did not understand Him and did not know God. If they had known God, they would have recognized Jesus as His Son; if they had really known Jesus, they would have known God also. (See John 14:9.)

It is quite plain that Jesus claimed God as His Father, and these men knew they could not call God before them as they would a man. Still they persisted in judging "according to the flesh" or "by human standards." They saw Jesus as no more than a human being;

and if He had another witness, they wanted to see Him in the same way.

With verse 20, John pauses to remind us that this was taking place at the heart of the temple activity. It was at the location where the offerings were placed. Some months later, Jesus saw a widow put in her mites at this place (Mark 12:41-44). Even though the sayings of Jesus incensed the Jewish leaders, they did not dare seize Him there. The place was crowded with people, including many enthusiastic followers of Jesus, who might have made trouble for the police. A little earlier, police had been sent to arrest Jesus, but had come back without Him (John 7:45, 46).

A little later, the leaders tried to arouse a mob to stone Him, but instead, the crowd protected Him as He slipped away (John 8:59).

Very briefly, John explained why Jesus could remain safe in spite of the fury of the rulers: His time had not yet come. Willingly He would give His life six months later, but not now. So in verse 21, we see Jesus continuing His talk in the midst of His furious enemies.

Now the light cast its shadow. If they did not accept Him, they would die in their sins. At first, *sin* is singular: "You will die in your sin" (John 8:21). Their sin was their rejection of God's Son. Because they rejected Him, they could not follow where He was going. Later, sins is plural (John 8:24), for if they did not have Jesus as their Savior, all of the wrongs would need accounting for.

"Will he kill himself?" (John 8:22). With this question, the Pharisees tried to avoid the suggestion that they would kill Him, and at the same time suggest that He would be separated from them by His own suicide. In the Jewish belief, such a sin would put Him in the depths of Hades, lower than they would ever go. Jesus retorted that He was from above (John 8:23), associated with Heaven and God, but they were from below, associated with this world and its prince, Satan.

Who Are You, Anyway? (25-30)

It seems that these people were trying to draw from Jesus a clear statement that He was divine. Then they would say he was a blasphemer. They would seize stones to stone Him, and perhaps a crowd would join them. But Jesus did not accommodate them with the excuses they wanted. He said, "Just what I have been claiming all along."

He went on to inform them that a time was coming when they would know who He was. "When you have lifted up the Son of Man, then you will know [who] I am" (John 8:28). Jesus referred to His death, being "lifted up" on the cross. (See John 12:32, 33).

After his crucifixion and resurrection, His teaching would become clear. Even priests and Pharisees would be among His people (Acts 6:7; 15:5).

At the feast of Tabernacles before His death, nearly all the priests and Pharisees rejected His teaching; but among the common people, many put their faith in Him (John 8:30). They were more open-minded.

Those who did not believe refused to accept what they should have known. Jesus made that clear, and proceeded to sum up what they should have known about Him:

1. He had much to tell them about themselves. If they would listen, He could teach them how to judge rightly rather than by faulty standards (John 8:15). They needed to know right from wrong, the important from the unimportant, the spiritual from the fleshly, the believing from the unbelieving, the true from the false.

2. He was sent from God. This indicated who He was. He was the Son of Man, related to man, representative of man, the best of man all put together; but He was also the Son of God, the representative of God bringing the truth of God. Hindered by their prejudice, His enemies did not understand this. Later He would be lifted up to die on the cross, and then lifted up to sit at the right hand of God. Then even some of His enemies would understand what He had been saying and would know it was true.

3. Furthermore, God stands with Jesus. The two are together in power and authority. And Jesus does everything to please God. There is complete harmony. Doesn't this tell us who Jesus is?

If one desires the light, he must follow the light of the world: Jesus, God's Son.

PART TWO

The Truth

John 8:31-16:15

CHAPTER SIX

Set Free
John 8:31-10:42

All of life is a quest; but what are we looking for? Is it peace? Or happiness? Or is it love? Or freedom? None of these count for much unless they are founded on truth. But does just any truth lead one to these goals, or is it a special truth?

THE TRUTH THAT SETS YOU FREE (8:31-59)

If ever an age deserved Paul's description of the last days, it is ours: "Ever learning, and never able to come to the knowledge of the truth" (2 Timothy 3:7, KJV). Never has man accumulated so many facts, acquired so much know-how, and penetrated so far into the nearest reaches of infinite space; but in spite of this, he has left a wide trail of confusion, uncertainty, strife, and chaos. People are maimed and destroyed in war, others are intellectually set adrift without any sense of direction, and others are morally lost in crime and license. Man is in revolt, trying to cut all his moorings to the past.

Our age has turned from the desperate question of Pilate, "What is truth?" (John 18:38) to the still more desperate question, "Is there any such thing as truth?" College freshmen are growing accustomed to hearing cynical professors emphatically deny the existence of abiding truth and affirm that everything is relative, depending upon the time and place. This type of lecturer frequently continues by maintaining that if there were such a thing as truth, it would be impossible for man to know it; and even if man were to come to a measure of the truth, it is highly unlikely that he could communicate it to another mind. Is it any wonder that the world is experiencing rebellion and chaos? The life-style of the land has been removing the pin from the hinges of truth, and the doors of knowledge are falling from their place.

Know the Truth (31, 32)

Jesus stood in the temple area in front of a rebellious, skeptical crowd and told them that they could indeed know the truth and that the truth would make them free. This scene is a continuation of His sermon on the light of the world, but the people He addressed at this time are described as "the Jews who had believed him" (John 8:31).

Jesus had been speaking to a crowd (John 7:20) at the feast of Tabernacles (John 7:2, 14). This included people of Jerusalem (John 7:25) as well as a large number of pilgrims from many places of the world, gathered for the Jewish ceremonies of the week. The audience also included Pharisees (John 7:32), and no doubt representatives of the chief priests, who sent temple guards to arrest Him (John 7:32). The guards, however, failed to do so (John 7:45). The hearers were divided in their sentiment. Some accepted Jesus as the Messiah (John 7:41), others wanted to seize Him and see His preaching stopped (John 7:43, 44).

When in the middle of His sermon on the light of the world (John 8:12), Jesus directed His words to "the Jews who had believed Him," one wonders just what segment of the crowd is meant. People committed to Jesus surely did not have the hostile attitude or make the bitter attacks that are indicated in the following verses. Some suggest that the people described in this passage had only a shallow belief that quickly gave way to hostility and threats to kill Jesus. It seems more likely that Jesus spoke to those who believed, but the more hostile retorts came from those who disbelieved. The pronoun *they* may refer to the Jews in general. Some of them did believe Jesus. He urged them to remember His teaching and follow it in order to be truly free. Then some who did not believe Him retorted that they had always been free (John 8:33). But they were in the chains of sin.

Jesus said, "The truth will set you free" (John 8:32). Those words are used and misused to support innumerable causes. But before one is ready to grab this statement and make use of it, he must consider the rest of the package that Jesus handed out at the same time.

The way to freedom is set forth step by step. Before one is set free, he must know the truth. Before he will know the truth, he must be Jesus' disciple. Before he can be Jesus' disciple, he must hold to His teaching. Before he holds to His teaching, he must be a believer.

Before asking "what truth?" and "what freedom?" one must consider the verse that goes before: "If you hold to my teaching, you are really my disciples. Then you will know the truth, and the truth will set you free" (John 8:31, 32). "If you hold to my teaching!" The way to know the truth is to abide in Jesus' Word, to obey Him, truly to follow as His disciple. Not just anyone knows the truth. It is not learned in just any way, and not just any truth leads to true freedom.

"The truth will set you free." This is not just any truth used to justify any cause. This refers to the revelation of Jesus (compare John 8:36), the truth of the gospel. It brings deliverance from sin and its consequences.

In the New Testament, truth is something to be done as well as believed. "But he that doeth truth cometh to the light, that his deeds may be made manifest, that they are wrought in God" (John 3:21, KJV). When this is understood, a deeper significance is found in the words of Jesus as He prays that His followers will be sanctified in truth. (See John 17:17, 19.)

In the epistles, one finds continued use of *truth* in this deeper sense. Paul warns that man exchanged the truth of God for a lie, and worshiped and served the creature rather than the Creator (Romans 1:25). In a parallel way, he speaks of the truth of Christ (2 Corinthians 11:10) and the truth of the gospel (Galatians 2:5, 14; Colossians 1:5).

Truth is more than God's reliability and man's consistency with the actual. Truth is the revelation of God that makes known the way of salvation in Jesus Christ: "And you also were included in Christ when you heard the word of truth, the gospel of your salvation. Having believed, you were marked in him with a seal, the promised Holy Spirit" (Ephesians 1:13). The truth is the gospel, and the gospel centers in Christ. As He is the living water who brings and sustains life, He is also the living truth that provides the way and shows the way to true life. "I am the way and the truth and the life. No one comes to the Father except through me" (John 14:6). With this meaning in view, Paul warns of the last days, which will lack a "knowledge of the truth" through rejecting God's revelation and, specifically, His Son Jesus Christ. It is with this meaning that John records the words of Jesus, "You will know the truth, and the truth will set you free." This is not the philosopher's truth in the concepts of men, it is not the demonstrator's cry in a civil crusade, nor is this the metaphysician's dream of an ultimate reality, nor the scientist's truth in his laboratory. This is the truth of God revealed in Jesus Christ. The freedom He brings is not the general freedom of thoughts or rights, but freedom from the bondage of sin and death.

All Are Slaves (33-41)

One can think of many questions Jesus' hearers could have raised to gain further understanding, but they only voiced their resentment at the implication that they were slaves. They must be in bondage, according to Jesus, since He was offering to free them. To them this was outrageous. After all, they were the proud descendants of Abraham. "We . . . have never been slaves of anyone" (John 8:33). What an absurd claim! Had they forgotten

Egypt and God's deliverance from bondage? And what of their present plight? They were under the power of the Roman conqueror. They had no land they could call their own. They looked for a Messiah to deliver them; and here Jesus stood before them with an offer of freedom, and all they could do was to show their resentment.

They had missed the point again. Their worst enslavement was below the surface. "Everyone who sins is a slave to sin" (John 8:34). This cleared up the matter of their need for freedom. But what about the reference to Abraham? They said they were sons of Abraham, but Jesus was the Son of God, and here they were ready to kill Him. This did not sound like Abraham's representatives (John 8:37). They were taking a stand contrary to God and to Abraham. This could only associate them with the archenemy of God—the devil. He then must be their father. "On, no," they protested. "We are not illegitimate children. The only Father we have is God himself" (John 8:4 1).

The Jews said they did not need anyone or anything to set them free, but Jesus said they were slaves of sin. They could not be free by being descendants of Abraham, but only because the Son, having a special place in the household, could give freedom to the slaves.

The claims of Jesus are plain here. He claimed to be sinless, not a slave to sin as they were. He claimed to be the Son of God, and to tell of what He had seen in Heaven before He came to earth. He claimed to be able to free the slaves of sin.

Children of the Devil (39-57)

In his writing on principles of interpretation, Alexander Campbell included a section on "the listening distance." He insisted that to understand the Scriptures, a person must be standing within the listening distance or he will not be able to hear the message of the Scripture. 'God is the center of this area, and the individual's humility is the periphery. This concept helps in understanding what Jesus said to these Jerusalem critics. They were not in listening distance. "Why is my language not clear to you? Because you are unable to hear what I say" (John 8:43). By their rejection of Christ, they were removing themselves from God's circle and joining the forces of the devil. Rather than God, they made the devil their father. Physically, they had descended from Abraham; but they could not rightly claim him as their father. A son should behave like his father, and their actions were not like Abraham's. They were acting more like the devil; so he must be their father.

In denying this, the Jews used strong language: "We are not illegitimate children" (John 8:41). They may have meant simply that they were loyal to God and He was their true Father; but it is possible that they meant to suggest that Jesus was an illegitimate child. That ancient slander is still being repeated by unbelievers.

Jesus unmasked the devil for what he is, a murderer and a liar (John 8:44). He deceived Eve with his lies; he prompted Cain to murder Abel; and this has been his work all along. Jesus told the truth. When His hearers denied it, they associated themselves with the father of lies and performed his work. As they plotted to kill the one sent from God, they identified themselves still further with the one who was a murderer from the beginning.

"Can any of you prove me guilty of sin?" Jesus asked (John 8:46). He issued this challenge and made His point not only for that day but for the ages to come. If any had been able to convict Him of wrong, it would have been done that day; but no one contested His claim. The assertion that Christ was sinless was not an afterthought included in later doctrine. It was made by Jesus himself and repeated by inspired writers.[13]

Jesus spoke the truth. If the ones who hear Him cannot accept the truth, the conclusion is that they cannot really hear the words of God because they do not belong to God.

---

[13] See 2 Corinthians 5:21; Hebrews 4:15; 1 Peter 2:22; 1 John 3:5.

Jesus' statement that the devil was their father brought still further exasperation to the Jews. Angrily they said Jesus was a "Samaritan and demon-possessed" (John 8:48). Perhaps they had heard of His ministry with the Samaritans that is recorded in John 4:1-42. Perhaps they had learned that He had come through Samaria on His quick trip to arrive in the midst of this feast of Tabernacles. Perhaps they intended a slur about His obscure beginnings in Nazareth, or even a question of His birth. They may have been thinking that He did not follow all the traditions of the elders, which Samaritans also failed to follow. Or perhaps a Samaritan was the most hated being they could think of, and that was reason enough to call Jesus one.

Jesus ignored the charge of being a Samaritan and denied the charge of being demon-possessed. Then He came to a climax of His claims. "I tell you the truth, if a man keeps my word, he will never see death" (John 8:51). Once again, Jesus was not speaking superficially, not meaning physical death, which all will suffer. Below the surface lay the impending spiritual death, the second death (Revelation 21:8). This is the inevitable consequence of dying in one's sins. The one who follows Jesus will never taste of that death.

The Jews scoffed at this. Abraham died. The prophets died. Was Jesus greater than they? "Who do you think you are?" (John 8:53). They were pressing Jesus to say plainly that He was the Messiah and was divine.

Jesus declined to praise himself, but reminded the critics that God honored Him. God did this by giving Him the power to do miracles in the sight of all. Abraham had rejoiced to look forward to His day, and in this way, Abraham, too, was glorifying Him. At this, the unbelieving Jews scoffed again. To think of Jesus claiming to have seen Abraham!

Before Abraham was Born, I Am (58, 59)

One of the most powerful statements concerning the deity of Christ was given by Jesus himself at this feast of Tabernacles. Jesus and the Jewish leaders had been having a running debate that drove them further and further apart. Jesus had promised them that if they would follow Him and keep His word, they would never die. He spoke of spiritual death. True life in Christ is eternal life with the Father. But the Jews could not see this. They knew that Abraham died, and they would not believe that anyone could be greater than Abraham. To this, Jesus answered that Abraham knew of Jesus' coming and rejoiced to see His day. Does this mean that Abraham at that time of Jesus' speaking was witnessing Christ's life and rejoicing in it? Or does it mean that Abraham rejoiced in his own day because of the prospect of the coming Messiah? God had assured Abraham, "All peoples on earth will be blessed through you" (Genesis 12:3). Abraham rejoiced in his day through the promise and was rejoicing at that time as he was aware of Jesus' work. The verb tenses are past, however, and probably the reference is to Abraham's rejoicing in his own time. The New International Version favors this interpretation, reading, "Your father Abraham rejoiced at the thought of seeing my day" (John 8:56). But the point Jesus was making was that Abraham favored Jesus and His work, and some of these Jews were opposing Him. If they claimed Abraham as their father, they were denying their own birthright by rejecting Jesus.

This led to further ridicule from the Jews. Did Jesus really expect them to believe that He had been alive in Abraham's time or that Abraham had known Him? In all calmness, without the least egotism on the one hand or apology on the other, Jesus affirmed the plain fact He knew to be true: "Before Abraham was born, I am" (John 8:58).

This Gospel narrative began with a majestic declaration of the pre-existence and deity of the Word (John 1:1, 2). Here Jesus affirmed the same. By using the phrase *I am* instead of *I was*, He not only claimed to have had existence in Abraham's day, but also affirmed His eternality and His deity. "I am" was the name by which God identified himself to Moses (Exodus 3:14).

John records several times when Jesus plainly claimed to be God: "I and the Father are one" (John 10:30). "Anyone who has seen me has seen the Father" (John 14:9). Such a claim is here in our text: "Before Abraham was born, I am" (John 8:58). He not only said He had lived long before He came to earth as a human being, but also identified himself by the very name of God," I am" (Exodus 3:14).

"At this, they picked up stones to stone him" (John 8:59). They understood that Jesus was claiming to be God. The reaction of the unbelieving Jews proves it. Jesus was claiming to be God, and to them, this was blasphemy. It would have been blasphemy if the claim had not been true. Saying that it was not true, they picked up stones to kill Him. But Jesus walked from their midst as He had walked from another crowd at Nazareth under similar circumstances (Luke 4:29, 30).

His time had not yet come. He was the truth, but they rejected Him. But to those who received Him and held to His teaching, then and now, it is given to know the truth and be set free.

HOW BLIND IS BLIND? (9:1-41)

Have you ever read a book that has a plot within a plot? Action is going on at the same time in two different circles, and yet they are related. Have you ever heard a pianist play a complicated musical arrangement in which the left hand seems to be following a melody independent of the right hand, and yet the whole is one composition?

One day Jesus gave sight to a man who had been born blind. This was action enough for a thrilling story; but the account brings in another scene of action, and another type of blindness comes into view. It becomes evident that some blindness is blinder than other blindness. Just how blind is blind?

The Relevant Question (1-5)

Some questions are relevant to every age. No question is more seriously considered than the problem of suffering. Why does a person have a handicap in life? Why is there pain? Why must hardships plague the lives of men?

No one knows just how the question came up on that day when Jesus and His disciples were passing a blind man. Probably it was not long after the feast of Tabernacles (John 7:2, 14). If it happened at a different time, John may have put the account of it here because it so fittingly follows Jesus' preaching on the light of the world. We suppose the place was in or near Jerusalem, because the pool of Siloam was there. It may have been close to the temple, where the blind man could ask for offerings from the worshipers.

The last verse of John 8 says that Jesus was "slipping away from the temple grounds." Either at that time or at some later time "as he went along" (John 9:1), the blind man caught His attention. The disciples asked about the cause of his blindness, but Jesus told rather what would result: "that the work of God might be displayed in his life." Jesus added, "As long as it is day, we must do the work of him who sent me" (John 9:3, 4). As long as He was living on earth, He needed to use His time to accomplish the work allotted to Him. The same rule applied to His disciples then, and it applies to His disciples now. Night is coming, earthly days will end, and opportunities will cease for work in this world.

As long as Jesus was in the world, He was the light of the world (John 9:5). In a beautiful way, this joins the sermon of chapter 8 to the miracle of chapter 9, which brings a blind man to enjoy light for the first time. But besides physical light, there is spiritual light for the soul. This, also, Jesus supplied to the man who received his sight. Even now, Jesus continues to be a light in the world as His life is reflected in the lives of those committed to Him; but while He was on earth, the world enjoyed the direct rays of God's light in the person of His Son.

The Gospel says that Jesus saw the blind man, but the disciples asked the question. Did Jesus call attention to the man in such a way that the disciples were prompted to ask? Had they ever seen this blind man before? How did they know he had been blind from birth? Was the blind man aware of Jesus' preaching? How much did he know about Jesus?

These questions are not answered, but there are some probabilities. If the blind man begged daily near the temple, Jesus and the disciples had probably passed him repeatedly. Almost certainly, he had heard of Jesus. "Among the crowds, there was widespread whispering about him" at the feast of Tabernacles as it began (John 7:12), and interest must have grown as He taught (John 7:14, 15). The blind man may have been in the audience to hear some of His teachings. And perhaps Jesus deliberately paused near the blind man and waited for the disciples to notice him and ask the question that opened the way for more teaching and yet another miraculous sign.

This was the question: "Rabbi, who sinned, this man or his parents, that he was born blind?" (John 9:2). As we have said, the question of suffering is always pertinent. However, as is often the case, those asking it did not give all the alternatives. The disciples saw the problem as did the friends of Job in the Old Testament. Sin was the cause of suffering, they thought, and the worse the sin, the more severe the suffering. Job had objected strenuously to that answer. He was no worse than the rest, and look at his suffering! He suggested that suffering might be a discipline to keep a person from sinning rather than a punishment because of sin. Elihu added that suffering builds character, and we may be the better for it. But at the very outset, the book of Job shows another source of trouble. Satan is going up and down in the world, tempting and trying to bring all the hardship he can. He tests both the bad ones and the good ones. Job's suffering was a test from Satan.

Jesus swept aside the disciples' suggestions. This man's sin had not made him blind, and neither had the sin of his parents. Instead of discussing the cause of blindness, Jesus focused attention on its results. Because this man was blind, the work of God was going to be displayed.

The working of God's power is associated with the presence of His Son. While He is present in the world, it is day; for He is the light of the world. He was about to give a practical demonstration of this by bringing light to a man who had lived in darkness all his life.

The Extra Test (6-12)

The faith of people is constantly being tested directly or indirectly. When Jesus healed a person, He often found some way of developing or testing that person's faith. In this case, He used mud.

Why did Jesus make the mud with saliva and put it on the man's eyes? Was this necessary? Was it medicinal, or part of some magical routine? Was it customary? One cannot say it was customary, because healing a man born blind was not customary. Jesus did use spittle in giving sight to a blind man at Bethsaida (Mark 8:22-26) and in giving hearing and speech to another man (Mark 7:32-35). The clay was not medicinal, and it certainly was not magical. Nor is there any indication that it was necessary for any reason.

It probably did, however, help to draw the attention of witnesses of the miracle, and it helped to arouse faith and expectation in the blind man. It opened the way for a command to be obeyed: "Go, wash in the pool of Siloam." It might be hard for a blind man to find his way to the pool. He might miss some contributions if he left his post. Would he have faith enough to do what Jesus said to do?

John notes that the meaning of *Siloam* is "sent" (John 9:7). This was appropriate at this point, both because Jesus was sent from God and because the blind man was sent to the pool to wash his eyes. This was a challenge to his faith. He obeyed because he believed in Jesus. The pool of Siloam is situated south of the temple area. It is fed by a canal from the spring of Gihon. Its water was used in the ceremonies and processions of the feast of Tabernacles.

"So the man went and washed, and came home seeing" (John 9:7). No miracle could be described more matter-of-factly, but one can imagine the joy and exuberance that must have accompanied that first day of sight. How did it happen? The man gave credit to Jesus, but he did not know where Jesus was after the miracle (John 9: 10-12).

Now an extra testing began. Even those who had known him before were uncertain of his identity. Eyesight had made a new man of him. He looked like the same man, however, and his word convinced his acquaintances that he was the same man. Then came the next question. How had he gained his sight? He gave all the credit to Jesus. He could not tell them where Jesus was now, but he knew the man called Jesus had opened his eyes.

The Convincing Sign (13-23)

The testing grew more severe when the Pharisees came into the picture. Some of them pointed out that it was the Sabbath Day. Jesus could not be from God, they said. If he were, He would not have done that work on the Sabbath. (Both the healing and the mixing of clay may have been questioned.) Others, however, maintained that this miraculous sign could not have been done by an ordinary sinner. This must prove that Jesus had come from God and bore God's approval. As their debate grew more heated, they forced the former blind man to take a stand. What did he have to say about the one who had opened his eyes? His conclusion was that Jesus must be a "prophet," a specially inspired man of God (John 9:17).

Since the hostile forces could make no progress in this way, they tried another tack. They said the man before them had never been blind. They said there had been no miracle. They said this man was a liar and his whole story was a fraud. Perhaps some of them really believed this. They sent for the man's parents, well knowing that ordinary citizens would be intimidated in their presence. The parents were indeed frightened, but their testimony was nevertheless a powerful bulwark of the truth. They knew the man was their son, and they knew he had been born blind. As to how he had received his sight, they were unwilling to say anything. They knew the mounting opposition to Jesus. They knew what it was like to be put out of the synagogue and suffer separation from friends and relatives. So they said, "Ask him" (John 9:21).

Why did some of the people take the man to the Pharisees in the first place? We are not told. Perhaps some partisans of the Pharisees thought they should be told of this latest infringement of the Sabbath-day rules; or perhaps some friends of Jesus hoped the miracle would make the Pharisees stop their opposition.

The Pharisees' investigation, whatever or whoever started it, seems uncalled for. Certainly it was prejudiced and unfair. Still it has provided all posterity with the best of evidence that the miracle really happened.

Another Blindness (24-34)

Finding the evidence mounting against them, the hostile Pharisees decided to end the inquiry and fall back on their own authority to keep the story of the miracle from spreading. They summoned the former blind man again and tried this time to break down his testimony. He was an ignorant, uneducated individual, but recently a beggar, and they probably figured he would be no match for their inquisition. But he had the truth, a courageous heart, a bright mind, and a growing faith.

The examiners appealed first to his piety. "Give glory to God,' they said. 'We know this man is a sinner" (John 9:24).

Not long before, Jesus had challenged, "Can any of you prove me guilty of sin?" (John 8:46). No one had stepped forward to make accusation. Now, behind His back, some of the Jews were ready to declare Him a sinner because He had given sight on the Sabbath.

Obviously, the healed man was not convinced. He would not debate or pass judgment about who was a sinner, but he fell back on the fact he knew: "I was blind but now I see" (John 9:25).

At this point, it seems that the Pharisees were trying to convince the man that his sight had come from God, but not from Jesus. After all, Jesus had not even been there at the pool when he had begun to see. "How did he open your eyes?" they asked (John 9:26).

Now the man replied with the kind of answer they deserved. He had already told them once (John 9:10, 11), and they did not listen. Why did they want him to tell them again? Were they thinking of becoming disciples of Jesus? (John 9:27).

This triggered further attack, and they hurled insults at the healed man. They accused him of following Jesus, while they claimed Moses as their leader. "We know that God spoke to Moses, but as for this fellow, we don't even know where he comes from" (John 9:29).

The former blind man turned this caustic remark into an admission of their ignorance. Their refusal to accept Jesus gave evidence of a blindness far more serious than the physical dark-ness experienced before by this lone defender. Could they not see that Jesus had opened his eyes? God would not give such power to a sinner. That Jesus could do this unheard of thing, opening the eyes of a man born blind, was evidence that God was with Him (John 9:30-33).

The attackers could not withstand his logic. Jesus had declared at the beginning that this man could not be called a particularly bad sinner simply because he had suffered blindness from birth. But now the desperate attackers proclaimed him "steeped in sin" because they could not answer his arguments.

"And they threw him out" (John 9:34). John 9:22 tells us the Sanhedrin had determined to excommunicate from the synagogue any who recognized Jesus as the Messiah. Perhaps this man was the first victim of that cruel, unjust decision. When he was thrown out, he lost his privileges of worship and participation in the services of the Jews—and very precious privileges they were!

The Two Results (35-41)

Jesus, hearing that the man had been put out of the synagogue, returned to ask if he believed in the Son of Man. This man did not rush into an admission without understanding, however. He in turn asked for direct information: "Who is he?" (John 9:36). Jesus' answer was no less direct: "He is the one speaking with you" (John 9:37).

"Then the man said, 'Lord, I believe,' and he worshiped him" (John 9:38). This was one result: a man healed of physical blindness also gained the sight of Jesus as God.

Ancient manuscripts have variant readings in John 9:35. There is early and weighty testimony for "Son of Man," but numerous manuscripts have "Son of God." The "Son of God" reading seems to fit better with the following statement that the man worshiped Him. But "Son of Man" also can be acknowledged as a title of the Messiah, and it is a term Jesus frequently used of himself. Whether Jesus really said "Son of Man" or "Son of God" at this time, the man whose eyes were opened knew He was worthy of worship. So do we, if our eyes are open to the truth.

The second result was that those who rejected Jesus turned out to be blind in their souls. They denied this, but in their denial of Jesus and the denial of any blindness in their lives, they became responsible for their guilt.

Jesus compared the former physical blindness of the healed man with the spiritual blindness of the Pharisees (John 9:40, 41). They shut their eyes to the truth when they rejected God's Son. If they had realized how blind they were, they could have sought the light of Christ, and He would have taken away their sin. But since they boasted that they saw all things clearly, they would remain in their blindness and must answer for the guilt of their sin. Such blindness is the darkest kind, far worse than blindness of the physical eyes.

How blind is blind? Worst of all is the blindness that shuts out Jesus. This is far worse than a physical blindness that still allows the mind to see important truths. There are those who can see physically, but remain in sin because they are blind to Jesus. How blind is blind? If it is spiritual blindness that shuts out the Savior, it is blind as blind can be.

THE SHEPHERD LEADS (10:1-42)

The tenth chapter of John is introduced by the double *amen* in Greek, translated "Verily, verily" in the King James Version and "I tell you the truth" in the New International. Although this phrase occurs twenty-five times in John's Gospel, it nowhere introduces a new section. For this reason, one is led to look for a connection between this passage and what goes before it. Chapter 9 tells of a blind man who not only received sight for his eyes, but also found faith in Christ and sight for his soul. The end of the chapter tells us that Jesus pointed out the blindness of the Pharisees who rejected Him. Then comes chapter 10, with the tender and reassuring parable of the Good Shepherd. Although the former blind man had been put out of the synagogue, he belonged to Jesus' fold. The Pharisees were no more than thieves and robbers, or hirelings at best. Following the sermon, the remarks include reference to opening the eyes of the blind (John 10:21). This, too, links the passage to chapter 9.

A sheep pen or "sheepfold," as the King James Version has it, was usually surrounded by a stone wall. Several flocks might share a pen at night. One man could keep watch while the shepherds slept. Coming for his sheep in the morning, a shepherd would use the gate, but a thief or robber in the night might try to climb in another way.

The watchman provided security for the sheep, as did the fence. In studying the message of the parable, we need not try to find what these represent in our own experience. They may be only scenery against which we see the parable's message about the work of Jesus. It is striking that He is identified not only as the good shepherd (John 10:11), but also as the gate or door (John 10:7).

He calls his own sheep by name and leads them out. Living with the flock day by day as lambs grow into mature sheep, the Eastern shepherd literally knew each sheep by name. It is comforting to think that Jesus knows each of us as well. And the sheep knew their own shepherd's voice. In the East, three or four flocks may graze all day together; but there is no trouble in separating the flocks, because each follows the signal of his own shepherd. If one does not hear the message of Jesus and follow Him, the reason is obvious: He is not one of Jesus' sheep. When a false teacher comes into the flock and tries to lead the sheep astray, the ones who know the voice of Jesus will not follow the strange voice.

Shepherds handle their sheep in different ways. In America, a shepherd usually walks behind his sheep as he drives them in the right direction. In the lands of the Bible, however, even now as it was in Bible times, the shepherd leads his sheep. The shepherd speaks, and the flock follows his voice. He goes ahead to show the way, to protect from dangers, and to find the best in water and pasture. Another help for the sheep is the security of a fold for protection in the night, the cold, or the storm. The fold is entered by its gate, which symbolizes both the security of the fold and the freedom to leave its walls.

Jesus is both our shepherd who leads us and the gate of the fold that protects us.

The Lord Is My Shepherd (1-6)

This chapter records a sermon about a shepherd, sheep, and a fold. Jesus began this sermon with a type of parable. Some have said that the Gospel of John has no parables. It is true that the word used for parable in the other Gospels is not used in John, but a similar word with the same meaning is seen in John 10:6: "Jesus used this *figure of speech*, but they did not understand what he was telling them."

This parable began with a comparison between the shepherd and the thief. The shepherd enters the fold by the gate, is respected by the watchman, and is followed by the sheep. On the other hand, the thief climbs in by another way, he is unknown to the sheep, and they run from him.

The shepherd and his sheep are an illustration of God and His people. This idea was not new to the Jews when Jesus used it. In the Psalms, the Lord is the shepherd of His people Israel (Psalm 23:1; 80:1; 100:3) and also in Isaiah (Isaiah 40:11). False shepherds depict the false prophets leading Israel into apostasy.

If the people could understand the meaning of Jesus' figure, they would identify Jesus with the Lord and the shepherd. Those who were trying to steal the sheep, prey upon them, and lead them astray would be identified with Jesus' attackers, the chief priests and the Pharisees. Such thieves bring death, not life.

I Shall Not Want (7-10)

Jesus became more explicit when the people failed to understand. He said, "I am the gate for the sheep" (John 10:7).

The gate protects the sheep in the fold, and yet the sheep can go out to pasture. This is a combination of freedom and security. Jesus is the entrance to salvation. He keeps His sheep secure; no one can snatch them out of His hand (John 10:28), and yet they are free indeed (John 8:36). He made the promise that anyone who enters through Him will be saved.

"All who ever came before me were thieves and robbers" (John 10:8). This certainly does not refer to the Old Testament prophets. It may mean false teachers who led people astray after the close of the Old Testament period, or even in the very period that Jesus was living in.

"I have come that they may have life, and have it to the full" (John 10:10). This might be called the theme of Christ's life and message. In contrast with the thieves who came to steal, kill, and destroy, Jesus came to bring true life.

This was set down in the prologue of John's Gospel. Jesus is the source of all life, the light of man (John 1:4). It is life that goes deeper than the surface, it is life that penetrates beyond the material, it is life that outlasts time. The duration and quality of this life are beyond measuring.

Near the end of the book, John states that all these things are written that men may believe that Jesus is the Christ, the Son of God and may have life in his name (John 20:3 1). In the closing days of His ministry, Jesus said, "Jam.., the life" (John 11:25; 14:6). Those who have Jesus will not lack life.

Your Rod Protects Me (11-14)

Then Jesus said explicitly, "I am the good shepherd" (John 10:11, 14). A measure of how good the shepherd is can be seen in his willingness to die on behalf of his sheep. Jesus was, in fact, to lay down His life for His sheep. He died in their stead, that they might have life. The contrast this time is not with the thief, but between the owner of the sheep and the hired hand who cannot be trusted when danger approaches. The good shepherd will protect his flock, even to the giving of his life.

This is another saying that could not be appreciated until after the crucifixion of Jesus. The good shepherd is also the Lamb of God who takes away the sin of the world (John 1:29).

Through the Valley of Death (15-21)

Once again Jesus became more specific, more personal: "I lay down my life for the sheep" (John 10:15). He added that He had "other sheep that are not of this [flock]" (John 10:16). They also would listen to His voice and join His flock. There would be one flock and one shepherd. The disciples around Jesus at that time were all Jews. They were this flock. However, He had some sheep among the Samaritans also (John 4:39-42). Later many Gentiles would be won by the preaching of the gospel. All Christ's people would be one flock under one shepherd.

Important claims were made in this sermon. People other than Israel were to be included in the flock. Not only would Jesus lay down His life, but He would take it up again. No one would be able to take His life until He voluntarily laid it down. This was His command from His Father. His life would not end in death, but He would go through the valley and out the other side. Those who follow Him, putting their faith in the Good Shepherd, need fear no evil.

"The reason my Father loves me is that I lay down my life—only to take it up again" (John 10:17). Jesus laid down His life on the cross, and He took it up again in the resurrection.

Once again the Jews were divided. Some maintained He was raving mad, driven by a demon. But there were others who insisted that no demon or person possessed by a demon ever opened the eyes of the blind.

He Restores My Soul (22-30)

A new scene began at John 10:22. The feast of Dedication had arrived. This was in the month of December, about two months after the end of the feast of Tabernacles (John 7:37). Jesus was again in the temple area speaking to the crowds. This time, He was in Solomon's colonnade, where there was some protection from the cold weather.

The sermon on the Good Shepherd serves as a bridge between the discourses at the feast of Tabernacles (John 7:14-9:41) and the action described at the feast of Dedication (10:22-39). It is difficult to say just when the Good Shepherd parable was given, but the motif of the sheep continues into this discourse at the feast of Dedication. Some of the Jews gathered around Jesus and asked for a plain statement telling whether He was the Christ or not. This may have been intended to trap Him into making a rash statement that would ignite the final flame to engulf Him; but on the other hand, many people friendly to Jesus must have been wishing for a plain statement, too. Even John the Baptist had asked for one (Matthew 11:2, 3). Jesus had made such statements to individuals (John 4:26; 9:35, 37), but He had refrained from a public announcement that would rouse the authorities to violent moves.

In reply, Jesus pointed out that they had evidence enough to believe without such a statement. The miracles He had performed could not be denied, and they were done in His Father's name. In other words, if God was His Father, then He must be the Son.

This did not satisfy the questioners. Their trouble was that they could hear Him talking but not listen to what He was saying. His own sheep, however, hear His voice and follow Him. They were not of His sheep because they did not want to be. His own sheep, those who are fully committed to Him, have no doubts about who He is. These are given eternal life. ("He restores my soul.") They will never perish.

Furthermore, no one will be able to snatch them away from the hand of God (John 10:28, 29). Some would like to believe that once you have become a follower of Christ, it is impossible to be lost. This verse does not say that it is impossible to run away—only that no one can come and take you away. This is a comparison of the power of God and the power of Satan or any other power opposing God. No one has the power to steal a person from the fold. One must be aware, however, that he can remove himself. Unless a person remains loyal to Christ and His teaching, he has no promise of care within the fold.

Jesus did not promise to restore souls and preserve souls by himself alone. He included God the Father in His work. Then Jesus gave a plain statement, not that He was the Christ, but that He was divine: He made one of the strongest declarations of His deity that has been recorded: "I and the Father are one" (John 10:30). Each word of this affirmation is packed with meaning: "I" (not a title such as the Son of Man, but I personally) "and the Father" (not "my Father" or some ambiguous reference) "are" (not "is": the plural verb reflects the individuality of God and Christ) "one" (not masculine in gender, but neuter, denoting one unified being rather than one person).

In the Presence of My Enemies (31-39)

When Jesus said, "I and the Father are one," the Jews picked up stones to kill Him. One becomes more suspicious of the questioners now. Were they asking Him to make a plain statement so they would have an excuse to kill Him? He had come to His plain statement. He had given more than an affirmation that He was the Messiah. Jesus had made a claim of deity. They responded with a charge of blasphemy.

There were several ways blasphemy could be committed: (1) claiming to be God, (2) claiming to do what only God can do, (3) railing against God, (4) pronouncing the unpronounceable covenant name of God. The Jews accused Jesus of the first of these.

As the angry enemies made their move, Jesus said, "For which of these [miracles] do you stone me?" (John 10:32). That stopped them for a moment. They did not want anyone to think they were killing Jesus for doing good. Not for any of the miracles, they stormed, "but ... because you, a mere man, claim to be God" (John 10:33). There was no doubt about what Jesus meant when He said He and the Father were one. They said He claimed to be God, and He did not deny it. That was exactly what He claimed.

In reply, Jesus appealed to Scripture that used the term gods to apply to the judges of Israel. Psalm 82:6 speaks of human judges of Israel who served as representatives of God in judgment, and it gives them the honorable titles of "gods" and "sons of the Most High." Jesus was the one God set apart and sent into the world. If those human judges could be called by such exalted names, how much more was Jesus entitled to be called the Son of God! Again He called attention to the miracles. He was doing such things as the

Father does, things that only God can do. This was what He claimed to be.

Unable to answer His argument, the enemies again surged forward to seize Him, but He escaped their grasp. This had occurred on other occasions.[14] It may not have been miraculous. The dense crowd that usually surrounded Jesus would make it very difficult to pursue Him if He chose to slip away.

My Cup Overflows (40-42)

Then Jesus left Jerusalem, where the power of His enemies was centered. It was not yet time for Him to die; so He went to the area where John had baptized in the early days. Probably former disciples of John gathered again to hear Him. They found that all John had said about this man was true.

By now John had been beheaded by Herod (Matthew 14:6 12), but his witness lived on. Not all that he had predicted had been fulfilled as yet. Jesus later would die as the Lamb of God (John 1:29), and would baptize with the Holy Spirit (John 1:33). Still the people were sure Jesus was the greater one whom John had foretold (Matthew 3:11; John 1:15), "and in that place many believed in Jesus" (John 10:42).

---

[14] John 7:30; 8:20, 59.

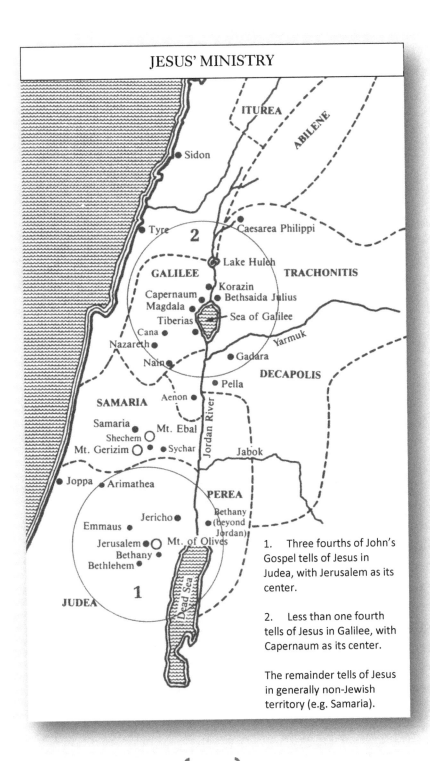

JESUS' MINISTRY

ITUREA

ABILENE

Sidon

Tyre

2

Caesarea Philippi

Lake Huleh

GALILEE

TRACHONITIS

Capernaum

Korazin

Bethsaida Julius

Magdala

Tiberias

Sea of Galilee

Cana

Nazareth

Yarmuk

Nain

Gadara

DECAPOLIS

Pella

SAMARIA

Aenon

Jordan River

Samaria

Mt. Ebal

Shechem

Mt. Gerizim

Sychar

Jabok

Joppa

Arimathea

PEREA

Jericho

Bethany (beyond Jordan)

Emmaus

Jerusalem

Mt. of Olives

Bethany

Bethlehem

Dead Sea

1

JUDEA

1. Three fourths of John's Gospel tells of Jesus in Judea, with Jerusalem as its center.

2. Less than one fourth tells of Jesus in Galilee, with Capernaum as its center.

The remainder tells of Jesus in generally non-Jewish territory (e.g. Samaria).

CHAPTER SEVEN

Life Again
John 11:1-57

Jesus worked many miracles to prove His claim to be the Messiah, the Son of God. In writing his Gospel, John chose a series of seven miraculous signs to show how this proof was used in the ministry of Jesus. He began with changing water into wine (John 2:1-11). A nobleman's son was healed in Capernaum, though Jesus was at Cana (John 4:46-54). Later, in Jerusalem, Jesus gave strength to a man who had been lame from birth (John 5:1-9). The feeding of the five thousand (John 6:5-14) was a miracle so striking that all four Gospels record it. In the night that followed, Jesus came walking on the water (John 6:16-21). Again in Jerusalem, Jesus gave sight to a man blind from birth (John 9:1-7). A climax was reached when Lazarus was raised from the dead (John 11:1-44).

A FRIEND IN NEED (11:1-6)

The raising of Lazarus was a climax in several ways. Although a miracle is a miracle, and one may be just as impossible as another without the power of God, nevertheless some miracles are greater than others. To raise a man from the dead is ultimate. Besides this, however, another crisis was at hand. The resistance of the Pharisees against Jesus and His ministry had come to a turning point. They must accept Jesus for what He claimed to be, or they must retire to the sidelines and become mere spectators, or they could increase their campaign against Him to meet the mounting proof He was placing before the people. The Pharisees and chief priests chose to go all out against Christ, "so from that day on they plotted to take his life" (John 11:53).

This brought a climax in the lives of Jesus' followers. Was their faith strong enough to stand the test? Thomas said, "Let us also go, that we may die with him" (with Jesus—John 11:16).

Many have wondered why this miracle is not recorded in the Synoptic Gospels (Matthew, Mark, and Luke) as well as in John. If it presents a climax in Jesus' ministry, they reason, it ought to be included in more than one of the records. The explanation lies in the different plans of the writers. Matthew, Mark, and Luke centered their attention on the ministry of Jesus in Galilee until they came to the events of the final week of His life. This was one way of keeping their accounts short so that more people would read them. Writing later, John apparently intended to tell some of the significant events that had been omitted. He included Jesus' early work in Judea, plus periodic activity in Jerusalem at later times. One of the events he recorded was the raising of Lazarus near Jerusalem.

Some have suggested that the raising of Lazarus did not actually happen, but that the story arose long after Jesus was gone. One should point out that resurrection miracles do occur in the Synoptics (the raising of Jairus's daughter in Mark 5:22-43, and the raising of a widow's son at Nain in Luke 7:11-15). These were important miracles also, but John does not include them because, for the most part, he chose material that had been omitted in the Synoptics. The minute details in John's account indicate that the record is true, the report of a reliable eyewitness.

A Friendly Family (1, 2)

Bethany was a town less than two miles east of Jerusalem. Jesus probably stayed there often during some of the week-long feasts at Jerusalem (Matthew 21:17). We know of one home in Bethany where He was a welcome guest (Luke 10:38-42). There were a brother and two sisters. The brother's name was Lazarus, which is a variant form of Eleazar and means "God helps." We know nothing about him except what we learn from the Gospel of John. (There seems to be no connection between this Lazarus and the beggar with the same name who appears in Luke 16:19 31.) The two sisters were Mary and Martha. They also appear in Luke 10:38-42. It is supposed that Martha was the older, because the home is called hers and because of the responsible role she played as the hostess. But Mary won praise for her devotion to Jesus as she sat and listened to Him in their home. She is identified as the one who poured perfume on the Lord and wiped His feet with her hair (John 11:2). This incident is told in the next chapter. It seems strange to find it mentioned here before it has been recorded, but we must remember that it was well known to Christians through the records of Matthew 26:6-13 and Mark 14:3-9. Still, John went on to tell about it in chapter 12, perhaps to note the time of it in his record. It was six days before the Passover, but Matthew and Mark did not record that.

This Mary of Bethany is not to be confused with Mary Magdalene, nor with Mary the mother of James and Joseph (Matthew 27:56), nor with Mary the mother of John Mark (Acts 12:12). And, of course, she was not the mother of Jesus.

In the Gospel records, Mary and Martha appear in three incidents: a dinner in their house (Luke 10:38-42), the raising of Lazarus (John 11:1-44), and a dinner in the house of Simon the leper (John 12:1-8; Matthew 26:6-13; Mark 14:3-9). In these accounts, Martha seems to be the manager, serving the meals and attending to details of arrangement, while Mary seems to be the contemplative soul concerned with higher values than physical care and comfort. From the slight indications we have, it seems that this was a family of considerable means and influence. There was a home large enough to accommodate guests like Jesus and His disciples. There was a tomb of cave-like proportions. Lazarus was honored in death by a considerable number of mourners.

Lazarus became ill, and the sisters sent word to Jesus, "Lord, the one you love is sick." Jesus had recently left Judea after numerous attempts to arrest or kill Him (John 10:31, 39). The sisters did not ask Him to come back where He would be in danger; but they knew His healing power, and it is obvious that they hoped He would save their brother's life. Even though Jesus loved Lazarus, Martha, and their sister, He stayed where He was for two more days before going to Bethany. Jesus was in "the place where John had been baptizing in the early days" (John 10:40). It was "across the Jordan"; that is, on the east side of the river.

Those who delivered the message must have been disappointed when Jesus made no move to help. Mary and Martha must have been even more disappointed when their messengers returned and reported that Jesus had said, "This sickness will not end in death" (John 11:4). Perhaps Lazarus was already dead when the messengers brought back that report. What Jesus meant was that Lazarus' days on this earth were not yet over. The death he suffered was only temporary. But Jesus' hearers did not understand this. Neither did they understand what He meant when He added that Lazarus' sickness was for the glory of God and His Son.

We must not imagine that Jesus was not concerned about Lazarus and his grief-stricken sisters. To prevent such a mistaken conclusion, John added, "Jesus loved Martha and her sister and Lazarus" (John 11:5).

Then why did He wait two more days before He did anything? The reason is not given, but we can conjecture what it probably was. Many people in Jerusalem knew Lazarus (John 11:18, 19). No doubt some of Jesus' bitter enemies knew messengers had been sent to Him. If he had gone back with the messengers, those enemies probably would have been waiting for Him, and there was no feast-day crowd to protect Him. It was not yet time for His violent death; so He wanted to come at a time when He was not expected. The delay meant two added days of grief for the sisters, but it also meant that the resurrection miracle would be that much more irrefutable both then and through the ages.

Another factor may have figured in Jesus' delay of two days. The message was almost a request from a family He loved. While Jesus was often quick to respond to appeals from strangers, it is notable that He did not yield so quickly to those who were near and dear to Him. His mother once suggested that He do something about the wine supply at a wedding feast (John 2:3-11). His brothers once told Him He should go to Jerusalem to the feast of Tabernacles (John 7:3-10). In each case, Jesus rebuffed the suggestion but later did what was suggested. Since Lazarus and his family were so close to Jesus, perhaps this is another case where Jesus delayed action to make it clear that He was not subject to a schedule designed by men, even His closest friends, but only to the will of God. His compassion called for action, but wisdom and submission to God required waiting.

A CONCLUSIVE SIGN (11:7-44)

Lazarus Is Dead (7-16)

After two days Jesus said to His disciples, "Let us go back to Judea" (John 11:7). This was like walking into the jaws of death. Judea was where deadly enemies were waiting for Him. Instantly, the disciples protested. Jesus' enigmatic reply in John 11:9, 10 suggests that there is a favorable time for every good work, and now was the time when Jesus could make a quick trip to Bethany and get away again without falling into the fatal trap of His enemies. Thus He could continue the work He wanted to do in His day, and still postpone His death until the appointed time.

Jesus explained that Lazarus was asleep, but He was going to awaken him. In both Jewish and Greek circles, sleep was used in a figurative way to mean death. But the disciples took it literally. If Lazarus had fallen into a natural sleep, they said, that was a good sign. He would get well, and there was no need for Jesus to go to

FOLLOW THE SIGNS

The Gospel of John is not only known as a Gospel of belief but as a book of signs. Miraculous deeds of Jesus are recorded in order to show the role of these acts both in the conviction of those who were present and those who would read of these signs in John's witness for all the coming years. These mighty deeds were evident signs for the power of Jesus and the truth of His message.

When one begins to watch for these signs, he can see the mounting proof of Jesus' claims throughout His ministry. These episodes are given each time with definite results of increased belief which is the overall purpose of John's writing this Gospel narrative. If one accepts the historical notes, the spiritual significance, and the witness to the immediate results, the reader must end this narrative with his own assent to believe.

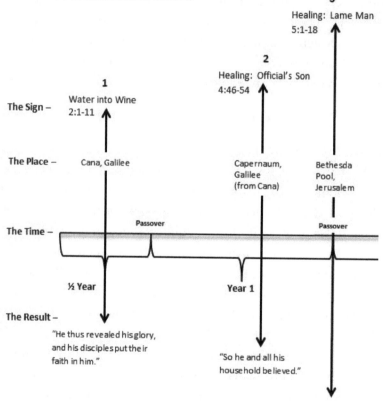

Some would claim a contradiction between John and the Synoptics in that John presents the miracles of Jesus as given in order to produce faith whereas the Synoptics require faith on the part of the person in need before the miracle can be worked (Matthew 13:58, Mark 6:5). Instead of a contradiction, however, this shows different stages of belief. Before the miracles (the Synoptics), an individual normally manifests some element of trust in Jesus, but after the miracle (John), his faith is manifestly increased by this clear evidence of Jesus' power.

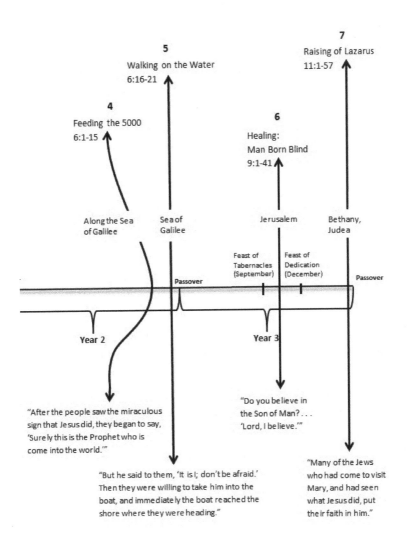

Bethany. Jesus then said, "Lazarus is dead.... Let us go to him" (John 11:14, 15).

Thomas, who was also called Didymus (meaning "Twin"), spoke out for the disciples. With words of courage and wholehearted commitment, he expressed his willingness to go to Judea and die with Jesus. Thus, he gave one example of what Jesus talked about later: "The man who hates his life in this world will keep it for eternal life" (John 12:25).

Disappointment but Hope (17-37)

Little Bethany was full of sorrow when Jesus came. Even from Jerusalem, friends had come to join the mourning. Someone saw Jesus coming and ran to tell Martha. She went to meet Him before the other mourners knew He was coming. Jesus did not work the miracle upon Lazarus without first challenging the living as He probed into their faith. Martha showed her disappointment by saying that Jesus could have done something if He had been there, but she showed her faith and hope by saying that He could still do something if He chose to ask God.

Jesus' reply, "Your brother will rise again," must have stirred her hope still more, but still she was cautious, not wanting to hope for too much. Of course, Lazarus would rise in the general resurrection at the last day. But could Martha hope for something more than this, something nearer? Dare she hope that Lazarus would rise that very day?

Jesus then delivered another "I am." Not only is He the bread of life, the light of the world, and the Good Shepherd; He is also life itself. And not only is He life, but He is the resurrection and the life: He is life in spite of death. And this life is true life. Essential to true life is belief in Jesus. Even if a believer dies, He will live forever in Christ.

"Do you believe this?" Jesus put the question directly to Martha, and it was a hard question. She could not understand all that Jesus meant. Her brother had believed in Jesus, and he was dead; yet Jesus said, "Whoever lives and believes in me will never die" (John 11:26). How could that be? But Jesus did not ask if she understood; He asked if she believed, and she did. "Yes, Lord, I believe that you are the Christ, the Son of God, who was to come into the world" (John 11:27). That covered everything. Understood or not, whatever the Christ said was true. Such was the faith of Martha.

When Mary came at Jesus' summons, we are told only a little of what she said, but we see an outpouring of deep emotional grief. Mary wept, the friends with her wept, and Jesus wept. Why did He weep? Knowing the future as He did, He had ample reason for grief. He knew of His own suffering coming soon, but He did not grieve for himself. He knew that Lazarus' place in Heaven was better than on earth. Jesus did not grieve for him. The grief that started His tears at this moment was the intense grief of those about Him. When they saw Jesus weeping, they said, "See how He loved him. Could not he who opened the eyes of the blind man have kept this man from dying?" So the time had come for another great demonstration of what Jesus could do.

Life Again (38-44)

Jesus asked where the body had been laid, and they took Him to the tomb. This was no easy moment for Jesus. Once again, He was deeply moved. He ordered the stone taken from the entrance of the cave-like tomb. Practical Martha quickly objected that the odor of decomposition would fill the air, but Jesus promised that if she believed, she would see the glory of God. All might see the miracle, but only the believers would see the glory of God.

"Father, I thank you." With these words, Jesus began a prayer. It was a prayer of thanksgiving before the event, and expressed the purpose, "that they may believe that you sent me" (John 11:41, 42).

In the silence that followed His brief prayer to God, Jesus raised His voice and called for Lazarus to come from the tomb. He came out, grave clothes and all. That Lazarus was able to come out, bound as he was with the grave clothes, may have been a miracle within a miracle.

Jesus, practical as always, ordered that he be released from the tightly wound cloth. Lazarus was free and his body filled with life.

REACTION (11:45-57)

Faith, Fear, and Plots (45-53)

This miracle was so convincing that many of the Jews who had been in doubt now believed in Jesus (John 11:45). Some of them reported to the Pharisees, perhaps hoping to convince even those who had been most bitter in opposition. If that was their intention, they failed.

The raising of Lazarus only strengthened the Pharisees and chief priests in their determination to get rid of Jesus. His coming to the area may have taken them by surprise, but as soon as they learned of it, they called an emergency meeting of the Sanhedrin, the ruling council of the Jews. There was but one question on their agenda. It was not a question of whether or not a resurrection miracle had happened or what it meant if it had happened. It was a question of how to stop Jesus, whoever He was and whatever He was doing.

Obviously, Jesus' popularity and His power with the crowds were growing. The restless people were longing for the promised Messiah, and most of them expected Him to lead them in winning freedom from the Romans, who ruled over them. If Jesus would plainly and publicly announce that He was the Messiah, armed rebellion might start, whether He wanted it or not. The ruling Jews reasoned that the Romans would come to punish the whole nation if disturbances continued and rebellion arose. Such a rebellion, they were sure, would be crushed, and they (the Jews who were in power at the time) would be removed from office because they had not been able to maintain order.

It was better that one should die, the high priest said, than that the whole nation perish. His words were more truly a prediction of what was going to happen than he realized, for—as John informs us—"he did not say this on his own" (John 11:5 1).

God spoke through Caiaphas, even though the high priest did not know it. Jesus would indeed die for the Jewish nation, "but also for the scattered children of God, to bring them together and make them one" (John 11:52). This would include Gentiles as well as Jews.

"So from that day on they plotted to take his life" (John 11:53).

Withdrawn but Imminent (54-57)

Since it was not yet time for Jesus to give His life, He again left Jerusalem, and once again the plots of the Jewish leaders were frustrated. But as the Passover approached, the people gathering in Jerusalem were expecting Him to return. The chief priests and Pharisees gave orders for His arrest, but still the people looked for Him. He had brought life to the physical body of Lazarus. Who could deny that He could bring life to the eternal spirits of God's people?

CHAPTER EIGHT

The Way of the King
John 12: 1-50

How can you tell who is a king? By the way he talks? By the way he is dressed? By the way people treat him? By the power and authority at his command?

WHAT MAKES A KING? (12:1-19)

Three things complicated the recognition of Jesus as king during His earthly ministry. First, His kingdom was not like kingdoms in this world. It could not be measured in miles or identified with a visible palace. It was a spiritual kingdom; and a king without an earthly throne was hard to recognize. Second, Jesus had not made public claim to His kingship. His kingdom was not what people expected, and opposition mounted so strongly against Him that Jewish leaders were ready to take His life in order to stop His acceptance. Jesus talked about the kingdom and about himself. Some had reached the conclusion He was the Messiah; and He had affirmed this to individuals, but not by way of public announcement to the crowds. Third, Jesus had a timetable to keep. He must have a period to instruct the multitudes in order to correct their false ideas of the Messiah. Then, too, the Jewish leaders might attempt to thwart His ministry and take His life if He pressed His claim too soon and too clearly. He must not allow His ministry to be ended before He was ready.

Strong indications pointed toward Jesus' kingship. He may not have dressed like a king, but the only valuable belonging we know about was a piece of clothing. At His death, the soldiers decided not to destroy His seamless garment (John 19:23, 24). As for the way He talked, the people noted immediately that He did not speak as the scribes, but as one having authority (Matthew 7:28, 29). His power was undeniable. He could work miracles of healing and had control even of the wind and the waves.

Such a man must be a king. Some had even tried to make Him their king openly, but He had foiled their attempts (John 6:15).

Now, however, the time had come in this final week of His earthly ministry to accept publicly the way of the kingdom. He was anointed. He was acclaimed in a triumphal entry. He was sought after by people of other nations. He laid down His injunctions. Just for a little time, people were treating Him as a king. In the midst of all this, however, Jesus gave warning of coming death, of suffering before the victory. Jesus came in the way of the king, but not in a way the world expected.

Anointed (1-8)

The last phase of Jesus' ministry before His death began with a feast. This dinner, a kind of community affair, was given in His honor at Bethany.

John answers concisely the basic questions of good reporting: When? Where? Who? What?

One would surmise that the day indicated is Saturday evening. It was six days before the Passover (John 12:1). If the Passover fell on Thursday (with Jesus' death on Friday, as indicated in Mark 15:42), then Saturday was the day of this event that came six days before the Passover. It was permissible to have guests for dinner on the Sabbath. Even the Pharisees did that (Luke 14:1). It may be that Jesus arrived in the vicinity the day before, and that news concerning His arrival had spread through Jerusalem. Jesus' association with Lazarus and the miracle of Lazarus' resurrection led to the chief priests' plans to kill Lazarus as well as Jesus (John 12:9, 10). Jesus may have come from Jericho the day before, arriving at Bethany about the time the Sabbath began at sunset.

The town of Bethany is specified as the place. It was situated less than two miles southeast of Jerusalem, on the eastern slope of the Mount of Olives. The feast was given by those who wished to honor Jesus. The ones most important to the narrative are named by John: Lazarus, Martha, and Mary. Lazarus was the one whom Jesus had raised from the dead, and the honor given Jesus may have been associated with gratitude for this miracle. John specifies that Lazarus was one of those reclining with Jesus at the table, while Martha was serving. These facts would not be noteworthy if the feast was at their home, so the mention of them seems to suggest that it was elsewhere. This harmonizes with the other Gospels that name the home of a certain Simon as the setting for this feast (Matthew 26:6; Mark 14:3).

During the feast, an anointing occurred. The practice of anointing the head played an important role among the Jews. *Priests* were set apart by anointment. For instance, Aaron, as he was installed as high priest, was anointed by pouring the holy oil on his head after his robing but before the sacrifice and consecration (Leviticus 8:12). Then he was anointed again after the sacrifice (Leviticus 8:30). Anointing also played a part in the appointment of a *king.* David is an example (1 Samuel 16:13; also 2 Samuel 2:4; 5:3). When an individual was set apart to the office of *prophet,* anointing was used at times. For instance, Elijah was told to anoint Elisha (1 Kings 19:16). The servant of the Lord was anointed to preach (Isaiah 61:1). Christ referred to this passage and identified himself as the fulfillment of Isaiah's prophecy (Luke 4:18-21). It is not recorded that Jesus was literally and ceremonially anointed with oil before that time, but *anointed* is used figuratively to mean He was chosen, designated, appointed. In this metaphorical sense, various ones whom God chose for various purposes were called anointed ones: the patriarchs (Psalm 105:15), the Persian King Cyrus (Isaiah

45:1), and perhaps the whole nation of Israel (Habakkuk 3:13). The very word *Christ*, which is the Greek translation of the Hebrew *Messiah*, means the anointed one (Psalm 45:7; Hebrews 1:9).

Another practice common in Palestine, and in Egypt as well, was the anointment of a dead body in preparation for burial (John 19:40; Mark 16:1). The ointments and spices were applied externally to the body in the Palestinian practice.

Among the Jews, it was also a custom to apply ointments to the exposed parts of the living body before going out into the hot sun. This was a daily use.

On monuments in Egypt, one finds an example of a host anointing his guest upon arrival for a feast. This must have been a common practice in Palestine as well, for Jesus rebuked Simon the Pharisee when he neglected the anointing as Jesus came to eat in his house (Luke 7:46).

At the event in Bethany, Mary provided special honor to Jesus as she anointed Him. We read about this occasion in Mark 14:3 9 and Matthew 26:6-13 as well as in this passage in John. Although Mary is not named in the Synoptic accounts, the details are so similar that it is impossible to escape the conclusion that their reference is to the same occasion.

Matthew and Mark say the woman anointed Jesus' head, but John says Mary anointed His feet. Understanding that both the head and the feet were anointed helps to clarify the picture of what happened. Probably Mary approached with the intention of anointing His head, but when this was completed and some ointment was left over, her humility and love, with her desire to use all the ointment, led her to anoint the feet of Jesus as well. She had not anticipated the need of a towel to wipe away the excess, so she used her hair for that purpose.

In many cases, anointing with oil was a simple gesture of honor to welcome a special guest. It becomes evident, however, that in this case, the anointing was more than a simple gesture. Mary used a precious ointment that was worth as much as a year's salary. It was a pound of pure or genuine nard, a fragrant ointment used both as perfume and unguent. It may have represented Mary's life-long and cherished savings.

John centers attention on the anointing that occurred at the feast. Four features stand out in the account: (1) the pound of pure (or liquid) nard was very costly; (2) Mary anointed Jesus' feet, which was not the ordinary practice; (3) she wiped His feet with her hair instead of using a common cloth; (4) the whole house was filled with the fragrance of the perfume. The mention of that last detail is one indication that the author himself was there and was impressed by the memorable fragrance.

The genuine nard spoken of may have come from an aromatic herb grown in the Himalayas between Tibet and India. Its transportation was expensive. It was in an alabaster jar (Mark 14:3), probably not the softer gypsum, but the oriental onyx or onyx marble. This, too, was expensive. Mary was not using what was left from another occasion. She broke the seal of the bottle and used the contents for this very anointing.

Judas criticized her action, pointing out that the ointment could have been sold and the proceeds used to feed the poor. It seems that everyone sided with Judas—everyone but Jesus. Jesus defended Mary's action. She had anointed Him for burial. This gave additional meaning to this particular anointing. The time had come for the mounting hostility to launch a final action. Death was closing in. It was evident to all that Jesus and His enemies were now on a collision course. Either total victory or a dismal death loomed ahead. Jesus had repeatedly warned His disciples of His coming death. Now this act of anointment was directly associated with it.

Jesus' approval of Mary's act did not scorn the need of the poor. Rather, it pointed out the coming climax to the whole of human history and the need for proper attention to the person and work of Christ. This anointment would be one added gesture to draw needed respect through ages to come.

John also noted another objection to Judas' suggestion. Judas was a thief. If the ointment had been sold and the money designated for the poor, he could have stolen some of it, for he was the treasurer of the group of disciples. It was no small operation to provide the necessities for thirteen men. This required a common treasury, and Judas was the one who supervised it. No doubt, he had ability and the confidence of the other disciples, but the fact remains that he was a thief. This must have been a vital factor in his fate as the traitor who betrayed Jesus.

The very anointing of Jesus supplied a fitting introduction to the final phase in His ministry. He was about to announce himself as king by entering the capital city amid the plaudits of the people (John 12:12-19). He was God's anointed, the *Christos*, the Christ. He was anointed to preach glad tidings to the poor, but He was also anointed as the King. He did not speak of this at the supper in Bethany, however. He said rather that He was being anointed for His burial, for His death was at hand.

Anticipated (9-11)

Word quickly spread along the route to Jerusalem that Jesus had arrived in Bethany. Those who saw Him told others, and the message ran through the city like wildfire, for everyone was looking for Jesus (John 11:55-57). It was no long trip from Jerusalem to the town just on the other side of the Mount of Olives. People came from the city, people en route to Jerusalem stopped along the way, people who were already settled early for the coming Passover now hurried to Bethany. All were coming to see Jesus and also Lazarus. After all, Lazarus was living proof of resurrection after death. He had been in the grave for four days, but now was alive and well.

The chief priests could not endure the continued presence of Jesus or the living testimony of Lazarus. They determined that Lazarus must be killed as well as Jesus.

Acclaimed (12-16)

On the next day after the feast, the first day of the week, Jesus made His entry into Jerusalem. All four Gospel writers describe the scene. Each has his own details to offer. John specifies that "they took palm branches" as they went out to meet Him. Branches of palms and other trees were used in the feast of Tabernacles, originally to make shelters to be lived in for a week (Leviticus 23:40, 42).

From their association with the happy festival, the palm branches became symbols of rejoicing for other festivals and special occasions.[15]

The triumphal entry of Jesus is so called because it resembled the triumph of a conquering general or the acclamation of a king ascending his throne. It was marked as such an occasion by the manner in which Jesus entered Jerusalem riding on a donkey. This was no ordinary way for a pilgrim to come to the Passover celebration. It was also marked by the reception He received. The palm branches spread before Him were reminiscent of victorious Simon's triumphal entry into Jerusalem when the Syrian rulers were expelled in the second century B.C. The shout of welcome was "Blessed is he who comes in the name of the Lord! Blessed is the King of Israel!" The first part of it associated Jesus with Psalm 118, and the happy people added "the King of Israel" to proclaim Jesus more plainly as the Messiah. To cap the climax, John called this event the fulfillment of prophecy in Zechariah 9:9, which also plainly proclaims the King. It was indeed the way of the King as Jesus made public His true identity.

The crowd shouted "Hosanna," which means "Save, I pray."

Only after telling of the happy welcome does John mention the donkey. This does not mean that Jesus yielded to the enthusiasm of the crowd and consented to mount the animal and enter Jerusalem as a triumphant king. He had already made arrangements with His

---

[15] Maccabees 13:51; 2 Maccabees 10:7; Revelation 7:9.

disciples and probably with others to secure the animal (Mark 11:1-7).

Matthew 21:2 makes it clear that there were a donkey and her colt, but Jesus used the colt. Jesus chose His own time and place to make public His claim to be King. He was not a conquering general on a warhorse, but a special kind of king, the prince of peace. He came on the colt of a donkey, and this had been prophesied in Zechariah 9:9.

The time had come! The great crowd of people joyfully proclaimed Him as their King.

Empowered (17-19)

It seems strange that the disciples could not see the meaning of all this at the time. Not until Jesus was glorified did the import of His triumphal entry and the fulfillment of the prophecies become apparent to them. Jesus had been anointed by Mary, but it is doubtful that she recognized the fuller meaning of her action until Jesus made her defense (John 12:7). Jesus was acclaimed by the people as King and Messiah, but it is doubtful that they recognized the significance of the fulfilled prophecy. However, one thing was evident to all. Jesus had raised Lazarus from the dead. He had worked miracles in the sight of the crowds. He was empowered from on high. He was a King with Heavenly authority.

Different elements were represented in the crowd that met Jesus on His entry into Jerusalem. There were those who had been present at the raising of Lazarus. They were repeating again and again what they had seen. Then there were those who had heard the reports and had gone out to see Jesus and Lazarus for themselves. But also there were those who feared for their own positions. These Jewish leaders, the Pharisees, now said to each other that something must be done, and immediately. "Look how the whole world has gone after him" (John 12:19). This was both ironic and truly prophetic. In days to come, Jesus would send His people to win a world much wider than that of Jerusalem (Mark 16:15).

Jesus' way was not the course of an earthly king. He must suffer and die before the ultimate victory. Therefore He could say to His followers: "Deny [yourself], take up [your] cross and follow me" (Matthew 16:24). This is the way of the King of kings. It is the only way.

A MATTER OF LIFE OR DEATH (12:19-50)

Some questions are purely academic. "What was the price of fish in London in 1892?" Probably the answer to this question does not change many lives today. Innumerable questions are asked that can never be settled. "If Grouchy or Ney had followed instructions, would Napoleon have won at the battle of Waterloo? If Napoleon had won, what would have been the consequences?" No one can really say what would have been if the actual happenings had not occurred.

Other questions are practical but really not very important. "Shall I take the expressway and go a longer distance but get there quicker, or shall I take the shorter route but take more time?" But then, both roads lead to the same place.

Some questions, however, are a matter of life or death. "Shall I pull the trigger of a gun aimed to take a life?" "Shall I disregard the doctor's warning that I must take certain precautions or else expect an early death?"

Then there are questions that relate to eternal life and eternal death. They are not related to man's physical being, but are matters of the inner man, matters of spiritual depth. What is the condition of a man's soul? Jesus said, "Do not be afraid of those who kill the body but cannot kill the soul. Rather, be afraid of the One who can destroy both soul and body in hell" (Matthew 10:28).

Facing Death (19-22)

Jesus faced death as He came to Jerusalem for the Passover. He knew it. The Jewish leaders had threatened to take His life. The disciples were undergoing a tremendous struggle within themselves. They were deadlocked between a confidence in the power of Jesus and a fear rising from His repeated warnings that He must die. The people also sensed the climax. Which would it be? Would the Jewish leaders win, bringing death to Jesus? Or would the Messianic hope in Christ be victorious and wipe out all opposition?

The climax seemed to draw closer yet each day. From the other Gospels, one learns that Jesus cleansed the temple on the day following His triumphal entry (Mark 11:11-17). This was followed by a day of questions (Matthew 21:23-24:1) as the Jewish leaders tried to trap Jesus by His own words (Matthew 22:15). Tension and hostility were high as the Sadducees and Pharisees plotted to take His life.

The temple area during these hours of furious debate is the most probable setting for the incident John records next, the request of the Greeks who wanted to see Jesus.

Who were these Greeks? One cannot be sure whether they came all the way from Greece or from some close Hellenistic area such as the Decapolis. But at least we know they were among the people who came to worship at the Passover.

At the beginning of Jesus' life, Wise-men from the East represented the Gentile world as they brought Him homage. Just before His death, Greeks from the Gentile world came seeking Him. These preliminary contacts seem to carry hint of the Gentiles' inclusion in the gospel invitation yet to come. Why did they want to speak with Him? Did they want to propose some philosophical puzzle? Or perhaps they wanted to give Him a warning about the hostile opposition that must lead inevitably to death unless in some way its course was altered. Perhaps it was more than a warning they wanted to give Him. They may have been ready to suggest a solution for the dilemma. Perhaps they wanted to issue Jesus an invitation to go with them to their home area and begin a new ministry there. They may have been ready to promise He would be better understood and appreciated and would be relieved of the threats of death that constantly hovered over Him in the land where He was living.

Rejecting Escape (23-28)

Of course, such suggestions are speculative, but some hint of a Greek proposal that Jesus flee may be found in the reply the Master gave. Oftentimes Jesus did not directly answer a question, but gave a sermon in which one finds both the direction of the question and the message the inquirer needed. For example, there was a time when a man in Jesus' audience interrupted the Master and asked Him to make his brother divide an inheritance with him (Luke 12:13). Jesus answered that He had not come for that purpose. But then He proceeded to preach a sermon against covetousness. This was what the man needed.

On this occasion, when the Greeks wanted to see Jesus, we are not told of the reason for their request or of a specific response to them, but the incident introduces Jesus' sermon on life and death.

These Greeks were proselytes to the Jewish faith, or at least "God-fearers," else they would not be in the temple area in this week of the Passover. But they were of Greek descent, not Jewish. Their approach to Jesus was through one of His disciples. Jesus had reached such prominence that perhaps they thought it would be presumptuous to walk up to Him personally with their request. Perhaps their request was one they did not care to make in public, and they wanted to draw Him aside. Or perhaps the time was so crucial and the peril so great that they felt this necessitated withdrawal.

They chose to approach Jesus through Philip, a disciple with a Greek name. His family must have had some connection with Greek people, else they would not have given him such a name. He could be expected to be more sympathetic with the Greeks. Philip then went to Andrew, another disciple with a Greek name. Perhaps Philip felt that Andrew was close to Jesus and could more fittingly deal with the Greeks' request. Perhaps Philip did not want to take full responsibility for presenting such a request to Jesus. Probably it was not unusual for people to want to see Jesus, but this request came from Greeks. Would Jesus welcome them? His mission was to Israel (Matthew 10:5, 6). Before this time He had told the disciples to preach only to "the lost sheep of Israel" (Matthew 15:24). Later the gospel was to go to all mankind, but the disciples did not yet understand that.

To "see" Jesus was more than to view Him. The Greeks wanted to interview Him, to get to know Him personally. Jesus' answer may seem surprising as we read it. It seems to be addressed to Andrew and Philip, but He spoke to instruct the crowds and give reply to the Greeks.

Finding Fulfillment (23-36)

If they came to suggest escape from danger, Jesus would not take the way out they had in mind. If they came to promise popularity and glory to Him, Jesus made it clear that He sought Heavenly glory rather than a poor earthly substitute. His glory would come through doing the will of the Father. Physical death is not the end, but introduces a fuller life, a richer order of things. The Gospel of John makes it clear that this eternal life can begin for the individual while he still lives in the world, but only after a death to his old, selfish self. Furthermore, a person does not save his life by seeking to escape physical death.

Jesus showed a relationship of death and life that transcended man's quick view of it. The first example was from nature (John 12:24). The seed must be put into the earth and die before it can reach a fuller form of life and have a fruitful accomplishment.

The seed grows and produces many seeds. The example then was extended to the lives of the disciples (John 12:25, 26). Honor will come to the one who serves well, not the one who seeks to spare himself or to satisfy selfish motives. But finally, Jesus gave himself as an example (John 12:27, 28). His own life must be given as a supreme sacrifice, and the time was now close at hand. He was not about to look for some way of escape. Rather, He looked to the Father to confirm His will by glorifying the name of Jesus.

A few months earlier, Jesus' enemies had not been able to arrest Him because His time had not yet come (John 7:30; 8:20). But now His hour was at hand, and we read this again and again (John 12:23, 27; 13:1; 16:32; 17:1). It was time for Jesus to be glorified by being raised from the dead and exalted at the right hand of the Father. He would come to that glory by way of torture, crucifixion, and death.

"Now my heart is troubled" (John 12:27). This seems to be a simple statement of fact. In John 14:1, we see that Jesus used the same word in urging His disciples not to be troubled. He wanted to spare them the kind of turmoil His own soul was experiencing. But He knew personally what it was to be torn by the prospect of death in physical agony, and the torture of bearing the sins of all mankind upon the shoulders of one who had known no sin in His own life.

In the King James Version, "*Father, save me from this hour*" is punctuated as if it were a simple request that Jesus might escape the time of torture and death leading to glory. It seems better to read it as punctuated in the New International Version. "*Father, save me from this hour*" then appears as a part of Jesus' question. Out of His troubled heart, He asked, "What shall I say? 'Father, save me from this hour'?" But instantly He rejected that possibility. "No, it was for this very reason I came to this hour." All His earthly life had been leading up to this time when He and the Father would be glorified together. He would not seek to escape the pain that would lead to glory. Turning away from such a request, He voiced the sincere desire of His heart: "Father, glorify your name!" His earnest wish was to bring glory to God, regardless of the cost.

A voice came from Heaven giving assurance of this glorification. God had glorified His name in all the miraculous works of Jesus and in all His Godly teaching. He would glorify it again by bringing Jesus back from death with redemption for all mankind.

The people did not understand the words spoken, but they realized that a sign had been given in response to Jesus' prayer. Some said an angel had spoken to Him. Others thought it had thundered.

To the listening people Jesus said, "This voice was for your benefit, not mine" (John 12:30). In the manner of speaking common among the Hebrews, the meaning of *not* is limited. Jesus' statement may well be translated, "This voice was not for my benefit alone, but for yours also." To Jesus, it gave assurance of glory; to the people, it at least indicated God's presence.

At Jesus' baptism, the voice of God had been heard (Matthew 3:17), and at His transfiguration, it had been heard again (Matthew 17:5). Now in this hour when His death approached, God's voice again was heard. The future glorification referred to would include the death, resurrection, ascension, and Heavenly exaltation of Christ, as well as the world-wide proclamation of the gospel.

Though the people did not understand it, the voice was for their benefit. It was a source of strength to those who had faith, and at the same time it offered a test of their faith. Jesus was the conqueror over Satan and death. "The prince of this world will be driven out. But I, when I am lifted up from the earth, will draw all men to myself" (John 12:3 1, 32). John felt his readers would need an explanation of Jesus' words (John 12:33), but evidently the people then present understood that Jesus was speaking of His death. However, they thought the Christ was to live and rule forever. They must have known that He called himself the Son of Man, for He did it often. So they asked Him to explain himself. Just who was He?

Again, Jesus' response did not so much answer their question as it answered their need. They needed to put their faith in Him while they could. As for being "lifted up," Jesus would be lifted up from the earth to die on the cross. But He also would rise from the grave and be lifted up in resurrection. Finally, He would be lifted up from the earth to ascend into Heaven. When this was accomplished, He would draw all men to His person. This verse does not say that all men would respond to the drawing power of Jesus. As a magnet uses its pulling power, some objects are moved and some are not, depending on the resistance of the object drawn. Jesus urged, "Put your trust in the light while you have it, so that you may become sons of light" (John 12:36). Then Jesus slipped away from the crowd.

Warning of Tragedy (37-43)

In writing the Gospel, John stopped to point out that even though Jesus had performed miracles, taught with authority, and lived a blameless life, the people as a whole were unwilling to commit their lives to follow Him. There were those who believed in Him with an intellectual assent, but were not willing to make their belief known (John 12:42). They were afraid of the rejection of men; so they preferred to reject Jesus.

This rejection was foretold in Isaiah 6:10; 53:1. This does not mean that God did not want Jesus' hearers to repent, nor that He forced them to hardness of heart against their will. It means that their resistance to God's revelation was foreknown and that rejection of God's truth leads to a hardening of the heart and a block in the understanding.

One should not think the action was performed in order to match the prophecy, but rather the prophecy was given because God was predicting what He knew would certainly come to pass. The foreknowledge of God is accurate and true. The prophecy did not force the fulfillment, but rather the prophecy was given to explain that God knew in advance the unbelieving hearts and the blinded eyes and the failure to turn to Him. Isaiah said these things in his time because he saw the coming glory of Jesus and the unbelief of men. This is a matter of life or death; this is a matter of salvation or destruction.

Is it merely a matter of intellectual belief or unbelief? John went on to give an example of Jews who believed what Jesus said; but for fear of condemnation from other men, they did not act upon their belief and commit their lives to Jesus.

Seeing the Light (44-50)

Jesus contrasted the darkness of unbelief and sin with the light of His own life and teaching: "No one who believes in me should stay in darkness." He then closed His teaching of the multitudes with the solemn warning that they would be judged for eternity by the word He spoke (John 12:47-5 1).

The Gospel of John tells more that Jesus said to His disciples, but these are His closing words to the crowd. He pleaded with them to come out of the darkness into the light of God's Word. Jesus did not come that first time to condemn the individual who is lost, but to offer an invitation to him. However, if he resists that invitation, the very words Jesus has spoken will condemn him at the last day. These words are not the words of Jesus alone. He brings the message of His Heavenly Father. Accept the person of Christ and the words of His mouth. This is a matter of life or death. It is a matter of eternal life or eternal death.

CHAPTER NINE

Final Truths
John 13:1-14:31

Sometimes the disciples faced situations too heavy for them to bear—especially near the end. The rush of closing events brought to the disciples demands beyond their strength.

TOO HEAVY TO BEAR

Circumstances demanded that one of them wash his fellow-disciples' feet. But each one felt this was too much to be asked, to lower himself to this type of service. Another burden was added when they were told that one of them was going to betray Jesus. Who would it be? Could any one of the Twelve be guilty of this? It was too much even to think of such a betrayal.

Then Jesus warned them He was going away. This thought was too much to bear. To be separated was bad enough, but to be told they could not come where He was going—that was too much to endure.

Peter insisted he was ready to lay down his life for Jesus. To offer his own life was not too much. But Jesus warned him, "Before the rooster crows, you will disown me three times!" (John 13:38). This seemed too heavy to bear.

Jesus told them these things so they would realize their own weakness. He wanted to be there to help them. He showed them by His example how to wash the disciples' feet. The Master provided the challenge of His own life. He showed a willingness to perform for His servants anything that was needed. He offered His love as the answer for loads too heavy to bear. His disciples must learn this love for one another. He warned Peter of coming denials so that Peter might have strength on another day to rise above the failures of the day before. Without Jesus, there are loads too heavy to bear; but with the example and help of Jesus, a way is made possible.

A Demonstration Lesson (1-17)

A lesson that is acted out in real life makes a lasting impression, especially when that lesson is given at a crucial moment in a person's life. The setting of this lesson is important. The disciples had been disputing about which of them was the greatest (Luke 22:24). On the other hand, the mood of Jesus was one of love. And the occasion was a feast where Jesus and His disciples were present.

The question arises as to whether John here describes the Passover feast or a meal that preceded the Passover. He opens his record of this episode with the phrase "before" the Passover (John 13:1).

This does not mean, however, that the evening meal described afterward is not the Passover feast. Rather, John is saying that before the Passover, Jesus knew His time had come to leave the world; and before the Passover He had loved those who were His own in the world, and this love was to continue to the end.

Knowing that He would be crucified the next day, Jesus did all He could to prepare His beloved disciples for that tragic ordeal. Thus, He "now showed them the full extent of His love" (John 13:1).

John 13:2 says, "The evening meal was being served." This is a better translation than, "Supper being ended," as the King James Version has it. The time indicated was during the meal rather than after the meal was finished.

From the description that follows in the thirteenth chapter of John, one would conclude that the Passover Feast itself is recorded there. In the Synoptic Gospels, one reads of a Passover feast that is specifically designated by that name.[16] In the Gospel of John, one finds discussions and events that are identical with those described in the Synoptics' record of the Passover. Although the washing of feet is not recorded in the Synoptic Gospels, it has an understandable connection with the discussion of Luke 22:24-27. The problem of who was the greatest may very easily be related to who would accept the lowest position and provide the service of washing the feet of those present.

At the same feast, Jesus announced His coming betrayal. The description of this event is in Matthew 26:21-25; Mark 14:18-21; Luke 22:21-23; John 13:21-30. The element of surprise in the disciples is reflected in all four Gospel narratives. Both Matthew and John name Judas as the traitor. Likewise, both the Synoptics and the Gospel of John relate that Jesus at this feast predicted the denials of Peter.[17] All these similarities indicate that John is telling about the same Passover meal that is recorded in the other Gospels.

One is extremely disappointed to find the disciples disputing on such an occasion about which one was to be the greatest. This whole discussion may have been precipitated, as some have imagined, because Judas had the audacity to rush forward and take a seat of honor next to Jesus. From our perspective, it seems that Peter might have been expected to fill that place, but we recall that James and John not long before had been asking for places above Peter's (Mark 10:35-40).

Whatever triggered it, there was a discussion about the order of rank among the disciples (Luke 22:24).

With this problem in mind, who would fill the role of a servant and wash the feet of the guests? Jesus had designated the ones to prepare the feast (Luke 22:8), but He did not assign anyone to wash the others' feet. Who had enough love to undertake the task? It

---

16 Matthew 26:19; Mark 14:16; Luke 22:15.
17 Matthew 26:33-35; Mark 14:27-31; Luke 22:31-34; John 13:37, 38.

should not be done by coercion, but by desire. It called for a willingness on the part of an individual to give complete service.

This was not a predicament deliberately manufactured for this occasion. It was the custom of the time that a host would provide his guest with water and a servant to cleanse his feet before a formal feast. The streets were dusty and dirty, the sandals were open, and the feet needed cleansing even more than the face and the hands. But Jesus had no literal slaves in His group. He had only companions and friends. Not one of them was willing to fill the role of a servant. So Jesus clad himself in a towel, took a basin, and proceeded to wash their feet himself.

As Jesus came to Peter, He met opposition. Peter let Jesus know his disapproval: "You shall never wash my feet" (John 13:8). But one who would fellowship with Jesus must accept His help as well as recognize Him as Lord. Jesus replied, "Unless I wash you, you have no part with me."

With customary wholeheartedness, Peter then insisted that not only his feet but his whole person be cleansed. If this was the condition of fellowship, he wanted his fellowship to be complete. But Jesus said He needed only to wash the part of him that was in need of washing. He added, "And you are clean, though not every one of you" (John 13:10). This was a riddle for the disciples to think about. When John wrote the record much later, he added the solution. Judas was the one who was not clean.

After Jesus had finished, He taught the lesson: "You call me 'Teacher' and 'Lord,' and rightly so, for that is what I am. Now that I, your Lord and Teacher, have washed your feet, you also should wash one another's feet. I have set you an example that you should do as I have done for you" (John 13:13-15).

The application of the lesson was not left as a riddle for the disciples to guess. Jesus stated it in plain terms. To the disciples, the words *Teacher* [or *Master*] and *Lord* meant more when applied to Jesus than when used of anyone else. He was a teacher with divine words, and He was Lord with divine power. With all His humility, Jesus said quite plainly and directly that they were right in addressing Him as "Master" and "Lord." Certainly, if the Son of God is willing to stoop to perform such a menial task, His followers should be willing to undertake anything for Him and for each other. "No servant is greater than his master" (John 13:16).

The question still remains, however, whether Jesus commands us to duplicate the *act* or to observe the *principles* that He laid down. Was He inaugurating the practice of feet-washing to be observed through the centuries, or was He giving a teaching of humility, love, and service in whatever way the opportunity arises?

In determining the meaning of this example, several factors are involved. One must remember that the washing of feet before a meal was a common practice in the time and place where this incident occurred. It was not thought of as having a religious significance such as baptism had. In the second place, one looks in vain to find it among the steps of salvation taught by the apostles in the early church. Furthermore, there is little mention of the practice in the history of the early church. Widows were commended for their good deeds, and among these was the washing of the feet of the saints (1 Timothy 5:10). But this does not give assurance that the practice was intended to be more than a way of meeting the need of that time. In other times, the same humility and love might be acted out in other needed services supplied by devoted Christians. Jesus completed the lesson with the observation, "Now that you know these things, you will be blessed if you do them" (John 13:17). It is the practice of the principle and not the motions of washing of feet that fulfills the lesson taught at this last supper.

A Life Gone Wrong (18-30)

Jesus again brought the attention of His disciples to the presence of one among them who was not a true part of the group. His words here about the "chosen" (John 13:18) do not have reference to the elect saints, but to the chosen apostles. One of them was to fulfill the prophecy of Psalm 41:9: "He who shares my bread"—that is, one who eats the same food and has a personal, close fellowship—"has lifted up his heel against me" (John 13:18). Violently, he has lifted his foot as an animal lifts his hoof to kick. (Or, perhaps, he has lifted his foot to shake off the dust as a symbol of rejection.)

Jesus had already affirmed that although they were clean who were at the feast, not every one of them was (John 13:10). Here He pointed out the one who was to betray Him. Several reasons can be seen for foretelling the betrayal: (1) to show that Jesus was not tricked by the deceit of Judas, but knew what was coming; (2) to prepare the disciples for the failure of a Judas; (3) to force Judas to a final decision. He could still repent if he wished, but if he determined to go through with the betrayal, he would be compelled to leave the group now. Then the Lord's Supper and the closing discourses could be received by the faithful, unhampered by the presence and remarks of a betrayer.

When they heard the prediction that one of them was actually to betray Jesus into the hands of His murderous enemies, they looked incredulously at one another. It is to the credit of these disciples that each one wondered about the possibility of his own apostasy rather than naming some other person as a likely traitor. This also indicates the full acceptance of Judas by the other disciples and their lack of the least suspicion of him. But somewhere along the line, Judas had gone wrong.

Some modern fiction writers attempt to heroize Judas, but this is a perversion of the Scriptural account. No amount of conjecture concerning the motives of Judas in betraying Jesus can change the clear-cut declaration that before the betrayal, Judas was already a thief (John 12:6). God chose Judas to betray Jesus, but God did not ask or compel him to do what he did. God merely knew what choices Judas had made and would make.

Not by any compulsion or coercion from Heaven, but by his own free will, Judas committed himself to walk the way of dishonesty and selfishness and rebellion against God. By his own free will, he rejected the teaching and example and person of God's Son.

To make the prediction complete, Jesus said He would give the betrayer a piece of bread dipped in the dish of gravy. Yet, even when a sign was given to identify the traitor, the disciples were not sure who he was (John 13:22-30). Two factors help to explain this. One, if Judas was seated beside Jesus, a piece of bread could be handed to him quite unobtrusively, and perhaps only John heard Jesus tell the meaning of that gesture. This may be an indication that Judas had indeed presumed to take the seat next to Jesus. Another factor is the complete confidence the disciples had in Judas. He must have been a man who displayed a pleasing and confident personality rather than a sullen, villainous appearance that artists often use to depict the traitor. Apparently, the disciples trusted Judas as fully as they did anyone else in the group.

When Judas took the bread, three things happened in rapid succession: (1) Satan entered into him. The devil had already prompted Judas to follow the course he was taking (John 13:2), and Judas had turned his back on God and had chosen the wrong way. He had been planning the betrayal of Jesus before and had already received the thirty pieces of silver, sealing his deal with the enemies. He was only waiting for an opportunity to hand Jesus over (Matthew 26:14-16). But apparently, Judas was still struggling with himself in indecision. Now he passed the point of no return and allowed Satan full control. (2) Jesus told him bluntly to do quickly what he was going to do. Judas then realized Jesus knew who His betrayer was. This was a moment to repent, but Judas gave himself more fully to the devil instead. (3) Judas left the room immediately. Tragically, John adds, "And it was night" (John 13:30). Night indeed for a life that had chosen darkness!

A Life in the Balance (31-38)

Freed by the departure of Judas, Jesus went on with the words He was anxious to share with His disciples: *glorification* (John 13:31,

32), *departure* (John 13:33), and a *new commandment* (John 13:34). His glorification meant His death on the cross, but also His resurrection from the dead and His ascension on high. Furthermore, He would be glorified through coming centuries in a growing host of men and women redeemed from sin and death and destined to life everlasting. All this glory would be shared by the Savior and the Father, who sent Him. Departure was a time of sadness, but even if the disciples could not follow at the time, they would follow later (John 13:36). The new commandment was love for one another. It would hold them together and mark them as disciples of Jesus. Even so are we bound together and marked today.

Peter could not stand the prospect of separation from Jesus. He was ready to follow right then. He burst out, "I will lay down my life for you" (John 13:37). How little he knew of the events to come that night! But Jesus knew, and He gave Peter warning. Before the rooster would crow in the morning, Peter would deny his Lord three times. Despite his claim of loyalty, Peter must bear not only the prospect of separation, but also the dreadful prospect of denial, of doing the very opposite of what he desired.

What a burden to be added to all the others! But what tipped the scales in Peter's favor was his faith in Christ, the love he had learned from the Master, the repentance he was willing to make in his commitment. The difference between Judas and Peter was that Judas, with burdens too heavy to bear, betrayed the only one who could really help him. But Peter turned to this one when he found he was unable to bear his burdens by himself. Jesus is the only way.

IN SPITE OF EVERYTHING (14:1-31)

As one drives along the shore road in Haifa, Israel, he passes a strange sight. It's a ship resting in dry dock in a roadside park. It stands as a monument to remind passersby of the courage and daring of a shipload of desperate Jewish refugees who ran the British blockade, and in spite of everything made the shore. The name given to this ship is a Hebrew word meaning "in spite of."

This is what can be written over the fourteenth chapter of John: "In spite of everything." Surely in these difficult final hours, Jesus could be expected to have a sad and mournful message about His departure from His disciples, His coming agony, His shameful treatment, and His death. But He did not. In spite of the unknown to man, Jesus could give guidance in the only way. In spite of going away, He could send another Comforter. In spite of conflict, He could provide peace. In spite of separation, Jesus could promise to return. Jesus is the victory in spite of everything.

Jesus was giving His words of farewell to His beloved disciples in the closing moments of this gathering in the upper room. A deep chasm separates the final farewell of a Christian from that of an unbeliever. Catullus, a Roman poet of the first century before Christ, put the pagan's feeling into words when he gave his closing remarks over the fresh grave of his own brother:

> But lo! these gifts, the heirlooms of past years,
> Are made sad things to grace thy coffin shell:
> Take them, all drenched with a brother's tears,
> And, brother, for all time, hail and farewell.

For him, nothing was left.

Socrates, however, believed there was more; but he did not know what. "Now the time for my departure has come. Our paths go separate ways; you are to live and I am to die. Which is better, God only knows." But Jesus taught us how to say farewell without the emptiness of Catullus or the uncertainty of Socrates. From Jesus' words to His disciples we learn the path to take.

Assurance: Trust in God (1-6)

Jesus told His disciples to stop the turmoil in their hearts. They could have peace and assurance if they would just trust in God and trust also in His Son Jesus. After all, death is not the end. Jesus, by His death and resurrection, was going to prepare a place in Heaven for all the people of God.

Jesus said the disciples already knew the way to the place where He was going. Thomas objected to that. He did not even know where Jesus was going, he said, so how could he possibly know the way? Then Jesus gave further assurance. He himself was the way. If one knows Jesus, he knows the way.

First of all, Jesus tells us not to be shaken, not to be afraid, not to let our hearts be troubled (John 14:1, 27). This word for troubled comes from a Greek word denoting a heavy sea in the midst of the wind and the storm. The injunction to put our faith in God may have several connotations. The Greek word means "believe," but it also means put your trust in, and this includes "commit yourself." In this context of Jesus' closing words to His disciples when He was about to be betrayed, the word *trust* has a particular significance. All three meanings have their place; but if a choice has to be made, at this point there was a crucial need for trust along with belief and commitment. There is no doubt that these disciples believed in God. Although at times they might question His action or His reasoning, they had no doubt about His existence. But now, in the face of tragic events and loss of a loved one, of shattered hopes and constant peril, Jesus urged them to trust in God and to trust also in Him, God's one and only Son. Jesus assured them they need not worry about Him. He would be actively engaged in preparing a place for His disciples, His followers; and in this place that would be prepared, there would be room enough for any who would come. And if we are to be together in the future, then this earthly parting is not the end. Catullus is wrong.

Guidance: Follow Jesus (7-15)

The disciples plied Jesus with questions. "Where are you going?" "How do we know the way?" Through all these questions, Jesus is the answer. He is the way.

Still Philip had a request. If he could just see God, this would give the positive evidence needed in such times of trouble as he and the other disciples were about to experience. Worry would end if He would just appear to them. But Philip missed the whole point. God had appeared to them in Jesus.

Furthermore, the disciples would be able to work in the future as Jesus had worked. They would do even greater things than Jesus had done, for now Jesus would be with His Father to see to it that all things were done to bring glory to God. The disciples would not do greater miracles than Jesus had done; but they would proclaim the good news of His death and resurrection, they would help to establish His kingdom on the day of Pentecost, and they would carry the gospel beyond Palestine and the Jewish race to offer salvation to all mankind.

Jesus promised to answer the disciples' prayers, but it was a conditional promise. It applied only to requests made in His name, and it was linked to the statement, "If you love me, you will obey what I command" (John 14:15). Requests made in the name of Jesus must be in harmony with His will and His command. Anyone can claim to love Him, but one who violates His teaching has neither love for Jesus nor promise of His help.

The New Covenant does not have detailed rules and regulations like those in the Old Covenant, but it has principles to be followed, actions to be taken, and explicit directions to be obeyed. If one seeks to twist these, change these, or neglect these, he shows that he has no love for God. If he obeys them gladly, his love is evident.

This is one of the strongest affirmations Jesus made concerning His deity: "Anyone who has seen me has seen the Father" (John 14:9). The words that Jesus spoke were words from the Father. The works that He did were works of the Father. Look at the very evidence of the miracles themselves. Furthermore, if a person follows Jesus with faith in Him, "he will do even greater things than these, because I am going to the Father" (John 14:12).

Assistance: Accept Another Comforter (16-27)

An added assurance was given at this time of departure. To give added strength and guidance in His absence, Jesus promised to pray on behalf of His followers that they might receive another counselor who would never be taken away. The King James Version reads "Comforter" instead of "Counselor." The Amplified Bible suggests other possible translations: "Helper, Intercessor, Advocate, Strengthener, Standby." The Greek word is sometimes spelled in English letters as *Paraclete*. Basically, it means one who stands alongside another: for example, one who aids him in a court of justice or pleads his case under any circumstances, or one who gives advice in some difficult situation. Christ had been the advocate for these disciples. Now, on the eve of His departure, He was giving them a promise: they would not be left alone, but another advocate would come to assist them, and this new Paraclete would never leave them.

This Comforter would be the very Spirit of truth. When Jesus was gone, it would not be the depth of the disciples' learning, their intelligence quotient, or the extent of their scientific investigation that would assure their grasp of truth; it would be their humility, faith, and love as they turned to God. Looking to God, they would receive His Paraclete. He would teach them, and they would record His teaching for us.

Jesus said He would not leave them "comfortless" (John 14:18), according to the King James Version. The Greek word translated "comfortless" is the word from which our word *orphan* is derived; so the New International Version reads, "I will not leave you as orphans; I will come to you." This might be taken to mean that Jesus would come to them after His resurrection. Again, it might be interpreted to mean that He would come with His power from on high at His second coming. It seems that a third possibility is the most likely: He would come to them in the other Comforter, the Paraclete, the advocate who was to be sent after Jesus' departure from this earth.

Soon Jesus would die, and the world would see Him no more. But He would be resurrected and bring into view eternal life—so His people would live also and He would be with them.

Jesus had earlier presented love as the source of obedience (John 14:15). Here He turned the picture around and showed obedience as the sign of love (John 14:21). A true disciple loves Jesus and obeys Him: he is loved of God; he is loved also of Jesus; to him Jesus makes himself known. Thus, Jesus comes to one who looks to Him in love and obedience.

Judas Iscariot now has gone, but another disciple was named Judas. He was known also as Thaddaeus, and the King James Version gives him the added name of Lebbaeus (Matthew 10:3). This one asked, "But, Lord, why do you intend to show yourself to us and not to the world?" (John 14:22).

As was often the case, Jesus seemed to ignore the question, but at the same time gave the answer. He spoke of love and obedience. To see Jesus after His departure, one must love Him and obey Him. If one rejects Jesus, he will not know the way, for Jesus is the way, the only way.

Jesus gave the added assurance that the Holy Spirit, the Comforter, the Counselor, would come to them. With the coming of the Holy Spirit, both Jesus and the Father also would come to stay. He would make sure the apostles would know all they needed to know; He would teach them all things and would remind them of everything Jesus had said to them (John 14:26). These words provide a good description of the guidance granted to those who wrote the Scripture. They were not allowed to trespass into realms of error, but were taught and reminded by the Holy Spirit about those things that were to be preserved.

Jesus left peace with His disciples. How could He say there was peace when all the world seemed ready to crush Jesus, His teaching, and all His followers? But peace with God is different from peace with the world. In fact, if we are to be at peace with God, there must be enmity against the world. (See James 4:4.) And though we may be engulfed in physical or mental strife, there can be peace of soul that rises above all the din and conflict of the world. In spite of everything, a Christian can know peace. This, however, is not peace with Satan. It is not the peace at any price that the world demands. It is peace on God's terms.

Promise: Watch for Jesus' Return (28-31)

Another note of assurance Jesus left was this: "I am going away and I am coming back to you" (John 14:28). He assured His disciples that they should not be discouraged because the place where He was going was really better than the place where He was with them. They should think less of their own loss and more of Jesus' gain. The Father was there, and He was greater than the Son, though the Son also was fully God.[18]

Jesus warned that the prince of this world, Satan, was on his way. He was coming right at that time. He might seem to be victorious in the death of Christ; but really, said Jesus, He has no effect on me. Jesus was going to His death voluntarily. Jesus assured His disciples that Satan could not have his way with Jesus.

The world must learn a lesson from Jesus. It must learn the necessity of love for the Father and obedience to His commands. Jesus emphasized that this had been His own program in life. He wanted to show the love of God and to "do exactly what my Father has commanded me" (John 14:31).

The final words of John 14 are "Come now; let us leave." This probably referred to leaving the upper room where Jesus had been communing with His disciples. The teaching in chapters 13 and 14 was delivered in the upper room, but Jesus continued His talk with the disciples as they walked through the streets and as they proceeded to the Garden of Gethsemane.

---

[18] See 1 Corinthians 15:27, 28; 2 Corinthians 8:9; Philippians 2:6-11; Hebrews 12:2.

In spite of everything, Jesus walked His own way to the very end of His earthly life. In spite of everything, He gave hope and assurance to His disciples. For His way does not stop at the end of earthly life, but continues to the Father in resurrection, ascension, and eternal victory. Even so, come, Lord Jesus.

HEAR THE SERMONS

Jesus preached to the multitudes; He taught and exhorted individuals in private conversations. The Gospel writers added meaning to Jesus' sermons as they described the setting, and at times pointed out the fulfillment of prophecy. The miracles are recorded with a message each time.

1.	New Birth	3:1-36
2.	Water of Life	4:1-42
3.	The Divine Son	5:19-47
4.	The Bread of Life	6:22
5.	The Life-giving Spirit	7:1-52
6.	The Light of the World	8:12-59
7.	The Good Shepherd	10:1-42
8.	The Farewell Discourses	13-17
	At the Last Supper	
	On the Way to Gethsemane	
	Jesus' Prayer of Intercession	

CHAPTER TEN

Truths of Promise
John 15:1-16:15

As Jesus walked along through the moonlit streets of Jerusalem, He continued to talk to His disciples. They were on their way to Gethsemane. This was Jesus' last opportunity to be alone with His disciples before His death. He still had many things to tell them, and some things He said as they walked along were unexpected. The last words of encouragement in the upper room were in keeping with a final farewell, but now He turned to an unexpected challenge and warning. The lives of His followers must bear fruit, and Jesus used the figure of a grapevine to make His point.

GOOD FRUIT COUNTRY (15:1-27)

From the Israelites' first approach to the promised land, grape clusters were important. As a part of their report, the spies brought back a huge, single cluster of grapes carried on a pole between two men (Numbers 13:23). They also brought pomegranates and figs. Through the centuries, the land of Israel continued to produce grapes, and the vine was exalted as a symbol.

Ezekiel wrote that disobedient Jerusalem would be destroyed like a useless vine (Ezekiel 15:1-8). Isaiah taught that Israel was the vineyard of God, but it brought forth wild grapes instead of good ones (Isaiah 5:1-7). Jeremiah announced that the noble vine, Israel, had become degenerate (Jeremiah 2:21). Hosea warned that judgment would come upon Israel, a selfish vine that produced fruit only for itself (Hosea 10:1, 2).

Jesus also used the figure of the vineyard. He warned of the fate of those who cared for a vineyard but refused to share the fruits with the owner (Matthew 21:33-45). They even killed the owner's son when he was sent to the vineyard. Jesus' hearers gave their own answer as to what should be done to these husbandmen: "They say unto him, He will miserably destroy those wicked men, and will let out his vineyard unto other husbandmen, which shall render him the fruits in their seasons" (Matthew 21:41, KJV). This pictured the fate of a nation that did not bring forth the fruits expected of it. God would take away what He had entrusted to it, and grant it to a people who would bring forth the fruits.

In the Sermon on the Mount, Jesus taught that "by their fruit you will recognize them" (Matthew 7:20).

During these closing hours before Jesus' arrest, the immediate surroundings may have introduced the figure of the vine. The house where Jesus and His disciples had kept the Passover may have had more than one vine growing on its outside walls and around the windows of the upper room. Jesus may have noted them as they were leaving the house. Or they may have walked through the temple area where a golden vine ornamented the entrance to the proud sanctuary Herod had built.

> The temple had its doors also at the entrance, and lintels over them of the same height as the temple itself. They were adorned with embroidered veils, with flowers of purple, and pillars interwoven; and over these, but under the cornices, was spread out a golden vine, with its clusters hanging down from a great height, the size and the workmanship of which was a surprising sight to the spectators.[19]

Jesus may have drawn attention to these golden clusters as He walked through the temple area with His disciples. To reach the

---

[19] Josephus, Antiquities of the Jews, xv, 11, 3.

Mount of Olives, they passed over the Valley Kidron, where fires of vine prunings may have been burning. As they approached the Mount of Olives, vines may have been growing along the way. Then, too, they had just come from the upper room where the Lord's Supper had been instituted with its "fruit of the vine." Any of these or several of these may have contributed to the vividness of Jesus' figure.

As one travels the roads in Queensland, Australia, he is struck by the fact that he is going through good fruit country. This is obvious because of the well-tended orchards and the heavy production of fruit on the trees. But a person will suddenly pass from a good section to bush country that produces nothing worthwhile. One wonders about the difference. These fields have the same good soil, the same amount of water and sun, but there is a difference. What makes the good fruit country? Healthy plants plus good care are needed, plus God's increase, but Jesus taught still more about the essentials.

The Essentials (1-4)

In Jesus' instruction to His disciples, He was careful to tell them what would be essential to a productive life. He taught the lesson of the vine.

First, the branch of the vine must bear fruit, or it will be cut off and destroyed. But second, Jesus pointed out that to bear fruit, a branch must be joined to the vine. Togetherness provides nourishment, growth, and ultimately the fruit. Another essential for the lesson is that Jesus is the vine. Notice that He did not represent himself as the stalk or stem, but the vine, the whole vine. The branches, the roots, the stalk—all of these are parts of the vine. And His followers were the branches. This lesson remains true today. To be a part of the good fruit country, the branches must be bearing fruit; and to bear fruit, the branches must be joined to Jesus.

Israel, the corrupt vine of old, has been replaced. Jesus is the true vine. In Him, Israel, including people of all nations, can find the real source of life and fruit. Those who become Christians and who remain in Christ (or *abide* in Him, as the King James Version has in John 15:4) are the Israel of God (Galatians 6:16).

The Only Way (5-8)

How can a branch maintain its healthy, fruitful existence? God helps in this by keeping the good branch pruned. The Father is the gardener. Sometimes we feel that hardships are cutting us back so much that we cannot function at our best as followers of Christ. On the other hand, one must recognize that by this very pruning, the fruits of the branch are increased.

A minister bought two trees from the same lot. He gave one to his neighbor, and he and his neighbor planted the trees close to one another on opposite sides of the fence. The trees grew together, they were of the same age, they had the same water, they had the same sun, they had the same soil; but the minister noted that his neighbor had two or three times as much fruit as he had. The only difference he could discern was that his neighbor knew how to prune the tree and keep it cut back. The minister had no knowledge about such things, but he determined to learn from his neighbor for future improvement.

Even those who are bearing good fruit will find that God cleanses their lives and enables them to bear still more. The pruning may be painful, but the result is worth all the pain (Hebrews 12:11).

Besides God's pruning, there is also man's work and attitude. Two features stand out in Jesus' picture of this healthy branch. The branch that is bearing fruit had high regard for the Word, and gains strength and guidance through its truths. The healthy branch also is the one who spends time in prayer, and through his communication with God he maintains the oneness with Jesus Christ that is essential to life and vigor. Faithfulness is the only way the branch can maintain his relationship to the vine.

Who are the fruitless branches? Jesus could have referred to the Jewish people, for they had failed to bring forth fruits worthy of the people of God. They were about to crucify God's Son. But the truth Jesus taught here was not confined to the first century. People still reject Jesus, they still fail to witness for Him, they still fail to render service that can be recognized as Christian fruit. God is still pruning His vineyard. God recognizes people for what they are and removes the unfaithful. Their names may be carried on church rolls, but not in the book of life. Fruitless branches may deceive us, but "the Lord knows those who are his" (2 Timothy 2:19). He is not deceived.

The pruning is not completed when the fruitless branches are removed. Those branches that bear fruit are also trimmed and shaped, disciplined so that they will bear more fruit. For the Christian, this process is continual.

The disciples to whom Jesus spoke had been pruned already (John 15:3). With three years of teaching, He had removed some of their worldly aspirations and some of their disregard for others so that they would be better fitted to produce the kind of fruit He desired.

Cleansed and made ready to bear fruit, the disciples must remain in Jesus. They must be faithful to His person and His teaching, for it is impossible for the branches to bring forth fruit of themselves. They must receive the life and power from contact with the vine.

Jesus had used many figures of speech referring to himself: "I am the bread of life" (John 6:35); "I am the gate" (John 10:7); "I am the good shepherd" (John 10:11). Here He said, "I am the vine" (John 15:1, 5). To this He added, "You are the branches." This refers to individual disciples, not to different groups that would divide the unity of the church into denominational segments. The union of Christ and His disciples is vital for the bearing of fruit.

If one remains in Jesus, this means that Jesus' teaching will remain in him. His whole being will be dedicated to doing Christ's will and accomplishing His purposes. Under these circumstances, his every prayer will be in accord with the will of God and the teaching and presence of Jesus. Besides, he will devote himself to the accomplishment of what he asks, and what he asks will be granted.

Our greatest problem is in failing to trust God's promises and to do His will.

What Fruit?

What is the fruit that the branch is responsible for bearing? Is it the number of souls that are led to Christ in a year's time? Is it the amount of money that is given to help the needy and those in distress? Is it the effort and attention that are given to the proclamation of the gospel in foreign lands? Is it special work among young people to provide guidance and strength in that crucial age of decision? Or is it the love and mercy that are shown to senior citizens who have grown weak in physical strength and short in alertness, but need love and care in the twilight years of their lives?

Not one, but all of these are included in the fruit expected from the life of a Christian. Even the deepening of one's own spiritual consciousness and closeness to God is part of the fruit of effective discipleship. A Christian may be lacking in one area, but that does not mean that he is bearing no fruit in other areas. It is wrong to feel that a total judgment can be seen at the end of each year in statistics that are published by a congregation. Only the Gardener, God, can give a true estimate of the fruit in a person's life.

The Attendant Circumstances (9-17)

In Greek grammar, there is a special designation for participles that supply "attendant circumstances" for the action of the main verb. But whether we use Greek or not, we can see that almost any action is attended by various circumstances. When we go through good fruit country and see a tree producing a bountiful crop, we feel sure the attendant circumstances are favorable. The water, the sun, the soil—each is doing its part.

In talking about the productive vine, Jesus mentioned some attendant circumstances. The branch is not only joined to Jesus, but has the attendant circumstances. The branch is not only joined to Jesus, but has the attendant circumstance of love. "As the Father has loved me, so have I loved you. Now remain in my love" (John 15:9).

But besides love, there is obedience. This too is an attendant circumstance to the fruitful vine. "If you obey my commands, you will remain in my love, just as I have obeyed my Father's commands and remain in his love" (John 15:10). Jesus listed still another circumstance that invariably accompanies the fruitful Christian life. This is joy: not a fleeting moment of lightheaded glee, but a deep-seated joy that comes from Heaven. Jesus spoke of it as His joy. "I have told you this so that my joy may be in you and that your joy may be complete" (John 15:11). This is one of the favorite themes of the Gospel.

Finally, Jesus gave this tender assurance: "You are my friends if you do what I command" (John 15:14). Jesus' followers are no longer servants, but truly friends in whom He confides and to whom He brings every love, joy, and consideration. These are the circumstances in which the vine with its branches flourishes. Just as the fruitbearing branch needs rich soil, sunshine, and rain, so the Christian needs love, obedience, and joy. Jesus assured the disciples in that solemn hour that He loved them just as the Father in Heaven loved Him. His love would be unfaltering and eternal; but they might not be equally strong and constant. Therefore, He added, "Now remain in my love." In other words, "Stay in the shelter of my love at all times." If we love Jesus, we will keep His commandments. On the other hand, if we keep His commandments, it is evident that we are abiding in His love.

Despite the tragic hour that lay ahead, Jesus was able to speak of joy. He had said previously, "Peace I leave with you." Now He said, "That my joy may be in you and that your joy may be complete." This is a joy that the world cannot know, even as the peace that Jesus left is a peace the world cannot know. This is a joy of complete self-surrender and love toward God. In the process of coming to completion, this joy includes suffering, service, and the noble self-surrender of the disciple to his Master. This joy every Christian can and should know as he serves his Lord.

Earlier in the evening, Jesus had given a new commandment: "Love one another." Now He repeated it. This is the summation of all the precepts and all the commandments that He has left with us. It begins in a love for God and a love for Jesus, and it extends to loving one another. We learn this love from Jesus: no one has greater love than the one who lays down his life for his friends. In love, the servant of Jesus becomes His friend. John 15:16 uses the limited negative common among the Hebrews: *You did not choose me* means "not only did you choose me, but I chose you, too."

The World (18-25)

There are other attendant circumstances that are not so pleasant. They do not aid the growth of the tree, but the growth goes on in spite of their presence. Jesus warned that the world hated Him and would hate His people also. Furthermore, the world hates the Father. We cannot expect better treatment for the servants than for the Father or the Master. As Jesus endured persecution, we as His servants must expect persecution from the world (John 15:18-25).

Disciples, then, should not be surprised at meeting resistance from the world. Worldly people hated Jesus, and they hate His followers, also. The Christian loves his enemies, but often they respond with hate. The world loves those who belong to the world. A Christian wrote to Diognetus in the second century, "The world hates the Christians, though it has suffered no evil, because they are opposed to its pleasures." If a man answers Christ's call, he no longer belongs to the world, and the treatment he receives will be no better than that given to Christ, his Master.

The basic reason for this treatment is that worldly people have turned away from the Father. They have rejected the one true and living God. If Jesus had not come, they might have continued in worldly ways because they saw no alternative. But now that Jesus has come and shown the way, they are without excuse. Jesus did nothing but good, and His miracles are plain evidence of divine power; but still the godless and selfish people hate Him and hate the Father as well.

The Counselor (26, 27)

Jesus again assured His disciples that He had still further assistance to give them. He would send a Counselor, or Comforter, the Spirit of truth. (See John 14:16, 17.) Sent by Jesus, the Spirit would go out from the Father, and He would give further testimony about Jesus. Furthermore, Jesus said, "You also must testify" (John 15:26). This is part of the fruit of this vine.

Jesus continued to mix warnings, encouragement, and instruction in preparing the disciples for the time He must die. Though the world would hate them, the Paraclete would be there to stand in truth against the attacks of the world. The Spirit would be sent from the Father. He would testify in the written Word. But the disciples must be witnesses also. They must tell what they had seen and heard while they were with Jesus. Christ gave them encouragement because the Spirit was coming, but He gave them the challenge because they themselves would have to give their testimony of historical facts and personal experience.

In good fruit country, the message of the gospel is heard in clear testimony with love, obedience, and joy. The branch must be securely joined to the vine, Jesus Christ. This is the only way.

THE PROMISE OF THE SPIRIT (16:1-15)

As Jesus' hour of suffering and death approached, His concern for the welfare of His disciples increased. He did not want them to despair. He was anxious for their faithfulness. They must remain in complete harmony with Him. They must be true to His word. They must be faithful in the face of all temptation, persecution, deceit, and false teaching.

Threats to Faithfulness (1-4)

In these final discourses before Jesus' death, He was attempting to prepare His disciples for the trials ahead. In John 14, He offered comfort; in chapter 15, He presented admonition; and here in chapter 16, He included prediction. To know something of what the future holds gives a strong boost toward meeting the occasions when they arrive.

First, Jesus warned them about going astray. This word in the Greek is associated with being taken unawares. One translation renders this, "So you may not be trapped." The disciples must beware of unsuspected entanglement.

Jesus warned them that they would be put out of the synagogue. Their former friends would ostracize them. They must be ready to endure sadness from loss of fellowship.

Persecution was in store for the disciples. The Spirit was not coming simply to help them conduct a life along the smooth and uneventful course of existence. He would come to uphold lives beset with the most severe types of hardship. Those who hated Jesus would hate His followers.

The hour would even come when the disciples' lives would be in jeopardy. Men would kill them and glory in the deed.

Ignorance would be the ground for much of the wrongdoing. The persecutors simply would not know God, and neither would they know Jesus Christ. These men would be so twisted in their minds that the killing of Christians would seem to them to be an offering of sacrifice to God.

Rejection of Jesus Christ is of necessity bound to rejection of God. God and Christ are one, and a person cannot spurn either of them without turning his back on the other. And the world cannot persecute Christians without rebelling against God.

Another hardship that must be faced would be the absence of the visible person of Jesus. Not only would the disciples miss His guidance, but they would become objects of the persecution that Jesus had drawn to himself when He was visibly in their midst.

Jesus had not spoken of these things while He was with His disciples day by day. But now He was going away and would not be at hand to strengthen and advise as He had done in the past. They needed additional help for the time when those future occasions would become a reality. To be forewarned of those periods of persecution was to be forearmed.

The Role of the Spirit (5-7)

Earlier in the evening, Peter and Thomas had asked about where Jesus was going (John 13:36; 14:5), but now they were no longer asking. Jesus had indicated that He was going to the Father's house, but they did not know where that was. Instead of asking more details about the future, the disciples were simply depressed at the prospect of being separated from Jesus. They were filled with grief. To offset this, Jesus encouraged them with teaching about the Holy Spirit.

Jesus sought to fortify the lives of His disciples by warning them of what was coming, and He also encouraged them through the promise of a Helper. This Helper was identified as the Spirit of truth (John 14:17; 16:13), and also as the Holy Spirit (John 14:26). Jesus explained, "Unless I go away, the Counselor will not come to you; but if I go, I will send him to you" (John 16:7). What was the role of the Holy Spirit? How could Jesus say He had not yet come, but would come only after Jesus' own departure?

One is informed of the presence of the Spirit at the very beginning of time. Genesis 1:2 says, "And the Spirit of God moved upon the face of the waters" (KJV). The Hebrew word for *Spirit* means primarily wind or breath, and so does the corresponding word in Greek. At the creation of man, God "breathed into his nostrils the breath of life; and man became a living soul" (Genesis 2:7, KJV).

This calls to mind the later time when the resurrected Jesus breathed on His disciples and said, "Receive the Holy Spirit" (John 20:22). The Spirit through the ages has brought life. "The Spirit of God has made me; the breath of the Almighty gives me life" (Job 33:4).

Besides life, the Spirit brought power to perform different tasks. For example, in giving instructions for the tabernacle, the Lord said of Bezaleel, "I have filled him with the Spirit of God, with skill, ability and knowledge in all kinds of crafts (Exodus 3 1:3). In the Old Testament period, the Spirit not only brought life and power, but He also brought the message of God. Micah affirmed, "But as for me, I am filled with power, with the Spirit of the Lord, and with justice and might, to declare to Jacob his transgression, to Israel his sin" (Micah 3:8). David declared, "The Spirit of the Lord spoke through me" (2 Samuel 23:2).

The Old Testament predicted that the Messiah would be accompanied by the Holy Spirit. "The Spirit of the Lord will rest on him—the Spirit of wisdom and of understanding, the Spirit of counsel and of power, the Spirit of knowledge and of the fear of the Lord" (Isaiah 11:2). In a unique way, Jesus was born of the Spirit (Matthew 1:20). At His baptism, the Spirit came in a special way (Mark 1:10). Speaking to the people of Nazareth, Jesus applied the words of Isaiah to himself: "The Spirit of the Lord is on me, because he has anointed me to preach good news to the poor" (Luke 4:18). In His death and resurrection, Jesus received power from the Spirit in moments vital to the fulfillment of His work. "Christ, who through the eternal Spirit offered himself unblemished to God" (Hebrews 9:14). "The Spirit of him who raised up Jesus from the dead . . ." (Romans 8:11).

During the ministry of Jesus, the apostles were already enjoying the powers granted by the Spirit. "He called his twelve disciples to him and gave them authority to drive out evil spirits and to heal every disease and sickness" (Matthew 10:1; cf. 12:28).

That there are different manifestations of the Spirit is evident, but the Spirit was not given in His fullness until Jesus had completed His work on earth. "By this he meant the Spirit, whom those who believed in him were later to receive. Up to that time the Spirit had not been given, since Jesus had not yet been glorified" (John 7:39). Following His resurrection, Jesus did breathe upon them, and His disciples received the Spirit in another token measure of the full gift (John 20:21, 22). This was another manifestation of the Spirit, but not the fuller manifestation yet to come, for even after this, Jesus could say, "I am going to send you what my Father has promised; but stay in the city until you have been clothed with power from on high" (Luke 24:49). Additional words of Jesus at the scene of His ascension indicate a yet future aspect to the Spirit's being given in full measure: "For John baptized with water, but in a few days you will be baptized with the Holy Spirit" (Acts 1:5). This was fulfilled on the Day of Pentecost, as recorded in the second chapter of Acts: "All of them were filled with the Holy Spirit and began to speak in other tongues as the Spirit enabled them" (Acts 2:4).

But what could the Holy Spirit do? What advantage would the disciples have when He was with them? Jesus summed up the activity of the Spirit by saying He would prove the world wrong in three categories: (1) sin, (2) righteousness, and (3) judgment.

The World Is Wrong (8-15)

The Greek word for prove wrong is more often translated "convince," "convict," "reprove," or "rebuke." Therefore, questions arise as to just what is meant, how it will be done, and what will be the result. There are differences between convincing a man, convicting him, rebuking him, reproving him, and proving him wrong. He may be proved wrong to others and refuse to admit it himself; but even if he is convinced of a duty, he may not act to fulfill it. If he is convicted of a crime, he must suffer the consequences even if he is not convinced that he has done wrong.

The word means more than a rebuke: it speaks of penetrating the conscience and registering a wrong as wrong. It is probable that all these meanings—convince, convict, rebuke, reprove, and prove wrong—are significant, and each one's significance varies with the individual. The results are varied. The whole world is proved to be guilty. Some are convinced of it, confess their wrong, and change their lives in repentance and submission, accepting the grace of God. Others are convicted, but persist in their hostility of God and His judgment.[20]

These three categories that Jesus specified—sin, righteousness, and judgment—revolve around the three leading figures in life's drama—man, Christ, and Satan. Sin has to do with man, and particularly with his faith or lack of faith in Christ. Righteousness involves Jesus, His ability to justify man, and the proof of His successful work seen in His ascension to the Father. Judgment directs attention to Satan, whose condemnation as the defeated prince of this world became evident when he failed to deter Christ from His redeeming work.

Jesus was speaking these words to the disciples on the very eve of the actions that made His teaching a reality. In the moment that Satan and the world brought the Son of God to death on the cross and thought they had overpowered Him, Christ used that very means to provide righteousness to man and condemnation to Satan. It was the turning point of all of human history, and the Spirit would come to convict the world of what was done.

The Comforter was to guide the apostles "into all truth" (John 16:13). The Spirit's understanding is not limited and partial. It is full, and it includes the correct relating of each truth with every other truth. In the Bible, one finds the work of the Spirit as truths are recorded according to the wisdom of the Spirit. "No prophecy of Scripture came about by the prophet's own interpretation. For

---

[20] For examples of results, see Acts 2:25-41; 7:54-58; 8:35-39; 1 Corinthians 14:24; Titus 1:13-16.

prophecy never had its origin in the will of man, but men spoke from God as they were carried along by the Holy Spirit" (2 Peter 1:20, 21).

This full truth of the Spirit is not subjective, arising simply from His own feelings: "He will not speak on his own; he will speak only what he hears" (John 16:13). As Jesus came bringing truth from the Father, so the Spirit also delivers the word of God and of the Son. Jesus said, "All that belongs to the Father is mine. That is why I said the Spirit will take from what is mine and make it known to you" (John 16:15).

The truth delivered by the Spirit is the "whole truth" and "nothing but the truth," not rising from self but from objective reality. It is also truth unlimited by man's ignorance of the future. Jesus promised about the Comforter, "He will tell you what is yet to come" (John 16:13). This was especially reassuring in a time of uncertainty and trial as Jesus and the disciples faced persecution and death. Hardship came as no surprise to the Lord because He knew the future as well as the past; and yet He could promise victory in the end. The Spirit would bring glory to Christ by corroborating His message and making it known to the disciples (John 16:14).

Jesus had much more to teach His disciples, but they were not yet able to bear it. Sometimes the phrase *too much to bear* means too much pain to endure, too much anguish to suffer, or too much pressure to live with. But here (John 16:12) the phrase seems to indicate things too deep for the disciples to understand. They must wait for the experiences of the coming days and the arrival of the Spirit, who would guide them to the truth. He would not simply explain His own feelings to them; He would deliver the message that He received from God and Christ. Among other things, said Jesus, He will tell you what is yet to come. This could refer to the stirring events of Pentecost and the establishment of the church, to the course of the Christians in that first generation, or even to the ultimate return of the Lord.

The message of the Spirit was to center upon Christ. The Spirit would bring glory to Christ; He would get His message from Christ; He would make known the things of Christ. This does not mean the Father would be left out, for all that belongs to the Father is also the Son's. The Spirit was to come to make the truth of the Father and the Son known to man. The Spirit himself is a person, not simply power or an impersonal entity of some kind. The *noun spirit* is grammatically neuter in Greek, but when a demonstrative adjective or pronoun is used, as in John 16:13, the gender is shown to be personal (masculine) and not inanimate (neuter). The Father, the Son, and the Spirit together bring truth to our souls.

Although the disciples did not then understand what was to come in the work of the Spirit, in this dark hour before His death, Jesus gave them assurance that the Spirit with His power of life and direction would be their Helper in the future.

The Friend in Court

The word translated "Comforter" or "Counselor" has many connotations that carry the depth of the word far beyond those two translations. The Holy Spirit is the Strengthener, the Helper. He is the Convincer. He is the Advocate who stands alongside to plead and argue our case and to instruct. He is our Counselor who suggests true reasoning to our minds, true courses for our lives to follow. He is in effect our counsel for the defense. In the very Greek word, there may be an indication of the legal function. C. K. Williams translates the word *parakletos* to mean "friend." One is reminded that legal terminology today includes the official friend in court. This may well add meaning to our understanding of the work of the Holy Spirit in the lives of the disciples and in our own lives today. Jesus assured the disciples that even though they were not to see Him much longer, it was to their advantage that He go away because after He was gone, they would have the opportunity to receive another Comforter, a true Friend in every way.

The same message comes through, whether to Zechariah, to Jesus' eleven disciples, or to His followers through the ages: "Not by might nor by power, but by my Spirit,' says the Lord Almighty" (Zechariah 4:6).

This is the only way.

PART THREE

The Life

John 16:16-21:25

CHAPTER ELEVEN

The Time Has Come
John 16:16-17:26

The gloom of death had settled upon the group of Jesus' disciples. This was the night before Jesus' crucifixion, and it was filled with intense apprehension. The disciples were plagued with doubt and uncertainty. They had reached the edge of despair. Jesus had warned them of times of weeping and mourning. They would be scattered as sheep without a shepherd.

FROM GRIEF TO JOY (16:16-33)

To turn grief into joy, Jesus pointed to the resurrection. "In a little while you will see me no more, and then after a little while you will see me" (John 16:16).

Commentators dispute over the depth of meaning in this passage. Was Jesus saying they would see Him in His appearances after His resurrection? Was He saying they would see Him in the person and work of the Holy Spirit from Pentecost on? Or was He saying they would see Him in His second coming at the end of time? Since the phrase *a little while* is used both of His departure and of His being seen again, it seems more likely that it refers to the few hours remaining until His death and then the few hours between His death and His resurrection.

The Gospel of John is noted, however, for its two levels of meaning. Perhaps this is another case where John records the words of Jesus with two levels in mind. Certainly Jesus had reference to

His death and resurrection. A more remote allusion to His second coming may have been intended as well.

The Resurrection in Prophecy (16-24)

A strong reassuring evidence that supports belief in the resurrection of Christ is the prediction of the event. This is not comparable to Babe Ruth's pointing to a place in the stands and then knocking his home run there; nor is it like the billiard player's indicating a certain pocket and driving the ball into it. Jesus not only predicted what would happen, but He predicted what is impossible with men: a resurrection from the dead. Time and again Jesus forewarned the disciples both of His coming death and of His resurrection. Following Peter's good confession of Jesus as the Christ of God, Jesus issued one of the clearest predictions: "The Son of Man must suffer many things and be rejected by the elders, chief priests and teachers of the law, and he must be killed and on the third day be raised to life" (Luke 9:22). On another occasion,

> Jesus took the Twelve aside and told them, "We are going up to Jerusalem, and everything that is written by the prophets about the Son of Man will be fulfilled. He will be handed over to the Gentiles. They will mock him, insult him, spit on him, flog him and kill him. On the third day he will rise again" (Luke 18:31-33).[21]

Such predictions were made not only by Jesus, but also by God's prophets hundreds of years before Jesus lived on the earth. After His resurrection, as He appeared to two disciples on the road to Emmaus, Jesus reprimanded them for lack of understanding: "And beginning with Moses and all the Prophets, he explained to them what was said in all the Scriptures concerning himself (Luke 24:27). Isaiah affirmed, "He will swallow up death in victory; and the Lord God will wipe away tears from off all faces." The veil of mourning spread over the nations will be removed (Isaiah 25:7, 8, KJV).

---

[21] See also Luke 5:35; 9:43-45; 12:50; 13:32-35; 17:25.

Both Jesus and the prophets before Him predicted His resurrection. It is also significant that following the resurrection of Jesus, the apostolic preaching continued to point to the importance of such predictions. Peter on the Day of Pentecost specified the Messianic prophecy from David:

> Therefore my heart is glad and my tongue rejoices;
>> my body also will live in hope,
> because you will not abandon me to the grave,
>> nor will you let your Holy One see decay.
> You have made known to me the paths of life;
>> you will fill me with joy in your presence
> (Acts 2:26-28; cf. Psalm 16:9-11).

Jesus did not dismiss the gravity of the coming experience. Indeed, there would be weeping and mourning. Even while intense sadness would grip His friends, the world—that is, the enemies of Jesus—would be rejoicing. To be rid of Christ, to have witnessed His end, would be a great relief to those who did not want to change their ways and who found Christ's presence a threat to their plan of things. This was not much comfort to the disciples. But then, Jesus said, "Your grief will turn to joy" (John 16:20). The very thing that would be grief to them would become joy. The cross stood for everything bad: pain, shame, punishment, and death. But this would be changed. Through its pain and suffering would come atonement and forgiveness of sins. Death was not the end; resurrection lay beyond. New life was not to be for Christ only, but for His people as well.

Jesus gave an illustration of how grief can turn to joy. A woman comes to pain and anguish at the time of the birth of her child. But once the child is born, she forgets the trials of labor and her life is filled with joy because of the new life that has been brought into the world.

The disciples were then in their period of grief, but the change of sorrow to joy would come when they would see Him again

(John 16:22). They would see Jesus after His resurrection from the dead. It would be evident that He had triumphed, and they would rejoice. No one could take away that joy. Although He would not continue with them in the same way He had lived among them before, nevertheless there would be positive contact. They would no longer be able to ask Jesus questions as they had in the past years of fellowship and instruction. Instead of asking Jesus, they would be praying to God in the name of Jesus. *In that day* (John 16:23) indicates the time between the Lord's ascension and His return. This would be a time when Jesus' people would lift their prayers to God. And God would hear them and respond generously to all requests made in the name of Jesus. The result of all this would be complete joy. That does not mean there would never be sorrow again; but once a person perceives what Jesus has done for him on the cross, there is a joy that abides despite all other conditions.

The Resurrection in Fact (25-30)

For all the predictions that had been given of Jesus' death and resurrection, the disciples still could not understand that such a dreadful experience as His death must be suffered nor that such an unlikely happening as His resurrection could transpire. Their mourning and their grief were to be real. But the victory was to be equally real. It took some time on that resurrection morning for the message of the empty tomb to penetrate their minds numbed with sadness. An empty tomb could mean that nothing had been placed there originally. But Nicodemus and Joseph of Arimathea, as well as the women who had watched them, knew that Jesus' body had been placed within the tomb. They knew that a stone had been rolled in front of the entrance.

Then, too, an empty tomb might mean that what had been inside had been stolen. But a Roman guard had been placed to make sure no one could remove the body. Without that guard, some might have believed the statement that someone took the body away. It is ironic that the Jewish leaders themselves once and for all had made such an explanation unbelievable. The chief priests and the Pharisees had gone to Pilate and said, "We remember that while he was still alive that deceiver said, 'After three days I will rise again.' So give the order for the tomb to be made secure until the third day. Otherwise, his disciples may come and steal the body and tell the people that he has been raised from the dead. This last deception will be worse than the first" (Matthew 27:63, 64).

Pilate had approved this plan and assigned the guard. One can be sure that upon their arrival at the tomb, the soldiers had checked to be positive they were not guarding an empty tomb. They had placed the seal of Rome across the stone that was replaced at the entrance, and with it they had put the mark of falsehood on any claim that the body was stolen. The testimony of the empty tomb became the more powerful because of the guard and the feeble lie they agreed to tell. They had seen the stone rolled back by an angel whose appearance was like lightening and whose clothes were white as snow. The soldiers had become so frightened they had fallen as dead men. When they recovered enough to report to the chief priests, they were given a large sum of money and told to say, "His disciples came during the night and stole him away while we were asleep" (Matthew 28:13).

Early in the morning, some women came to the tomb. Not even suspecting that Jesus was alive, they brought spices and ointments to place about His body. They, too, were frightened by the angel, but he invited them to see the place where Jesus had been but now was not. "He has risen from the dead," said the angel. "So the women hurried away from the tomb, afraid yet filled with joy, and ran to tell his disciples" (Matthew 28:7, 8).

The negative testimony of the empty tomb and the helpless soldiers is made sure by the positive testimony of the appearances of Jesus after He rose from the dead. Mary Magdalene saw Him first as He appeared to her in front of the tomb (John 20:11-18; Mark 16:9). Some other women saw Him as they hurried from the tomb to tell the disciples that an angel had said He was alive (Matthew 28:8-10). Simon Peter saw Him sometime during that day (Luke 24:34). Two friends of Jesus going to Emmaus came to realize who He was as He prayed over the evening meal (Luke 24:13-32). In the evening of that first day of the week, Jesus appeared to ten of His disciples in an upper room in Jerusalem (John 20:19, 20). A week later, He appeared to the Eleven, as Thomas was with the Ten.

Then the disciples went to Galilee as Jesus had told them to do. There He appeared to seven of them on the shore of the Sea of Galilee (John 21:1-23). He appeared to the Eleven on a hill that He had selected (Matthew 28:16-20). He appeared to more than five hundred people at one time (1 Corinthians 15:6).

Back in the environs of Jerusalem, He again gave the Great Commission before He ascended from the Mount of Olives (Luke 24:45-51; Acts 1:7-9). Then the disciples knew what Jesus meant when He said their grief would be turned to joy (John 16:20).

They lacked understanding of His predictions when He made them, and it took the resurrection, in fact, to bring them full awareness of the meaning.

Jesus admitted here that He had not been speaking in explicit, literal words. He had been using language with a meaning below the surface and not easily seen. This did not mean merely the illustration of a woman bearing a child, that was plain enough. But Jesus had been saying He was going away. He had said the disciples would not see Him for a little while, and then they would see Him. He was talking about His death and resurrection without directly using the words. This was not because He wanted to hide anything from the disciples. Earlier He had predicted His death and resurrection in the plainest terms, and just as plainly, they had rejected the prediction. It was one of the things they could not bear as yet (John 16:12). Now He was preparing them for the shock of His death by speaking in gentler terms of going away and coming back. But He said a time was coming when He would speak plainly. When His death and resurrection were accomplished facts, the disciples would be able to understand more. Then Jesus' words would come to them plainly through the Holy Spirit, and they would understand the message He would bring.

In that time, the disciples were to pray in Jesus' name, as we have seen in John 16:23 and 24. However, this did not mean that God was so cold and distant that He could not hear their prayers, and would listen only to Jesus. In plain language, Christ told them that God loved them. The word for love here is *phileo*, a warm, personal love resulting from their own belief that He had truly come from the very person of God. In plain terms, Jesus affirmed that He had indeed come from the Father into the world. The disciples could see Him in the world, and they were just as sure that He had come from the Father as they were that He was there with them. Then Jesus told them simply and plainly that He would leave the world and go to the Father. This language was explicit. It did not say how He would go—by crucifixion on a cross and ascension into a cloud—but it very plainly said He would go.

Now His disciples seemed relieved. This was plainly spoken. They did not need to look for some hidden meaning. They still did not know how all this was coming to pass, but they were confident that Jesus knew all things. When He said He had come from God, they were ready to take His word for it.

The Resurrection in Belief (31-33)

Jesus had said, "In that day you will no longer ask me anything" (John 16:23). This word for ask has two major meanings. It can signify a request for information to increase comprehension. On the other hand, it can signify a petition, a request for help or comfort or some material thing. The disciples had been wishing to ask for information (John 16:17, 18), but when Jesus was no longer with them, they would pray to the Father through the name of Jesus. The loving Father would respond by supplying their needs (John 16:23-28). Their grief would turn to joy and their scattering without purpose would turn to peace and victory, for Jesus would overcome the world in His resurrection (John 16:32, 33).

What must accompany the fact of the resurrection is belief in the resurrection. If a person does not believe, then the resurrection has no power in his life. This does not change the fact that Jesus had been raised, nor does it change the fact of the resurrection at the end of time when some will rise to eternal joy and some to eternal condemnation; but without faith now, the mere fact of resurrection leaves the grief of life unchanged and leaves the end of life without hope.

On this eve before Jesus' death, He exclaimed to His disciples: You believe at last!" (John 16:31). They were, indeed, facing the right direction. They had put their trust in Jesus. But they had a long way to go in comprehension. They understood that Jesus had come from the Father and lived among men. They understood that He was leaving the world and going back to the Father. They did not need to ask further about this. But though they believed Him, they did not understand about the coming death and coming resurrection. Even with the fact of His death and the fact of His resurrection, it was difficult for them to accept what happened. This made the prophecy all the more important when they studied it later. Jesus knew ahead of time what was going to happen. The prediction of the resurrection and the fact of the resurrection together provided a solid basis for their faith. But still they must believe. Before grief will turn to joy, there must be belief. This is the only way.

Jesus was glad, then, that the disciples had come as far as they had. But the struggle was not over. Jesus had to warn them of the scattering that would follow His arrest and death. They would be like sheep without a shepherd. Jesus would die alone, but His heavenly Father would not desert Him. Even His words, "My God, my God, why have you forsaken me?" (Matthew 27:46) would not mean desertion, but only agonizing separation for the moment.

After that cry, Jesus would still speak to the Father and commit His Spirit into the Father's loving hands (Luke 23:46).

In spite of what was coming, Jesus could offer peace in the midst of trouble. "But take heart! I have overcome the world."

WHEN JESUS PRAYED (17:1-26)

Whenever Jesus faced an important occasion, it seems that He went to His Father in prayer. Before He chose the twelve disciples, He prayed all night long (Luke 6:12). After feeding the five thousand and evading an effort to make Him king (John 6:15), He went into the hills to pray (Mark 6:46). Once He was on a mountain with three of His disciples, and as He prayed, He was transfigured with Heavenly glory (Luke 9:28, 29). His enemies came to arrest Him as He was at prayer in Gethsemane (Mark 14:32). Just before that, however, as He walked through the night with His eleven disciples, He paused to pray for them, for himself, for all believers, and for the world. This is the longest prayer of Jesus that has been recorded. From it, we can learn both about prayer and about Jesus himself.

There are different kinds of prayer. At least, there are different elements in prayer, whether they are put together in one prayer or offered in separate prayer. Too often, one comes to God in petition, asking for something, and forgets that prayer has other parts as well. Thanksgiving for what has already been given should never be neglected. Praise and worship must be included. Communion and promises are included in the privilege of prayer.

Jesus provides examples of these different elements in prayer. Adoration is seen in the opening of the model prayer. "Our Father which art in heaven, hallowed be thy name" (Matthew 6:9, KJV). Praise is heard as Jesus prays, "I praise you, Father, Lord of heaven and earth, because you have hidden these things from the wise and learned, and revealed them to little children (Matthew 11:25). Thanksgiving appears as the Master says, "Father, I thank you that you have heard me" (John 11:41). But on this night before His death, Jesus' voice was raised in heartfelt petition.

He Prayed for Himself (1-5)

Jesus turned from teaching His disciples to pray to His Father. After addressing His Father, He said simply, "The time has come." This was the hour of climax in all human history. God's Son had been sent to the earth for a special mission. This mission was nearing completion as Christ was about to make possible the redemption of man through the sacrifice of himself on Calvary.

In this prayer, Jesus began by making request for himself. The Son was near the completion of His humbling tasks, and now it remained for God to glorify Him. The Father would glorify the Son in His resurrection, His ascension, and the establishment of His church; and in these same events, the Son would glorify the Father, for the Son reveals the Father, and glory comes to God through all the Son is and does.

The prayer Jesus made for himself was packed with the very essence of His life and work. (1) God granted Him authority over all men. This was evident in the way He taught and con-ducted himself (Matthew 7:28, 29; 28:18). (2) Jesus has eternal life to give to those given to Him (John 11:25). (3) Eternal life is knowing God and Jesus Christ (John 14:11; 20:31). (4) God has been glorified on earth by the Son's completing His work (John 4:34). (5) The glory for which Jesus prayed was the glory He had with the Father before the world ever began (John 1:1; 8:58; 16:28).

Jesus' prayer for His Father to glorify Him was no selfish plea. He sought His own glorification so that He might further glorify the Father. He wanted to be glorified in order to fulfill the will of God and accomplish the task set before Him. His glory was to come through the cross, and His accomplishment was to bring salvation to mankind. His was the authority to give eternal life. To provide the way to eternal life was the purpose for which Jesus came into the world. The way to life must be opened by His death. Now as Jesus approached the culmination of all the tasks He had to perform on earth, He took the struggles of His heart and spread them before the Lord. The subject of His prayer included himself, although the whole tenor and purpose of His prayer was selfless, directed on behalf of all mankind and of all time. In Jesus' prayer, the truth of God's redemptive plan for all mankind shows forth. He is our high priest, and He prayed on our behalf even when He prayed for himself.

He Prayed for His Disciples (6-19)

One must note that in the prayer of Jesus recorded here, there is a widening circle of attention. Jesus first prayed for himself, then for His disciples, then for all those who would later be included among His followers, and finally for the world. The section that records His prayer for His disciples has its beginning with verse 6 and continues through verse 19. "*I am not praying for the world*" (John 17:9) means only this part of Jesus' prayer was not for the world. He was not excluding the world from all His prayers, but He was emphasizing that at this particular time, His petition was for His disciples.

The real distinction of the disciples of Jesus is their relationship to God and His Son. In this true relationship, the Father and Son are joint possessors of the disciples. Glory is brought to Jesus in the living testimony of lives dedicated to Him and to the faithful performance of His service (John 17:10). In this way, we may glorify Him in our own lives.

Now that the Son was leaving the disciples and going to the Father, the disciples would need these things in particular: (1) unity among the followers like the unity of the Father and the Son (John 17:11); (2) joy in full measure: not worldly joy but Jesus' joy (John 17:13); (3) protection: not a removal from the world, but a protection from the evil one (John 17:15); (4) dedication on the basis of the truth of God's Word (John 17:17); and (5) mission: as Jesus was sent, so He sent His disciples (John 17:18).

When Jesus introduced the apostles into His prayer, He first offered prayer *about* them rather than *for* them (John 17:6-8). He testified in the presence of God that the disciples whom God had granted to Him had been given the message that God wanted Him to give them, and that they were obedient to God's Word.

After Jesus prayed about the disciples, He then offered His prayer for them (John 17:9-19). He did not pray that God would take them out of the world in which they lived. They were not to become recluses, separated from the society of men. Rather, they were to live in the world, but not to succumb to the ways of the world. Jesus prayed that they would be protected from the evil one. They were to bear witness of the Lord Jesus Christ in the midst of the society of men, and they were not to yield to the temptation of the devil.

Jesus prayed that they would be set apart, sanctified, or made holy. This is not a miraculous second blessing, but a dedication to the ways of God—a dedication chosen by the individual and granted in the grace of God. Such dedication would be brought about by the truth revealed in God's Word. By obeying that Word, the disciples would be set apart for the service of the Lord, yet they were to labor in the midst of men. Christ's disciples must not comfortably occupy self-righteous ivory towers; they must go where the people are, see their needs, and patiently show them the way of life eternal.

He Prayed for Those Who Would Believe (20-24)

Jesus prayed for himself and for the eleven apostles gathered before Him. Then He opened His prayer for the church, the believers of all time to come. The word *church* is not used here, but its people are described as "those who will believe in me through their [the apostles'] message" (John 17:20). This included those living in Jesus' lifetime, those who would live in the early days of the church, and those who would live in coming generations as long as the world exists.

Jesus' prayer for these believers of coming generations was first that they be one as Jesus and His Father are one. He gave the purpose of this unity: "that the world may believe that you have sent me" (John 17:21). He gave the basis of this unity: the apostles' doctrine (John 17:20).

This refers to the message that was to be proclaimed by the disciples of Jesus, a proclamation of truths revealed from God. This message is recorded in Scripture and is still proclaimed. It includes not only historical facts that unfolded before the apostles' eyes, but also the meaning of those facts as God inspired those apostles to understand it and convey it to others.

This message is not a compendium of beliefs all people hold in common. It is not a consensus that men have arranged. It is not a message framed or approved by some human organization. It is simply the word that Jesus gave the apostles.

Belief in Jesus through this message—this is the basis upon which the hearts of those who follow the Lord should be united. The feeling or subjective view of individuals is not the basis of Christian unity, nor is the consensus of a group of persons. Jesus prayed that His people would be united upon the objective truth God had made known through His apostles. For all who believe in Jesus through that message, He prayed "that all of them may be one, Father, just as you are in me and I am in you. May they also be in us so that the world may believe that you have sent me" (John 17:21).

This unity for which Jesus prayed is the unity of individual Christians with one another and with God. No ecclesiastical setup is suggested, no organizational basis or effort. Jesus prayed for unity of Christians: a unity springing from the love of each person for God and for others who have accepted Christ. The desired unity is like the unity between the Father and the Son. Disciples of the Lord should enjoy a fellowship comparable to that divine relationship, a oneness of harmony, of love, of dedication, of complete awareness of truth and righteousness, and of identification with that which is perfect.

Naturally, there are areas where one opinion differs from another, but the differing opinions cannot be the foundation of unity. Opinions must be confined to their proper areas; they must not infringe upon those truths that God's Word makes explicit. In the explicit word of the inspired apostles is a solid base for Christian unity. Where the Scriptures speak, there is apostolic teaching; and both belief and obedience must follow. In opinion, there should be liberty. Where the Scriptures are silent, each person has the privilege to determine his preferred course. Thus the Christian finds unity in the essentials of God's Word, and freedom of opinion in the realms where God has not given directions.

Alexander Campbell put it this way:

> 1st. Nothing is essential to the conversion of the world but the union and cooperation of Christians. 2nd. Nothing is essential to the union of Christians but the Apostles' teaching or testimony. Or does he choose to express the plan of the Self-Existent in other words? Then he may change the order, and say — '1st. The testimony of the Apostles is the only and all-sufficient means of uniting all Christians. 2nd. The union of Christians with the Apostles' testimony is all-sufficient and alone sufficient to the conversion of the world.' Neither truth alone nor union alone is sufficient to subdue the unbelieving nations; but truth and union combined are omnipotent. They are omnipotent for God is in them and with them, and has consecrated and blessed them for this very purpose.[22]

No one can dispute the desirability and importance of unity among Christians, but one must question any suggestion that the work of evangelizing the world should wait until the unity of all Christians is accomplished. Perfect unity is a goal toward which the Christian must strive; but, like the perfection of each individual, it will remain an ideal not realized in its fullness short of Heaven.

---

[22] "Alexander Campbell, The Christian System (Cincinnati: Standard Publishing, n.d.), p. 87.

Why did Jesus desire this unity? He summed up its purpose in this brief phrase: "That the world may believe" (John 17:21). Christians divided and contradictory in message and in deed present a confused and unconvincing picture to the world. "Every kingdom divided against itself will be ruined, and every city or household divided against itself will not stand" (Matthew 12:25). But Christians who are true to the Father and to the Son are also true with each other. This is a mark of a true Christian, and it must be sought as a part of the Christians' purpose in life. Not only does the true Christian choose right against wrong, good against evil, and Jesus over Satan; he also chooses harmony and oneness with those who follow Jesus Christ. When there is such unity, then strength and witness are increased so that the world may see the devotion and love of a Christian for his brother and for the Master he serves. Seeing these, the world is more ready to believe.

The prayer for unity rises to its climax in verses 22 and 23. The glory that Jesus received from the Father came through the cross that He was about to endure. It came through His obedience to that which God had set for Him to do. Jesus stated that He gave this glory also to those who followed Him. This meant that they too must come to glory through suffering, service, and obedience to God and through reflection of God to others. The glory Jesus shared with His followers included the task to be done as well as the victory to be won. "I have given them the glory that you gave me, that they may be one as we are one" (John 17:22). Again the purpose of this unity of all Christians is emphasized: "to let the world know that you sent me" (John 17:23). And Jesus added one more bit of knowledge that a united church can convey to the world: the knowledge that God loves His people. A church bound together in fervent mutual love surely does much to assure the world of the love of God.

Earlier in the evening, Jesus had warned the disciples that He soon must leave them (John 14:1ff). He told them that His departure would be for their advantage because after He was gone, the Holy Spirit would come to them (John 16:7). He also promised that He himself would be living with them along with the Holy Spirit (John 14:18, 21).

Now, at the close of His long prayer, He asked not that He might be with them, but that they might be with Him. This seems to mean not upon earth, but in the Father's house where He was going to prepare a place for them (John 14:1-3).

There they would see His glory as never before, the full glory of His divinity. Thinking of that eternal glory, Jesus pointed also to His Father's eternal love: "because you loved me before the creation of the world" (John 17:24).

He Prayed for Unbelievers (21, 22, 25, 26)

Jesus closed His prayer with statements and not petitions. One statement concerned the world, which has two particular failings. The world does not know God, and it does not have that contagious love that is learned from Christ and shared by Christians. "Righteous Father, though the world does not know you, I know you" (John 17:25).

This knowledge of God is more than knowing the way of life. It is life. It is life eternal (John 17:3). Knowing God is more than knowing facts about Him. It is facing toward Him and receiving from Him the grace and power of His presence. It is linked to our knowledge of Jesus Christ. We cannot approach God except by the revelation He has made of himself, and He has revealed himself in His Son.

Through Jesus, one knows God and sees His love. Jesus prayed that this knowledge and love of God may be in His disciples as they live in the world. There is no other way to be transformed from the world into the kingdom of His love.

The mark of identification with the world is a lack of love for God, the Creator, and consequently a lack of love for man whom He created. Jesus wanted such love as God had for Him to be in His followers (John 17:26). He was asking something for His followers that is lacking in the world (John 17:14). The world does not accept Christ; it does not love God and man. This lack of acceptance and love leads to the sin and degradation, the selfishness and rebellion that have been bringing destruction to the souls of men through the centuries.

The center shifts from self to God as one leaves the world and comes to Christ. When the center shifts thus, one's activity becomes more involved in obeying God and in serving others. Such activity increases as one hears Jesus pray, "That the love you have for me may be in them and that I myself may be in them" (John 17:26).

Jesus prayed for all of us the night before He died on the cross. His prayer teaches the importance of communion with God, the necessity of accepting His Son whom He sent into the world, the oneness of the followers of Christ, the basis of this unity in the Word the apostles delivered from God, and the purpose that the world may believe. When Jesus prayed, He not only communicated with God, but also drew us closer to himself and to one another. In this closeness, we glorify the Christ who taught us to pray.

CHAPTER TWELVE

The Way He Died
John 18:1-19:42

WHY THEY ACCUSED HIM (18:1-40)

From the moment He was born in Bethlehem, Jesus was threatened. Herod tried to kill Him because, as the reigning king, he was afraid of a rival. Herod was jealous. He was selfish and cruel. He had a record of sin.

Satan continued to try to overcome Jesus. A special example is seen in the temptations in the wilderness after His baptism. When Jesus cleansed the Jerusalem temple early in His ministry, He drew the bitter enmity of the Jewish religious leaders (John 2:13-21). Legalists tried to stop His healing on the Sabbath (Luke 6:6-11; 13:10-17). They claimed Jesus blasphemed in declaring He could forgive sin (Matthew 9:2-8). And in Jerusalem, the religious leaders were waiting to take His life (John 7:1-25). Another Herod, Herod Antipas, threatened to kill Him in Galilee (Luke 13:31). The word was out for His arrest in Judea (John 11:57). Again and again, it was jealousy, selfishness, and cruelty that stood behind the attacks.

But how could they accuse Him who was without sin? What reasons could they give?

Why Judas? (1-11)

When Jesus finished His praying, He and His disciples "left" (John 18:1), crossing the Kidron Valley. Left where? At the close of chapter 14, one finds the words, "Come now; let us leave." This may be the time when the group left the upper room; and then chapters 15, 16, and 17 may have been delivered at various places along the Jerusalem streets on the way to an eastern gate by which they now left the city.

When they came to Gethsemane to arrest Jesus, it was Judas who betrayed Him. This is especially hard to understand—how a disciple who had been with Jesus for over three years could possibly turn upon Him and deliver Him to the men who would bring about His death. Some have tried to heroize Judas. They maintain that God had chosen him for this role, and Judas was only doing what he had to do. This overlooks the freedom of Judas' will and the foreknowledge of God. God knew that Judas would be a thief and a traitor, but God did not cause him to be either. Judas was both dishonest and covetous. He was ambitious and unscrupulous, so unscrupulous that he could approach Jesus at the moment of betrayal and greet Him with a kiss of pretended affection. He wanted power. When he became convinced that Jesus was about to die, he did not want to be on the losing side. He offered himself to the Jewish leaders who had power. His remorse at what he had done led only to suicide, not to true repentance and reformation of life. It was selfishness, possibly a kind of jealousy, and reckless cruelty that prompted the betrayer to act. He also had a record of sin.

Judas knew of the place where Jesus was accustomed to be with His disciples. To that place he led a mixed crowd of people. Some were Roman soldiers, for John used the technical word for the Roman cohort.[23] The full cohort usually numbered about six hundred men, but sometimes the word was used to denote a detachment of the cohort, such as a maniple, about two hundred men. Even this was a large number to be dispatched to arrest one man. One must remember, however, that earlier the temple guard had been ordered to arrest Jesus, but had failed to bring Him back (John 7:32, 44-46).

---

[23] *Seira* (John 18:3).

Besides the Roman soldiers, there were officials of the temple guard. These were Jewish soldiers or police. They were sent by the chief priests, who were Sadducees (Acts 5:17), plus some Pharisees. Probably those who sent the officers were members of the Sanhedrin, the highest ranking council among the Jews.

Those who came with Judas were carrying torches, perhaps resinous strips of wood bound together; lanterns, oil-fed lamps with handles for carrying; and weapons, including swords and clubs (Matthew 26:55).

John has already made it clear that Jesus knew what was in the mind of men (John 2:25). He was not forced to die, but willingly gave up His life (John 10:18). Jesus asked the crowd, "Who is it you want?" (John 18:4).

He promptly made it clear that He was the one they were looking for; but instead of advancing to take possession of Him, they drew back and fell to the ground (John 18:6).

In again telling them who He was, Jesus included a condition for His arrest. His followers must be allowed their freedom. This seems to have caused no concern. The crowd was there to arrest Jesus and no one else.

Peter whipped out a sword and cut off the ear of the high priest's servant. One must believe that Peter was not aiming at the ear, but at the head itself. Probably the victim dodged in time to save his life, but not his ear. Peter was told to put the sword away. Christ was not to be deterred from fulfilling His mission. He must drink of the cup His Father had given Him. John does not record the healing of the ear, but Luke 22:51 does.

Why Annas? (12-18)

The soldiers were encouraged when Jesus rebuked Peter and made no move to resist. They bound Jesus and led Him to Annas. Formerly, this Annas had been high priest. Perhaps he still held the supreme office in the Sanhedrin. He was highly respected by the Jews, while Caiaphas had official standing with Rome.

In this period, the Jews virtually had two high priests. Annas had held the office from A.D. 6 to A.D. 15, but he had been deposed by the Roman authorities. By Jewish custom, however, he was entitled to hold the place for life, and so the Jews continued to regard him as their high priest even while another carried out the official duties of the priesthood. The Romans who had deposed him had given the office to his son-in-law, Caiaphas. Thus Luke specifies that Annas and Caiaphas were in the high priesthood as the ministry of Jesus began (Luke 3:2).

Such was the prestige of the older man that the officials brought Jesus to him first. As the New International Version describes the proceedings, Annas was the high priest, and he first questioned Jesus about His disciples and His teaching (John 18:19). Probably messengers were going to awaken members of the ruling council and tell them to assemble as quickly as possible. Meanwhile, Annas conducted a preliminary examination, hoping to draw from Jesus some answers that could be used against Him in the major trial. The Gospel of John is the only one that records this particular hearing, and it does not tell what accusations were brought against Jesus. Apparently the questioning failed to bring out anything damaging to Jesus, and frustration and anger caused an official to slap Him in the face (John 18:22).

Basic reasons for the bitter enmity against Jesus may have gone unspoken both in this preliminary questioning and in the formal hearing before the official high priest early in the morning (Matthew 26:57-67). Jesus had driven out the cattle from the temple area, overturned the tables of the money changers, and interrupted the lucrative business of the Sadducees who had made the house of the Lord into a den of robbers. Jesus had aroused the jealousy of the religious leaders because He had taught the people as one having more authority than they. He had directly opposed them in their teaching because they emphasized the traditions of men as though they were the doctrine of God. He had exposed the scribes and Pharisees for what they were, hypocrites. He had vanquished them in each controversy when they had directly confronted Him. Why did they accuse Him? Jesus stood in the way of their own plans; He was a threat to their position and the status quo. Their enmity arose from jealousy, selfishness, and cruelty.

Why Peter? (15-18, 25-27)

Peter and another disciple came to the high priest's courtyard. One door gave access to the open area from which one could enter the porches and rooms. Probably the other disciple was John the apostle. He was able to gain admittance for Peter because he knew the girl at the door. Peter's first denial was made when the girl asked whether he was another of this man's disciples. The question was put in a way expecting a negative answer, and Peter fell into the trap. He replied, "I am not" (John 18:17).

Peter did not share in accusing His Lord, but he did deny Him. How could this be? Peter was Jesus' foremost defender. He was the one who drew the sword and struck out at the servant of the high priest in the Garden of Gethsemane. Peter was the most audacious, the most outspoken. How could he so soon deny that he had even known Jesus? He was concerned for Jesus' welfare. He was as anxious as ever for the personal safety of Jesus and the success of His program. His love for Jesus had brought him to the court of the high priest to see what fate awaited the Master. It took great courage to come to this courtyard of the enemy when most of the disciples were in hiding. Why then did Peter fail when he could have made his testimony count for Jesus?

The place had something to do with it. Peter was warming himself at the fire in the enemies' company (John 18:18). It was much easier to drift with the current than to pull against it. Then, too, the questions were put to Peter in such a way as to expect negative answers (John 18:17, 25). It was easy to say no. Besides, his life would be in danger if he were known as a disciple. In fact, the third time he was asked, the question was a challenge: "Didn't I see you with him . . . ?" (John 18:26). Peter may have been willing to die for Jesus, but how could he be of any help if he were killed or even arrested at this point? It seemed better to stay alive, even if by deceit. Furthermore, he had been rebuffed when he had tried to defend Jesus (John 18:11), and this led to uncertainty about what course should be followed. So Peter's reasons for denying Jesus were quite different from Judas' reason for betraying Jesus or the rulers' reasons for crucifying Him. Peter was not jealous, but he was confused and afraid. Peter was not selfish, he was not cruel, but he was very anxious to escape detection.

Why Caiaphas? (19-24)

The questioning before the high priest continued (John 18:19). Some would maintain this means that Jesus was now before Caiaphas, the official high priest; but it is more likely that Annas still could be called high priest and the action continued in his court until Jesus was sent to Caiaphas as recorded in verse 24. This did not necessarily mean going from one building to another. Perhaps He was led from one room to another along a porch near the fire. On that porch, He may have turned to look at Peter. This was after the third denial, and Peter immediately departed (Luke 22:60-62).

The Gospel of John records that Jesus was taken to Caiaphas (John 18:24), and the Synoptics tell us something of the trial held in his presence. The whole Sanhedrin, the ruling council, was assembling with Caiaphas. False witnesses were put forward to speak against Jesus, but their testimony was so contradictory that it had no value. Caiaphas resorted to questioning Jesus himself, hoping that He would make some rash statement that could be used against Him. Finally, the judges declared He ought to be put to death because He said He was the Christ, God's Son (Mark 14:55-65).

Unable to find a truthful witness against Jesus, His opponents sought false testimony. The two witnesses maintained that Jesus had said, "I am able to destroy the temple of God and rebuild it in three days" (Matthew 26:61). Jesus had not said exactly this. In

John 2:19, His words are reported: "Destroy this temple, and I will raise it again in three days." But John goes on to explain that the temple Jesus had spoken of was His body. "After he was raised from the dead, his disciples recalled what he had said" (John 2:21, 22). Even as twisted by false witnesses, however, that remark was not a crime worthy of death. Finally, the high priest charged Jesus under oath by the living God, "Tell us if you are the Christ, the Son of God" (Matthew 26:63). Jesus said He was, and Caiaphas maintained that He had committed blasphemy. If Jesus were not the Son of God, this accusation would have been true. But since He spoke the truth, it was a false accusation. Nevertheless, the assembled rulers declared that Jesus ought to be put to death (Matthew 26:65, 66).

Under the Sanhedrin's rules, no sentence of death might be delivered during the night hours. So the council waited till the break of dawn (Mark 15:1) to give legal approval to the decision made during the night. Jealousy, selfishness, and cruelty won. Jesus was convicted. He was judged "worthy of death" because He said He was the Son of God.

Why Pilate? (28-40)

The death sentence had to be approved by Roman authority. The land of Israel was part of the Roman Empire. In minor cases, the Sanhedrin ruled without interference from Rome, but it was not allowed to put anyone to death (John 18:31). Therefore, Jesus was taken to Pilate, the Roman governor. It was still very early in the morning.

The incredible insistence of the Jewish accusers mounts as we read from one instance to another:

1. The Jews would not enter Pilate's judgment hall because they did not want to be defiled and unable to keep the Passover. Since they would not enter the hall, Pilate came out to them.

2. When Pilate asked for the charges, the Jews impudently told him they would not have brought Jesus if He were not a criminal.

They had brought Him to Pilate only because they wanted Him executed by Roman decree.

3. When Pilate tried to release the king of the Jews, the accusers insisted that he release instead Barabbas, one who had taken part in a bloody rebellion. So Barabbas was released and bloody rebellion grew and grew till Rome wiped out the city of Jerusalem and ended the Jewish nation only forty years later.

The Jews would not enter the judgment hall of the Romans, but insisted that the Roman governor, Pilate, must come outside. The Jews did not want to be declared ceremonially unclean during the Passover celebration, for this would disqualify them for some of the meals and activities of the week. The word *Passover* can be used to denote (1) the Passover lamb (Exodus 12:21), (2) the Passover meal (Matthew 26:17), or (3) the Passover week (Ezekiel 45:21). Since the Synoptics make it clear that the Passover meal had been eaten the evening before, and the Gospel of John also records that meal, John 18:28 must refer to some other meal during the Passover week rather than to the Passover meal itself.

Pilate complied with the demands of the Jews and set up his judgment seat outside the palace. He could find no wrong in Jesus that would justify the death penalty. At first, the accusers did not mention the charge of blasphemy, but said Jesus was a rebel who claimed to be king (Luke 23:1, 2).

"Are you king of the Jews?" To this question of Pilate, Jesus replied that He was a king, but His kingdom was not of this world. If it were, He said, His disciples would fight and not allow the Jewish officials to bring Him thus to the governor (John 18:36, 37). Pilate knew this was true, for only a few days earlier, a great throng had hailed Jesus as their king (John 12:12, 13).

Unwilling to sentence an innocent man to death, Pilate thought of a plan that he hoped would free Jesus without antagonizing the Jews. It was customary to celebrate the Passover by mercifully releasing a prisoner. Pilate gave the Jews a choice—Jesus or Barabbas. This Barabbas was not a mere demonstrator for freedom.

He had been condemned as an insurrectionist and a murderer (Mark 15:7; John 18:40). Remembering how popular Jesus had been, Pilate must have thought the people would demand His release. However, the crowd before the palace that morning was controlled by the priests and Pharisees. It demanded death for Jesus and shouted to free Barabbas.

Luke tells that Pilate also sent Jesus to Herod, who had jurisdiction in Galilee (Luke 23:6-12). Since Jesus had come from Galilee, Pilate used this excuse to put the verdict in the hands of Herod. But soon Jesus was sent back to Pilate. Herod did nothing but add to the insults, attacks, and mockery.

The sins of man loom larger and darker as one sees why Jesus was accused. All of the evil of Satan and the jealousy, selfishness, and cruelty of wicked men were focused on taking the life of the only good, righteous, and perfect man who ever lived.

THE CRUCIFIXION AND ITS MEANING (19:1-27)

Historically, Jesus died by crucifixion under Pontius Pilate. But the way He died included more than the mode of His execution. He died to fulfill the will of God. No one took away His life; He gave it up. Jesus said, "I have power to lay it down, and I have power to take it again. This commandment have I received of my Father" (John 10:18, KJV). This was the purpose for which Jesus had come. But there was more to the will of God than an arbitrary whim. God did not will simply that Jesus die, but that He die for our sins (1 Corinthians 15:3). The way Jesus died atoned for the sins of man (Romans 5:9, 10).

This was the sacrifice of the Lamb of God that had been foreshadowed in the Old Covenant (Isaiah 53:7-10). "Look, the Lamb of God, who takes away the sin of the world!" (John 1:29). This figure of the lamb was not only in prophecy, but was to be used in glorifying Jesus in the Heavenly realms: "Worthy is the Lamb, who was slain, to receive power and wealth and wisdom and strength and honor and glory and praise!" (Revelation 5:12).

The way Jesus died also showed to man the very love of Christ. His death on the cross cannot be separated from the driving force of love both in the Father and in the Son. It was Jesus' love that kept Him there on the cross to the end. Because of this, the way He died becomes an example to man. It shows us the way of love and sacrifice for one another. We are not the perfect man that Jesus was. We are not the Redeemer; but we are followers, and Jesus shows us the way. It was a way that led to death, but this death brought new life. This seeming defeat brought eternal victory. This grief was turned to joy.

The Weakness of Pilate (1-16)

The eighteenth chapter of John records that Pilate tried one device after another to avoid condemning Jesus to death. First, he tried to return Jesus to the Jewish court. "Take him yourselves," he told the Jewish leaders, "and judge him by your own law" (John 18:31). They refused because they wanted the death penalty, and only a Roman edict could order that. Pilate declared Jesus innocent (John 18:38). The accusers insisted that He not only claimed to be king, but was stirring up the people all over Judea, starting from Galilee. Since Jesus came from Galilee, Pilate sent Him to Herod, who ruled in that area but was in Jerusalem for the Passover. Herod could get nothing from Jesus, and soon sent Him back to Pilate. Again Pilate proposed to release Jesus after he had beaten Him (Luke 23:4-16). When the Jewish leaders still insisted that He be crucified, Pilate recalled the custom of celebrating the Passover by releasing a Jewish prisoner. He gave the Jews a choice between Jesus and Barabbas. The crowd insisted that Barabbas be released and Jesus be crucified (John 18:39, 40).

"Then Pilate took Jesus and had him flogged" (John 19:1). The soldiers added some cruel torture of their own. Apparently Pilate hoped this punishment would appease the crowd outside His palace so they would be willing to let Jesus go. But when they saw Him battered and bloody, they still cried, "Crucify! Crucify!" (John 19:6).

In desperation Pilate said, "You take him and crucify him. As for me, I find no basis for a charge against him." The Jews then finally voiced their gravest charge. They said Jesus must die because He claimed to be the Son of God (John 19:7).

At this, Pilate was all the more worried. He did not want to execute an innocent man, but neither did he want the crowd before his palace to become a vicious mob. He did not want to anger the Jewish rulers before him, for they could seek revenge in various subtle ways. And now he had yet a new worry. He did not want to anger the gods. What if Jesus was indeed a son of one of them? One more time, Pilate rushed Jesus into the palace to ask Him, "Where do you come from?" (John 19:9).

COMPARE THE RESPONSES

The Gospel of John is more than an abstract record concerning belief in Jesus. It tells also how people responded when they were confronted with His teaching, His miracles, and His invitation to follow Him. Each was forced to make a decision. Some accepted in belief; some, refusing to believe, rejected Him. This chart assesses selected responses from the first chapter to the last. The upper half estimates the intensity of the acceptance in a scale from 1 to 10. The lower half registers the degree of rejection (-1 to -10). The disciples, led by the Twelve, show the reaction of this general group on sixteen occasions in the ministry of Jesus. These occasions are numbered and identified in the occasion key. The second string of responses indicates the reaction of different individuals associated in the record more or less related to the designated occasion. The intended individuals are identified in the key. The third string of responses plots the feelings of the crowds. These are different crowds on different occasions. A crowd in Galilee, at the feeding of the 5000 is different from a crowd in Jerusalem at the feast of Dedication, or at the Triumphal Entry, or at the trials of Jesus. The last string estimates the hostility of the religious leaders against the person and teaching of Jesus.

Three trends become immediately apparent at one's first glance at the chart:

(1) The disciples show a growing belief and commitment to the Master, but the course is marred by a deep depression, bewilderment, and grief at the crucifixion of Jesus. This is quickly offset by a soaring line to the top degree of conviction resulting from Jesus' resurrection event.

(2) The religious leaders are still more constant in their determined descent into their desperate opposition against Jesus. The chart shows the disciples of Jesus and the enemies of Jesus were headed for opposite poles from the outset.

(3) The Gospel of John tells the reader about selected individuals. It is a realistic report because some of these individuals accept Jesus and others reject Him. This accounts for the dramatic dips into disbelief and the comparable ascents into acceptance. The record tells of both. Different crowds and different circumstances affect the reaction of the crowds in a realistic way as well.

This chart is, of course, but one person's estimate of each situation. You might choose to differ on some of the details. But how would you rate yourself and your belief-response on a similar scale—both then and now?

	Occasions	Disciples	Crowds	References in John	Individuals	Religious Leaders
1	Baptism of Jesus	2	0	1:19-34	John the Baptist (10)	-3
2	Call of Disciples	5	0	1:35-51	Nathanael (8)	-3
3	First Passover	6	3	2, 3	Nicodemus (4)	-5
4	Jacob's Well, Sychar	5	6	4:1-42	Samaritan Woman (8)	-6
5	Signs in Galilee	7	6	4:43-54	Official of Capernaum (8)	-5
6	Sabbath in Jerusalem	5	3	5:16-41	Hostile Jews (-2)	-7
7	Feeding 5000	7	8	6:2-15	Little Boy (9)	-7
8	Bread of Life	5	-2	6:25-59	Peter (6)	-8
9	Jesus' Testimony	7	5	8:12ff.	Pharisees (-5)	-8
10	Jesus and Blind Man	8	5	9	Blind Man Healed (9)	-8
11	Feast of Dedication	7	5	10	Unbelieving Jews (-5)	-9
12	Jesus and Lazarus	8	6	11	Mary and Martha (10)	-10
13	Triumphal Entry	9	8	12	The Greeks (7)	-10
14	Betrayal	5	0	13:26-30	Judas (-5)	-10
15	Crucifixion	1	-5	19	Joseph of Arimathea (4)	-10
16	Resurrection	10	4	20, 21	Mary Magdalene (10)	-9

Occasion

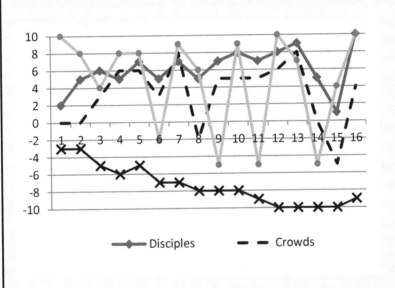

Disciples — — Crowds

Jesus replied nothing. Angrily Pilate reminded Him that He was ignoring the one who held the power of life or death. Then Jesus calmly said Pilate had only the power that God had given him. The one guilty of the greater sin was Caiaphas. He was supposed to be God's priest, but he had handed God's Son over to the governor empowered by God, and had demanded that He be put to death!

Once more Pilate tried to free Jesus, but now the accusers shouted that this would prove he was no friend of Rome. This was a clear threat. If Pilate let Jesus go, the accusers would report to the emperor that he tolerated a rebel who was stirring up insurrection and claiming to be a king. That threat was the final thing that made up Pilate's mind. He feared to condemn an innocent man, but he feared the Jews more. He feared the gods, but he feared the power of Rome still more.

Pilate brought Jesus out for the last time. Solemnly he took the judge's seat on the Stone Pavement, which probably was an open square in front of his Jerusalem headquarters. It was the day of Preparation (Friday) during the Passover Week. So early had the accusers brought Jesus, and so urgently had they pressed their demands, that now it was only about the sixth hour (six o'clock in the morning by the Roman method of noting time).

From the judgment seat, Pilate gave the Jewish leaders a last chance to modify their demand: "Shall I crucify your king?" They shouted back, "We have no king but Caesar" (John 19:15). One wonders if any of them remembered this forty years later, when Caesar's troops crushed their city and brought their nation to a halt.

The Sins of Man (17-27)

Not only was the death of Jesus necessitated by the sin of man, but even the way He died was due to the exceeding sinfulness of man. Jesus' death was entirely unjust. Pilate knew that Jesus was not guilty of any crime, let alone a crime deserving the death penalty. This is the reason Pilate again and again tried to acquit Jesus. Finally Pilate gave in to the demands for death, out of fear for his own reputation and position. How ironic it is that he did not save his reputation, but lost it for all centuries to come! The enemies had no real charges against Jesus. They accused Him of blasphemy; but if Jesus' claim to be the Son of God was true, it was not blasphemous for Him to make it.

People die in different ways. Many die of natural causes, either suddenly or after prolonged illness. Accidental death claims many lives in unexpected tragedy. Some people suffer violent death—in war or from sudden rage of adversaries or as victims of premeditated crimes. Others suffer at their own hands in suicide. All must die; but not many die for a specific purpose, and only a few lay down their lives for the benefit of their fellowmen. Only one has died for all.

Jesus went through the streets carrying His cross. He was crucified outside the city, as was the custom (Hebrews 13:12). John does not tell of the passerby who was drafted to take the cross the last part of the way. (See Mark 15:21.)

The label that Pilate used to designate the crime ("Jesus of Nazareth, the king of the Jews") gave insult to the Jews by declaring that their king was dying on the cross. This was Pilate's revenge on those who had forced his hand, and he refused to change it.

It was custom for the four soldiers responsible for a crucifixion to divide among themselves the possessions of the condemned. Jesus had only His clothing. It seems that the soldiers found some satisfactory way of dividing most of it, but the tunic was left over. This was a special garment, not made of several pieces sewed together, but woven in one piece. Since it was impossible to divide it without greatly reducing its value, the soldiers decided to cast lots to see who of the four would receive the whole garment. This fulfilled the prophecy of Psalm 22:18.

Jesus now committed the care of Mary to the disciple whom He loved, who must be John, the author of the fourth Gospel, and probably the son of Mary's sister, who also was near the cross. It seems quite likely that Jesus' mother's sister (John 19:25), Salome

(Mark 15:40), and the mother of Zebedee's sons—James and John—(Matthew 27:56) was the same person.

DEATH ON THE CROSS (19:1-42)

Jesus' death was unique. It was premeditated by evil men but planned by God. Jesus laid down His life, but it was not suicide. He allowed himself to die, but He did not take His own life. He was executed as a criminal, but He was innocent. He was a Jew, but He died in the most shameful, cruel manner of Roman punishment. He was but one man, but He died for all.

The way Jesus died was in fulfillment of His own purpose in living. He had come into the world to give His life a ransom for many. But one might ask, why must He die in this way to fulfill His purpose? One could reply that it was the will of God. Jesus did not come into this world to exercise His own desire and fulfill His own program apart from doing the will of God and following the direction of His Heavenly Father. But this leads simply to the next question. Why was it the will of God that His own Son die on a cross? One must conclude that it was an absolute necessity. Such a death in the midst of suffering and shame would never have been allowed if there had been any other way. Why was it necessary? The question leads one immediately to the sinfulness of man. Man, created with the freedom of will, has chosen to walk in a path of sin that leads directly to eternal destruction. It was in God's purpose that Jesus die for the redemption of mankind. This redemption was achieved in such a way that in one stroke Jesus died to show His love for every man, to atone for the sins of man, and to give man an example of the full extent of sacrifice for others.

First He Was Scourged (1-16)

Ordinarily, scourging was given as a part of the capital sentence. After the man had been condemned, he was beaten so severely that he would die more rapidly while hanging on the cross. John makes it clear, however, that Pilate was anxious to use the scourging to arouse the sympathy of the people. He hoped this would lead them to agree to Jesus' release. Along with the scourging, the soldiers plaited a crown of thorns and arrayed Him in a purple robe. This was a mocking parody of kingly splendor; and it served to increase the shame of the victims while it heightened the enjoyment of sinful men with their perverted sense of humor. But the people refused to be swayed by the sight of the beaten and ridiculed Jesus. When they continued their insistence, Pilate condemned Jesus to death.

He Carried His Cross (17)

When a criminal was to be crucified, it was customary to force him to carry his own cross to the place of execution. In accordance with the law that forbade crucifixion within the walls, Jesus was led outside the city.

He started out carrying His own cross; but from the exhaustion and extreme pain of the severe scourging just endured, plus many days of intense conflict, Jesus must have fallen beneath the load of the cross. Simon, coming in from the country, was forced to finish the task of carrying the cross to the site of execution (Mark 15:21; Luke 23:26). This place was called *Golgotha*, which in the Hebrew language means the place of the skull. In Latin, the translation is *Calvary*.

He Was Crucified (18-27)

The Gospel narratives do not go into detail in telling the reader just how Jesus was nailed to the cross and the cross was implanted in the earth. This is noteworthy. It shows that God is not anxious simply to arouse our sympathy, but He is anxious to draw a response in commitment and obedience.

There were several forms of crucifixion. A man might be nailed to the cross or he might be tied with ropes. The crosses themselves were of different shapes. There was a simple stake that had been used in earlier times. There was a cross in the shape of an X, there was a cross in the shape of a T, and there was the cross that traditionally has been thought to be the one used in Jesus' death. It is likely that the tradition is correct, for the record says that a sign was placed "above His head" (Matthew 27:37) with the statement of His supposed crime: "Jesus of Nazareth, the King of the Jews" (John 19:19).

That Jesus was nailed to the cross is clearly indicated in the record of His appearances after His resurrection. Thomas said he would not believe the Master was alive unless he could see the print of the nails and put his finger where the nails had been (John 20:25).

The death of Jesus was unjust. He was a man without sin dying on a cross on behalf of sinful men. Furthermore, His death resulted directly from the most heinous kind of sin, sin bringing torture and shame upon an innocent man. It was a death cruel beyond our comprehension. It was a shameful death between two thieves. Matthew and Mark refer to them as thieves or robbers, and Luke calls them malefactors or criminals. It seems evident that with deliberate malice, Jesus' enemies arranged to have these two crucified with Him. This would increase the shame of execution by associating Jesus in His death with such depraved criminals.

A figure struggling through the streets, bent beneath the load of the cross he was carrying, was no new picture to the world of the first century. A poet has said, "For those were crude and cruel days, and human life was cheap." A little more than a century before Jesus died, Alexander Jannaeus had given order for eight hundred of his enemies to be crucified. The wives and children of those men were massacred before their eyes as they hung on their crosses. Crude and cruel days indeed!

He Died (28-37)

In Psalm 69:21, one finds a prophecy of Jesus' thirst and the vinegar He was given. This drink probably was a sour drink that the soldiers had brought for their own use.

Other Scriptures were fulfilled when the soldiers broke the legs of the thieves but, finding Jesus already dead, they pierced His side with a spear. "Not one of His bones will be broken" (John 19:32‑34).[24]

Crucifixion was a shameful death. The cross had become the very symbol of the severest torture and ultimate horror. The Romans had a law that no Roman citizen could be crucified; no matter how despicable a criminal he might be. This end was too shameful for any Roman citizen to endure. But Jesus, the Son of God, died that way.

He Showed His Love

Jesus died in pain and shame, weighted with all the sins of mankind. For the Christian, however, the cross has come to have a significance entirely different. It is a symbol of love because God so loved us that He gave His Son to die in our stead and because Christ loved us enough to die for us. The cross is a symbol of redemption because through Jesus' suffering, our sins are forgiven. It is a sign of victory because even in that moment of shame, of torture, and of death, our Savior was winning freedom for all mankind. And through this suffering and shame, Christ came to glory.

> But we see Jesus, who was made a little lower than the angels, now crowned with glory and honor because he suffered death, so that by the grace of God he might taste death for everyone.
>
> In bringing many sons to glory, it was fitting that God, for whom and through whom everything exists, should make the author of their salvation perfect through suffering (Hebrews 2:9, 10).

As Jesus hung on the cross, He showed His love and concern for others. Even in His dying hour, He was concerned for His mother as she wept before His face. He committed her to the care of the disciple whom He loved (John the apostle), who stood beside her (John 19:26, 27). Apparently, Mary's other sons were not there. She would need care and protection. Her Son did not want Mary to be

---

[24] See Psalm 34:20; Zechariah 12:10.

alone. Jesus loves all mankind, but He loves and cares for each person in an individual way.

He Gave an Example of Sacrifice

Once again we see Jesus as He dies on the cross. His love constrains us to give ourselves for one another even as He gave himself for us.

> For Christ's love compels us, because we are convinced that one died for all, and therefore all died. And he died for all, that those who live should no longer live for themselves but for him who died for them and was raised again (2 Corinthians 5:14, 15).

He Was Buried (38-42)

The burial of Jesus was important to His loved ones because they did not want His remains to be desecrated. It was important to Jesus' enemies because they did not want someone to steal the body and later make false claims of a resurrection. It was important to all posterity that the body of Jesus be accounted for from the time of His death until the resurrection appearances of the same body. All stand in debt to Joseph of Arimathea and to Nicodemus, who had the courage to take the body of Jesus from the cross and place it in Joseph's nearby tomb. It was the Jewish day of Preparation (Friday), and the Sabbath was the next day (John 19:31). Joseph of Arimathea had been a disciple of Jesus, but secretly because he feared the Jews. He now asked Pilate for the body of Jesus.

This was no small favor he was asking. In cases of treason, the Roman government did not allow loving care for the body of an executed man. Even a mother could be denied the body of her son slain on a cross. As a final dishonor to a traitor, his body was simply taken to a refuse area or left to decompose along the road. In this case, however, Pilate readily gave the body to Joseph. This is one more proof that Pilate knew Jesus was innocent.

Joseph had a tomb ready for use—a fine tomb carved in solid rock. Such a tomb was designed to be used for a number of bodies.

Joseph probably had it prepared for himself and his family, but it had not yet been put into use. When Joseph offered his tomb for the remains of Jesus, he put his own life in jeopardy. If he revealed himself as the friend of a traitor, he would naturally be suspected of treason. Now, however, the love of Christ was so strong that he could not resist answering in sacrifice of self.

Nicodemus was another who followed the example of Jesus. He was one who had come to Jesus by night (John 3:1-21). Perhaps he, too, had been afraid to be a disciple of Jesus openly; but now he brought a mixture of myrrh and aloes, about seventy-five pounds. (The "hundred pounds" of the King James Version are troy pounds, about twelve ounces each.) Together Joseph and Nicodemus wrapped the body of Jesus with this fragrant mixture and left it in the tomb. Perhaps they expected to return when the Sabbath would be over and more spices could be purchased.

The way Jesus died is the greatest of challenges to the lives of men. It was submission to the will of God; it was atonement for the sins of men. It showed the love of Jesus and gave an example for all mankind. It was the only way.

CHAPTER THIRTEEN

The Dawn of New Life
John 20:1–21:25

No man can hold back the dawn. It cannot be hurried by anticipating it nor stopped by doubting. No one could keep Christ in the grave—not Satan, not death, certainly not men. When day dawned on the first day of the week and the tomb was empty, new life came to the words spoken as Jesus was born into this world: "Because of the tender mercy of our God, by which the rising sun will come to us from heaven to shine on those living in darkness and in the shadow of death, to guide our feet into the path of peace" (Luke 1:78, 79).

This was the dawn of hope. Women saw the empty tomb and heard the message of the angel.[25] They had new hope for the survival of Jesus, but that was not all. They also had new hope for themselves. Their welfare, their future, their relationship with God—all had been wrapped up in the life of Jesus. Now, if He was alive, their hope was alive, also. This might have been selfish if it had been a hope only for themselves. But it was a hope for all mankind, a hope for the weak and lost and helpless, a hope of salvation to replace the dread of destruction.

This was not only the dawn of hope, but also the dawn of resurrection. If Jesus was actually raised from the dead, then His resurrection would not be the only one. Others would follow. It was

---

[25] Matthew 28:5, 6; Mark 16:6; Luke 24:5–7.

truly the dawn of a new day. Even though the second resurrection has not yet occurred, it stands secure. The one who was raised from the dead has promised another resurrection by which all of His followers will be raised as well. Although other resurrections have occurred, Jesus alone has been raised to die no more. He is the first fruits; there is more fruit to come (1 Corinthians 15:20-23).

His resurrection is the dawn. In due time, as day follows dawn, our resurrection will follow the resurrection of Jesus Christ.

THE GOOD NEWS (20:1-18)

When the resurrection of Jesus dawned upon the understanding of His followers, there were immediate results. They ran to tell the message (John 20:2; Matthew 28:8). This was characteristic of that day. Everyone was running. The darkness had been so deep, and the dawn indicated such a beautiful day, that everyone was eager to spread the news.

A New Hope (1-9)

Mary Magdalene was the first to the tomb in the dawning. From the other Gospel narratives, one learns that she was not alone. Two of her companions are named in Mark 16:1. But it seems that Mary was in the lead. They came to finish preparing the body for permanent burial, not because they expected a resurrection. No hope of seeing Jesus alive on earth was left among them.

The first day of the week was still in darkness as these devoted women made their way to the tomb with spices to be placed about the body of Jesus. It would not be long before the light of day as well as the light of understanding and hope would burst upon them.

The Gospel of John follows the activity of Mary Magdalene alone, while the other Gospels speak of Mary the mother of James, Salome, Joanna, and others.[26] One wonders not only why Mary was given special prominence by John, but also why she was the privileged one who first saw the risen Lord. Whether one can

---

[26] Matthew 28:1; Mark 16:1; Luke 24:10.

answer this or not, Mary ran with news of the empty tomb to Peter and John. When John recounted the events of that first day of the week, he naturally gave an important place to the one who first brought the news to him.

Mary Magdalene's name indicates that she came from the town of Magdala, located on the southwestern coast of the Sea of Galilee. She was among those whom Jesus freed of demon possession (Mark 16:9; Luke 8:2). Some have described her as a very sinful woman before Jesus found her, but there is no good reason for thinking this or for identifying her with the sinful woman who anointed Jesus' feet (Luke 7:36-50). Rather, she followed Christ and contributed to the support of Him and His disciples (Luke 8:2, 3).

Mary was present at the death of Jesus (Matthew 27:55, 56), and she lingered to see the tomb where they laid Him (Mark 15:46, 47). Now she returned after the Sabbath to help bring more spices for Jesus' burial.

In the morning's early light, Mary saw that the stone was not closing the door of the tomb as she had seen it on Friday afternoon (Matthew 27:61). Her first thought was that someone had taken the body from its resting place, and she wanted to find help to do something about it. She ran to tell Peter and John. Why these two rather than some others? Perhaps because they were outstanding leaders among the apostles. Perhaps because they were the closest ones. In any event, Mary knew where she could find them, and she lost no time taking the news.

Left behind at the tomb, the other women heard an angel say that Jesus had risen from the dead. Then they, too, were running, running to find other disciples and give them the good news (Matthew 28:5-8).

Meanwhile, Mary Magdalene came to Peter and John. Breathlessly she said, "They have taken the Lord out of the tomb, and we don't know where they have put him!" (John 20:2).

John ran more swiftly than Peter, and often this is taken as an indication that he was younger. It is very probable that he was younger, but his speed can hardly be taken as proof. A swift man of thirty can outrun a slow man of twenty.

John, however, was not so bold as to enter the tomb immediately. "He bent over and looked in" (John 20:5). This is an interesting description of one who is *bent over looking intently* at something. He saw the grave clothes lying before him.

Simon Peter had no such hesitation. He rushed into the tomb for a closer look. What he saw has been described in different ways. One reader imagines that Jesus' body had emerged from the wrappings without disturbing them, leaving them still wrapped as they had been, but now collapsed because there was nothing inside. Another imagines that Jesus or an angel had removed the wrappings and folded them neatly. The record does not specifically confirm either of these suppositions, but merely says the disciples saw the clothes lying there. It does specify (John 20:7) that the head cloth was not with the others, but in a place by itself folded up (NIV) or wrapped together (KJV). This detail gives the impression of neatness and order. If the body had been stolen, the thieves probably would have taken the clothes with it; or if not, would have left them scattered about in disarray.

When the other disciple went inside, he saw the tomb, saw the grave clothes as they were, and saw that the body was not there— and he "believed" (John 20:8). What did he believe? Some say he now believed Jesus had risen from the dead. Others point out that the disciples did not believe that even Mary had said she had seen Him (Mark 16:9-11). There at the tomb, they say, John believed only what Mary had already told him—that the body was gone. It is not necessary to trace exactly the beginning and growth of belief in these two and the other disciples. Before another day dawned, most of the disciples would see the Lord himself (John 20:19, 20).

Of course, there were grounds for belief in a resurrection even before they saw the empty tomb. The Scriptures predicted it. John notes, however, that they still did not understand these prophecies (John 20:9). Jesus explained them that evening (Luke

24:45-47), and later, guided by the Holy Spirit, Peter used some of them very convincingly (Acts 2:24-36).

New Life (10-18)

Peter and John had come swiftly and probably were gone before a weary Mary made her way back to the tomb. She stood at the entrance, exhausted, alone, uncertain, and near despair. Reluctant to step into the gloomy interior, she bent down and peered through the opening as John had done when he had arrived. But this time, Mary saw two angels in white sitting at the two ends of the place where the body of Jesus had been.

This fine tomb, made for a prominent citizen, probably had its central chamber surrounded by niches in which bodies were to be laid for their last rest. But it may have had in the middle of the chamber a stone bench where a body could be placed for its final preparation with spices and wrapping. Perhaps the body of Jesus had been left on this bench over the Sabbath, awaiting final attention before being placed in its permanent niche. This place would be visible from the entrance and would also have room for one angel to be seated at the head and one at the foot of the collapsed grave clothes. The other women had already seen the angels, who were described as "men in clothes that gleamed like lightning" (Luke 24:4).

Mary was crying, and it seems that she was too numbed with sorrow to be as frightened as the other women had been. Apparently Mary was so drained by the sorrow of the past few days, so weighted by her present concern for the whereabouts of Jesus' body, so exhausted by the recent run to summon help, and so preoccupied in her own thoughts that she simply did not realize that she was in the presence of angels!

The angels broke the silence with a question: "Why are you crying?" She could only speak aloud the words she must have been saying over and over in her troubled mind: "They have taken my Lord away, and I don't know where they have put him"

(John 20:13). She was not expecting to see Jesus. The report she made later was not the result of wishful thinking. It was not the product of her imagination. Jesus' body was gone, and she could think of nothing but the logical conclusion, which later proved false, that someone had carried it away.

Did Mary hear a sound behind her? Did she see the angels looking past her to someone beyond? We do not know, but she turned around and saw Jesus standing there. She did not realize, however, that it was Jesus; she did not recognize Him. We need not suppose that His appearance was changed. Her tear-filled eyes, her distraught and stunned condition, and her knowledge that He was dead were enough to keep her from recognizing Him. Certainly it shows that she was not expecting to see Him.

She still had a singular concern: she wanted to know where the body of Jesus was. But thinking this was the gardener, she was hopeful that he really might know. She even added, "Tell me where you have put him, and I will get him." As though she would be able to carry His body from one place to another even if she knew where it was!

Then Jesus spoke her name, and this brought her back to her senses. Excitedly she cried, "Rabboni," which means Master or Teacher. Not only did she have new hope in her life, but she virtually had new life!

As the King James Version has it (John 20:17), Jesus then said, "Touch me not; for I am not yet ascended to my Father."

This is better translated in the New International Version, "Do not hold on to me, for I have not yet returned to the Father." The Greek phrase can mean "do not touch me," or it can mean "do not detain me." The latter sense is preferable, for Jesus on other occasions invited disciples to touch His resurrected form (Luke 24:39). He ate food as other human beings do (Luke 24:42), and He showed the disciples the print of the nails in His hands and feet (Luke 24:40; John 20:20, 24-28). Jesus' resurrected body was the same body that had been laid in the tomb. It was not because Jesus appeared in another form that Mary could not touch Him, but because He had so many tasks to accomplish and so short a time in which to do them.

Mark 16:9 tells us this was the first appearance of Jesus after He rose from the dead. Mary thus became the first messenger to go to the disciples with the glorious, exciting, awesome news. She had seen the Lord, and indeed, He was returning to God the Father.

Jesus is our living Lord because He conquered death. The tomb was empty because the bonds of death could not hold the Son of God. Not only was the dead body missing, but the living Jesus was seen and heard. The wages of sin is death (Romans 6:23), but more is involved in that penalty than the first death, the loss of physical life. There is a spiritual death that ends in the second death and eternal separation from God (Revelation 21:8). By Christ's victory, the forgiveness of sins is made effectual and man can be released from his former bondage to sin (Romans 5:17). Christ is our living Lord because He brings renewed life to those who are dead in sin. When Jesus greeted His disciples with "Peace be with you!" (John 20:19), He used familiar words; but they carried a deeper significance now. Since the resurrection, man can have a peace of soul never known before. Spiritual death is vanquished by conquest over sin. Because Jesus is alive, Mary had a new life ahead of her.

A New Message (1-18)

The death of Jesus had different meanings to different people. To the Pharisees and priests, it seemed their victory. A menace to their teaching and their power seemed to have been removed. To the soldiers, the crucifixion of Jesus was just another job to be done. No matter how many misgivings they may have felt, they accomplished their task. To the disciples of Jesus, His death brought despair. Hope fled from them as they scattered into the darkness at Christ's arrest. To Judas came a realization of his guilt, and as a result, he went out and hanged himself.

Then Jesus arose from the grave "with a mighty triumph o'er His foes." This too had different meanings to different people. The Pharisees and priests refused to admit His resurrection, for this admission would have been an admission of their own evil deeds. They had to concoct a lie and try to cover up the truth. They told the soldiers to report that while they were sleeping, someone had stolen the body (Matthew 28:13). In resisting the truth, they added still more wrongs to their deeds. But to the disciples, the meaning of Jesus' resurrection was very different. Their new hope was like a release from prison. Death is a prison no man can escape by himself. It is the wages of sin. But Jesus conquered death. Its bonds were not able to hold Him, and in His victory He promises freedom from sin and death to all who will accept His gift: "For as in Adam all die, so in Christ all will be made alive" (1 Corinthians 15:22).

To the disciples, the resurrection was a bright light in darkness: "The people that walked in darkness have seen a great light: they that dwell in the land of the shadow of death, upon them hath the light shined" (Isaiah 9:2, KJV). Without Jesus to bring light into our lives, we could not know where we are. We would not see the meaning of life now, nor have any promise of life hereafter. The risen Lord is the light of the world. He really lives today. He is a living proof of a living God.

The prompt reaction of Mary was to share this news with someone else. Through the hope and the light of the resurrection, power was supplied in the lives of the disciples. They pro-claimed the gospel with such force that it was said they turned the world upside down. This gospel can transform the world with its power. It needs to be proclaimed by one who himself is transformed by the hope and the life that Jesus' resurrection brings.

So included with the new hope and new proof, there was a new message to be preached. One cannot help noting that on the resurrection morning, Jesus' followers were continually on the run to take the news. Mary ran to the disciples, two disciples ran to the tomb, two others ran back from Emmaus (Luke 24:33). Jesus has commissioned us to keep on the run taking the good news. One finds all the joy, peace, and assurance beyond the reach of materialism in the message of the resurrection. Jesus in turn lays upon us the burden of making this known to others. "Peace be with you! As the Father has sent me, I am sending you" (John 20:21). Resurrection was the dawning of a new message.

The Belief that Counts Most (20:19-31)

John clearly states his purpose for writing his Gospel narrative. "But these are written that you may believe that Jesus is the Christ, the Son of God, and that by believing you may have life in his name" (John 20:31). Although secondary purposes have been suggested, this explicitly declared purpose is above them all. Some have noted the possibility that John was anxious to supplement material found in the other three Gospel narratives; and his choice of events fits this suggestion, for it is often different from that of the Synoptics. Others have noted an emphasis on the hostility of the Jews throughout the narrative. Still others have pointed out the Gospel's opposition to Gnostic teaching, as John shows clearly that the Word became flesh and dwelt among us as a man. Another note is the preliminary teaching of the Gospel concerning baptism and the Lord's Supper. This is done in an introductory way through Jesus' conversation with Nicodemus (John 3:3-8) and His sermon on the bread of life (John 6:30-58). All of these, however, must take second place to the primary thrust of the whole life and work of Jesus, culminating in His death, burial, and resurrection. To accept Jesus, one must recognize Him as the Messiah (in the Greek, Christ) predicted in the Old Testament. To accept Jesus, one must recognize the power of the resurrection; he must know Jesus as the Son of God and the Lord.

Stop Being Afraid, and See (19-23)

It was the evening of the first day of the week, the day on which Jesus arose from the dead. According to Jewish calculation, a new day began with nightfall. Some have suggested that this scene must have been after nightfall and therefore on the second day of the week. The meeting of the disciples was entered by two who had been more than seven miles away when it was "nearly evening" (Luke 24:13-35). *Nearly evening* is very indefinite, however, and it is quite possible that the two returned to Jerusalem before nightfall. Also, John at times used the Roman system of calculating time, which includes the evening with the day before. In any event, John clearly times Jesus' appearance to a group of disciples at the close of the first day of the week—that day of Jesus' resurrection (John 20:1, 19). The other Gospel writers also specify the first day of the week for the resurrection day (Matthew 28:1; Mark 16:2; Luke 24:1).

On the evening of that Sunday, the disciples were together in a house. Ten of the twelve apostles were there. Judas was dead (Matthew 27:3-5), and Thomas was absent from the group (John 20:24). However, others were gathered there with the Ten. Two who came from Emmaus had seen Jesus and then gone directly to the place where they had found the apostles "and those with them" (Luke 24:33). How many others were there, one has no way of knowing.

John indicates that fear and apprehension gripped the disciples. The doors were shut. This no doubt means they were locked for security.

The fact that the doors were locked for fear of the Jews gives a hint of the situation the disciples were enduring. They were afraid the circumstances surrounding the death of Jesus would lead to their own arrest and a similar fate. Certainly, there is nothing remarkable in their fear. It is more remarkable that they did not scatter to their homes in Galilee.

Jesus came and appeared in their midst. Many theories have been propounded to explain how He did this. Some who deny the miraculous are anxious to find a natural explanation. Some have suggested that Jesus used a ladder to enter a window, others that He descended from the roof, and still others that He slipped in with the men from Emmaus. All of this speculation is contrary to the record. On the other hand, some who maintain the deity of Jesus and accept the supernatural have suggested that this even shows Jesus in a new, spiritual body different from the body He had before His death. Certainly it was marvelous and miraculous that His body was now alive despite the deadly wound in its side, and certainly it was miraculous that this material body appeared in a closed room; but it is not necessary to suppose that the substance of the body was different from what it had been before. Jesus walked on the water in the body He had before His death; there is no reason to suppose He could not have appeared in a closed room in that same body. Both these miracles are beyond our understanding. We simply do not know how they were accomplished; but we need not conclude that either of them required a spiritual or glorified or unsubstantial body different from the one Jesus had before His death. The body He had after His resurrection was the same body that had been laid in the tomb. It still carried the marks of the nails and the wound of the spear. It was real, physical, substantial.

Thus, it is useless to conjecture how He came through the locked doors. John certainly considered it a miracle, but he does not attempt to explain how it happened. We should follow his example.

Jesus' first utterance to these that were assembled was, "Peace be with you" (John 20:19).

This was the conventional greeting of the East and still remains until this day. Yet there was special significance to these words. Anything but peace had been ruling in the minds and hearts of these men whom He addressed. But by His very presence and by His word, a wonderful peace was brought to them.

After His greeting, note what Jesus did next. He did not begin a discourse on existential philosophy, trying to convince His disciples that one can accept stories as true with religious significance when they are historically false. Nor did He attempt to prove to them a spiritual resurrection without a physical, bodily rising from the dead. Nor did He launch into a lecture comparing literal and figurative interpretation. He simply showed them His hands and His side (John 20:20).

This was the quickest way He could convince them that He was the same Jesus they had seen die on the cross and that He was really there and alive. It was a literal, physical, living body that He showed them. It was a body of flesh and bones, wounded by nails and spear, able to eat solid food (Luke 24:37 43).

By showing the disciples the hands that bore the marks of the nails and the side that had been pierced by the spear-thrust, Jesus assured them not only that He was a living being, but also that He was the very person they had known in the past—the one who had been their Master and Guide. The disciples were overjoyed upon their being thus convinced. This was what Mary Magdalene and others had told them, but they had felt it was too good to be true. The Gospel of Luke explicitly says, "And while they still did not believe it because of joy and amazement. . . (Luke 24:41).

It was not an easy task to convince these men that such a triumphal conclusion could come from such a tragic death. But He was telling them, "Stop being afraid, and just look and see that I am the same Jesus. See the print of the nails and see My side. Stop being afraid and see."

The use of words with double meaning has already been noticed in John's Gospel. Jesus' use of the word *see* is another example. There is a surface meaning and also one of deeper significance. Jesus showed them His hands and side, but He wanted them to understand the meaning of it all. He wanted them to see the victory over death, to see the resurrection of the body, to see the triumph over all the enemies of man. He wanted them to know the power and authority of the person of Jesus in their midst.

Having shown the disciples the evidence that He was their Lord, Jesus repeated His blessing of peace and gave them another statement of His commission (John 20:21).

The Great Commission was issued not once but many times, especially in this short period between Jesus' resurrection and ascension. Jesus told them He was sending them on a mission just as He had been sent. He breathed on them to impart to them the Holy Spirit.

Some have difficulty relating this passage with Jesus' saying that He must go away before the Spirit would come (John 16:7), and with the description of the coming of the Spirit in Acts 2. The difficulty may be resolved in either of two ways.

First, it may be possible that Jesus at this time did not actually impart the Holy Spirit to the apostles, but only repeated His promise that they would receive the Holy Spirit after Jesus' departure.

Second, one must remember that there are numerous manifestations of the Spirit. What occurred in this meeting of the disciples with the resurrected Lord was not the same as the baptism of the Holy Spirit described in Acts 2. The manifestation recorded in Acts 2 fulfilled the promise of Christ that the Spirit would come after His departure, but here in John 20:22, we may be reading of a different manifestation of the Spirit that was granted for special strength and guidance in that crucial hour.

What did the Holy Spirit do for the Ten at this time? The record does not say. Perhaps He gave them courage as they were hiding behind locked doors (John 20:19). Perhaps He guided them in the choice of someone to take the place of Judas (Acts 1:15-26).

Note, however, the statement of Jesus that immediately followed His mention of the Holy Spirit. It has to do with the forgiving of sins (John 20:23). How were these disciples to go about forgiving sins or not forgiving them?

When Jesus gave His commission to the disciples, it involved the proclamation of the gospel: "Go into all the world and preach the good news," or "preach the gospel," as the King James Version has it (Mark 16:15). When Jesus promised the Holy Spirit, this also had to do with the proclamation of the gospel: "He ... will convict the world concerning sin, and righteousness, and judgment" (John 16:8, NASB). Obviously, the Holy Spirit brought this conviction as the disciples preached the gospel. (See Acts 2:37, for example.)

So when Jesus referred to the forgiving of sins, it seems that this also was associated with the proclamation of the gospel. He was not saying that the apostles, or any future clergy, or the coming church, could actually by their own wisdom or power declare even one sin of one individual remitted. Rather, they were to preach the gospel. Through the proclamation of the gospel, one is brought to a decision to accept Christ; and if he does accept the Savior, his sins are forgiven. The opposite is true of those who reject Christ.

Stop Doubting and Believe (24-29)

In our time and place we cannot see the physical Jesus in the Judean hills or on the Sea of Galilee, but we can see Him on the deeper level that is just as real as the surface.

One is confronted with a problem, however. Can we actually understand Jesus if we have never seen Him as a physical human being? Thomas helps us with this problem. He was determined not to be swayed by wishful thinking. Others might be carried away by overactive imaginations to exciting hallucination, but not Thomas! He knew that in the end, all must face reality, and he wanted reality as his foundation. Even when others said they had seen Jesus, he was not willing to accept their testimony unless he could see the Lord with his own eyes and test His body with his own hands.

For some reason unknown to us, Thomas was not with the other ten apostles when Jesus came into their midst. No explanation of his absence is given. No intimation is left whether it was to his credit or his discredit that he was not among the people gathered in the room where Jesus appeared. What is quite sure is that he demanded physical evidence before he was willing to believe in the resurrection of Jesus. Thomas was frank about his doubt when the others told him they had seen Jesus. He knew Jesus had died. It seemed incredible that He was alive again. Thomas said he would not believe it unless he could both see for himself and add the test of touch to the assurance of his eyes. Wishful thinking would not influence him!

A week later, the disciples again were together on the first day of the week (John 20:26). This time Thomas was with them, and Jesus appeared again. In a similar manner, He greeted them: "Peace be with you." Then Jesus confronted Thomas and invited him to touch His nail-scarred hands and spear-torn side: "Put your finger here; see my hands. Reach out your hand and put it into my side. Stop doubting and believe" (John 20:27).

There is a difference between Thomas and us. He lived in a time when it was possible for him to test in this way, and it is not possible for us. But it is important to us to know that in that day when Jesus was raised from the dead, there were those who were anxious to test the surface as well as to plumb the depths. If the depths are real, the surface should be real as well.

Now the Gospel of John comes full circle. It began with the affirmation that the Word was God, and now the whole Gospel reaches its climax in the exclamation of Thomas as he acclaims Jesus, "My Lord and my God" (John 20:28). This is what the Gospel of John is written for, to lead an individual to believe that Jesus is the Son of God. Thomas shows us how one man came to that belief. He was not easy to convince, but he came to the full acceptance of Jesus Christ as God. This included belief in the resurrection and much more.

We are not told that Thomas actually reached out his hand to touch the nail prints and to examine Jesus' side. Some maintain that he did, others are as certain that he did not. Since the record does not tell us whether he did or did not, it is evident that the actual contact was not important. Thomas could believe without touching Jesus' flesh. We, too, can believe without finding a fossilized footprint of Jesus in the streets of Jerusalem. But lack of a footprint does not make Him unhistorical. We have the imprint of His life in ways innumerable down through the corridors of time. One need not witness a physical resurrection in his own lifetime in order to believe that Jesus was resurrected from the dead. On the contrary, one should expect something unique of the one and only Son of God.

Reading the words of Jesus to Thomas (John 20:29), one wonders whether Jesus was rebuking Thomas as much as He was challenging us: "Because you have seen me, you have believed; blessed are those who have not seen and yet have believed." Thomas both saw and believed. He tested the surface and accepted the depths. We give thanks because this very Gospel of John gives us testimony of the surface and points us also to the depths. It presents clear and sure evidence that Jesus lived and died and rose again, and the established facts provide sound basis for secure belief that Jesus is the Son of God.

Then another question is raised: Can't one omit the surface and simply leap to the depths? If one can no longer test the physical resurrection of Jesus in the laboratory of man's experience, can't one just accept some sort of spiritual resurrection without accepting the physical? Today, there are those who proclaim the resurrection of Christ, not as something that occurred in a historical, bodily way, but as something that came to be in the beliefs and musings of early Christians. After all, they reason, if Thomas was wrong in demanding to touch the body of Jesus, is it not wrong today to emphasize an actual bodily resurrection? Is it not more important to see the resurrection of Jesus as a victory over sin and death? What does it matter whether a body came back to life or not?

But is it possible to omit the one belief and leap to the other? In other words, can one deny the bodily resurrection of Jesus and still accept the power of the resurrection in the lives of individuals of the early church and the lives of believers today? Belief in Jesus is not a matter of accepting either one or the other. Belief in Jesus accepts both the bodily resurrection and the spiritual significance, both the surface and the depths. Jesus' challenge rings down through the ages of time: "Stop doubting and believe!"

Stop Dying and Live (30, 31)

By the testimony of his own eyes, Thomas was led to accept the victory of Jesus over death and sin, to recognize Jesus was the Lord Messiah and the very person of God. But Jesus promised a blessing on those who are led to the same conclusion by the reliable testimony of others. We can share Thomas' belief without seeing Jesus. For that very purpose, John wrote this record. There were so many miraculous signs that John could not record them all, but he recorded enough so that a reader may believe that Jesus is the Messiah, the Son of God, and by believing may have life in His name.

Why did God give miraculous signs, of which the resurrection is the climax? Why did John record them? These miraculous signs were given and recorded so that by this surface testimony, one may understand the eternal truths that lie beneath. The belief of Christians is summed up in the statement that "Jesus is the Christ, the Son of God." Then the purpose of that belief is summed up: "By believing you may have life in his name" (John 20:31). This is not a belief that is academic. This is not a belief that is subject to cultural tendencies. This is not a belief that has no consequences. This is a belief that is tied inextricably to eternal salvation. Those who do not believe are facing eternal death. On the other hand, the life of believers is special life as the children of God (John 1:12). Jesus came. Jesus was life, and that life was the light of men. Stop dying and live.

FOLLOW HIM (21:1-25)

The Gospel of John comes to a natural conclusion with the close of the twentieth chapter. John, however, has one more snapshot he wishes to share. An incident occurred on the Sea of Galilee (also called the Sea of Tiberias) and involved some matters that needed to be included before his book was ended.

The twenty-first chapter of John is like a chest packed with precious treasures. It provides beautiful scenes and expresses beautiful feelings, but issues stern warnings and inspires high hopes. This is a fitting close to the spiritual Gospel. This chapter, however, has drawn the attacks of numerous critics who choose to maintain it is not a part of the Gospel, nor written by the same hand.

All manuscript evidence points toward including this chapter at the close. The author gives a conclusion in 20:30, 31, but this does not forbid his adding an important scene and explanatory remark as a postlude. Especially one might expect this if there was some rumor that needed correcting. That the beloved disciple would live on to the Lord's return was a mistaken notion that was circulating among Christians. The fact that this chapter corrects this erroneous impression does not mean that another author must have written it; it is appropriate for John to include this correction himself. Other reasons will become apparent for including the incidents recorded in this chapter. It occupies a role that is vital to the whole Gospel of John.

No break in literary style occurs between the main body of the Gospel and the closing chapter. Some claim there is a difference, but U. D. Bloomfield shows conclusively that every chapter provides some differences from the others, and this closing one has somewhat less differences than some others.[27]

John's Gospel does not end with the resurrection of Jesus, but with a challenge to His disciples. It is not simply a challenge for belief, but a call for commitment. Paul's epistles give doctrinal teaching, but each leads to a "therefore" section with practical application of the truths presented. Lives are changed because of acceptance of Jesus and His teaching. Following Jesus demands action, a life that obeys Him. So John's Gospel not only presents the facts of Jesus' life, death, and resurrection, but ends with the challenge to Peter and to us to follow Him and feed His sheep.

Wherever He Leads (1-8)

---

[27] G. D. Bloomfield, John, Peter, and the Fourth Gospel (1934).

Jesus had left explicit instructions for His disciples to meet Him in Galilee (Matthew 28:16). So they went to Galilee; but when they got there, they did not find the resurrected Jesus. They waited for Him, but for a time they did not see Him. One evening, Peter declared he was going to fish, and six others decided to go with him. This need not mean they were returning to their old ways and rejecting Jesus for the business of fishing. Rather it may indicate they wanted to spend their time doing something useful instead of remaining idle while they waited.

They had met the first test: they had come to Galilee, and they were looking for Jesus. After they labored all night fishing and had caught nothing, another test came. A figure on the shore told them they should cast their net on the right side of the boat. As if these seasoned fishermen had not already tried every device they knew to bring in some fish! Still they had caught nothing. Could this voice from the shore actually help them?

This description of a miraculous catch of fish at the close of Jesus' earthly association with His disciples provides a beautiful parallel with the miraculous catch at the time He called some of the fishers to become fishers of men (Luke 5:4-10).

One wonders whether the disciples remembered that earlier scene when a voice called from the shore, asking if they had caught anything and then telling them to cast their nets on the right side of the boat. Why did they not recognize Jesus at once? Several reasons are possible. They were about a hundred yards away (John 21:8), and it was early in the morning (John 21:4). Perhaps it was scarcely light. Also, there is the possibility that Jesus did not choose to have His identity known prior to the catch. In one earlier appearance, to the two on the road to Emmaus, the witnesses at first were kept from recognizing him (Luke 24:16).

They had been watching for Jesus, but now they did not know Him as He called to them across a hundred yards of water in the dim light of dawn. But when they followed His instructions, and the nets were filled with fish, they knew this man was more than an ordinary man. It must be Jesus.

After the catch, it was John who first exclaimed, "It is the Lord!" (John 21:7). But it was Peter who jumped overboard to swim to Him. He had not time to bother with boats or fish or other disciples; he wanted to get to Jesus. This is one more indication of his genuine commitment to Jesus.

However He Provides (9-14)

Finally, the disciples came to the shore, dragging the fish 153 big ones. They found that Jesus not only was there, but had provided for them. A warm fire was burning and fish were already cooked for a satisfying breakfast along the beautiful shore of Galilee. Not the least of all these enjoyable details was the very presence of Jesus with His disciples once again.

Some people puzzle over the meaning of the number 153 for the fish that were caught. There is no indication that one should look for a mystical meaning to the number. John simply re-corded the fact, and not every fact has a hidden meaning. Here was a remarkable catch. There were 153 large fish.

The disciples accepted Jesus' invitation to have breakfast with Him. Many memories must have flooded their minds along with the memory of that earlier catch of fish, for they had often been with Jesus beside this lake or on it.[28]

John specifies that this was Jesus' third appearance *to His disciples* after He was raised from the dead (John 21:14). This ignores His appearances to Mary Magdalene, to some other women, to two disciples on the road to Emmaus, and to Simon Peter. Jesus had *twice* appeared *to a whole group of disciples* (John 20:19-29). Now, in Galilee, He appeared to seven of them, five of whom are named. Some have suggested that the other two were Andrew and Philip, who also were fishermen among the apostles. However, John does not even make it explicit that the unnamed two were two

---

[28] See Mark 2:13; 4:1-9; 5:1-13; 6:30-51.

of the eleven apostles. Probably, the whole group of the apostles was waiting in Galilee to meet Jesus at a time and place He had appointed (Matthew 28:16).

Whatever He Demands (15-17)

The New International Version labels this paragraph, "Jesus Reinstates Peter." This may be too strong and too official an inference to be drawn from the scene that it records. Peter al-ready had been in a private interview with Jesus since his three denials (Luke 24:34). He did not need an official reinstatement in this meeting by the lake. What he needed, both for himself, for the other disciples, and for all posterity was a warm, personal assurance and injunction from Jesus that would offset the public reports of his denials. This is what we are given as we read Jesus' repeated question, Peter's repeated declarations of love, and the repeated command for him to carry on the Master's work.

After they had eaten their breakfast, Jesus asked Simon Peter, "Do you truly love me more than these?"

What did Jesus mean, "more than these?" The words were spoken on the shore of the Sea of Galilee, where Peter had his home. There he was surrounded by beloved companions, and beside him were the fishing boat and well-filled net. It would seem Jesus was asking whether Peter would put love of Him before all else in this world. The call of the fishing lake, the call of the physical blessings of this world, even the call of close fellowship with his loved ones—all were included.

It seems unlikely that Jesus was saying only, "Do you love me more than these other disciples love me?" That may have been a part of the question, however. Peter had claimed that he would never forsake Jesus, even if all others would (Matthew 26:33). It would be fitting for Jesus now to ask, "Do you still claim to be more devoted and loyal than anyone else?" After that affirmation of loyalty, Peter had denied the Lord three times. It may be that Jesus was recalling those denials as He three times asked about Peter's love. But there was more than that in His question.

It seems unlikely that Jesus was asking only, "Do you love me more than you love these disciples?" This too may have been a part of the question. Some of these disciples had been neighbors and partners of Peter before they knew Jesus. They had been drawn closer through three years of following the Master. Their fellowship had been fused in the fire of grief at His death and lifted in joy at His resurrection. But still, devotion to Jesus must be above any devotion to companions.

It seems unlikely that Jesus was asking, "Do you love me more than you love the boat and net and fish and sea?" Peter long before had left these to follow Jesus. Though he had re-turned to them that night, probably that was merely to use his time well until Jesus again was ready to use it.

It seems more likely that Jesus was including everything in His question. "Do you love me more than home and family and friends and living?"

The words used for *love* in this passage are two in number, and they change back and forth. The first two times He put the question, Jesus used the word *agapao*, and Peter replied with *phileo*. The third time Jesus put the question, He changed from the word He had been using (*agapao*) to the word Peter had been using all along (*phileo*). *Agapao* is the word used of God's love for all mankind, a deep unselfish love extended while we were yet sinners. It is also used of the deep, selfless concern we ought to have for all mankind, even for the enemies who hate us most bitterly. *Phileo* is used of the personal, warm, affectionate type of love: such love as we have for our own families and intimate friends. It is used of God's love for His own Son (John 5:20). If we are to carry out our Lord's commission, we need both kinds of love; and we need love not for Jesus only, but also for all those He loves. We need a warm, personal affection for those we know personally; but we also need a deep, unselfish, sincere, abiding concern for all the lost of the world. Impelled by such love, we find joy and satisfaction in giving them the joyful news of Christ and His resurrection. These loves lay on each Christian a burden of concern for the physical welfare of his fellow man as well as care for his spiritual state. But *phileo* is the warm, personal love Peter wanted to express to Jesus.

Jesus noted Peter's grief because Jesus asked him the third time, "Do you love me?" The three times may have been intended to parallel the three times Peter had denied his Lord in that sad night before the crucifixion. The denials had been made in answer to questions asked beside a fire in the courtyard of the high priest, a fire surrounded by enemies of the Lord. This declaration of love came beside a fire on the beach in the midst of fellow disciples. Would Peter's love hold firm when he was again in the midst of enemies? He must have resolved that it would—and it did!

In Jesus' replies, He first said, "Feed my lambs," then, "Take care of my sheep," and then, "Feed my sheep." The difference between *lambs* and *sheep* in this case is probably the difference between young converts, newly introduced to the ways of the Lord, and mature Christians, the sheep of His pasture, who also need care and shepherding.

Whenever He Calls (18-23)

After three times giving Peter his task, Jesus added a warning of coming times of trial. Once before, Peter had been warned of failure and denial, but not this time. He would not deny again, but Jesus warned him of the kind of death he would suffer.

As a young man, Peter had dressed himself and gone wherever he wanted; but later someone else would dress him and lead him where he did not want to go. John explains that this was a warning of the kind of death that would come to Peter. The Greek word translated "dress" can mean "gird" or "bind." "Stretch out your hands" may have reference to crucifixion, or it may speak of putting forth the hands to be bound in arrest. The expression was often used to describe crucifixion in early Christian writings. This was to be Peter's fate. In later years, he would be bound and led away to execution.

Peter's death is not recorded in Scripture; but there is ancient testimony that he was crucified, and that by his own request, he was hung on the cross with his head downward because he felt unworthy to die as his Lord had died.[29]

John says Peter was to glorify God by his death. In witnessing for Jesus Christ, one witnesses for God and glorifies God. Sometimes this is costly to the one who witnesses. He may sacrifice much for the sake of his testimony. He may be persecuted, even killed. In such a case, God is glorified the more, for the faithful witness shows that loyalty to God is dearer than life itself.

On the other hand, this glory given to God reflects glory upon the one who bears witness. The honored name *martyr* comes from the Greek word meaning to bear witness. If tradition is correct, Peter became a Christian martyr. In his death, he glorified God, and God has glorified him. After this warning of trials to come, Jesus gave Peter the clear instruction, "Follow me."

Before his denial of Jesus, Peter had asked the Lord where He was going. He had been informed that he could not follow at that time. On that occasion, Peter had replied that he would lay down his life for Jesus. That was when Jesus had given the warning that Peter would deny Him thrice instead of following (John 13:36-38). But now the denials were behind, and so was the death of Jesus. The resurrection was proved, and victory lay ahead. Peter's faith and love were confirmed. With full warning of Peter's martyrdom, Jesus was ready to give the climactic final admonition, "Follow me." Peter, in turn, was ready to give full dedication to the way Jesus pointed out.

"Following Jesus" is the briefest summary of the Christian life. This includes faith, obedience to God, service to man, and

---

[29] Eusebius, Ecclesiastical History iii, 1, 1.

surrender of self. It entails sacrifice and suffering, but it brings gladness and satisfaction. It makes this life worth living and gives promise for the world to come.

As Jesus walked with Peter and gave him these words of admonition and warning, Peter saw the disciple whom Jesus loved (the apostle John, we have concluded) following along. We are not told what prompted Peter's next question. Was there a trace of jealousy? Was it plain curiosity? Was it a genuine concern for John's well-being? In effect, Peter asked what was going to happen to John. Jesus replied in the direct way that Peter needed. Simon's attention had wandered again. He should not be thinking of John's role in life; Jesus was talking to him about his own prospects. The Master simply replied that Peter's real concern should not be the outcome of John's life, but the commitment in his own life: "If I want him to remain alive until I return, what is that to you? You must follow me."

From this saying of Jesus, a rumor went out that John would not die before the Lord would return. Jesus was not saying what lay in the future for John, but He was saying Peter need not be concerned about that. (In effect, He told Peter that it was none of his business what happened to John.) Peter should be concerned about the injunction Jesus had given him, "Follow me." This is the only way to the true life.

However It Ends (24, 25)

The Gospel of John ends with a decisive endorsement of the author. It identifies him as the disciple whom Jesus loved. Then it adds, "We know that his testimony is true" (John 21:24). To know what the *we* refers to would be rewarding. Some say it is the author himself, using an editorial *we*. Others think the Ephesian elders who were well acquainted with John added their endorsement.

Finally, John adds his own personal closing note. Even when his book is added to those of Matthew, Mark, and Luke, the four writers have only begun to tell all that could be told about Jesus.

But what it tells is important to every man, and it is reliable. Describing the death of Christ on the cross, John adds, "The man who saw it has given testimony, and his testimony is true. He knows that he tells the truth, and he testifies so that you also may believe (John 19:35).

Much is accomplished in this closing chapter of the Gospel of John. Far from being an unnecessary appendage added later by another writer, it is a helpful conclusion that ties some dangling parts into the unified whole.

First, it gives added assurance of the resurrected Lord and His activity in Galilee. We see Him loving His people and caring for them.

Second, it gives added assurance of Peter's repentance and restoration. This counters the tragic glimpse of Peter in his denial of Jesus in the courtyard of the high priest (John 18:15-18, 25-27). If that were the final glimpse, one would be left with a feeling of disappointment and uncertainty. Peter had run to the tomb and had been with the disciples at Jesus' appearing; but by including this closing tender scene along the shores of the Sea of Galilee, John assures us again of the reinstatement of this ardent apostle. Here we see Peter accepted by Jesus and fully determined to follow Him.

Finally, the false rumor about John is cleared up. What was said and what was meant is helpful for all posterity. It warns us today not to be too curious about the destiny of our brethren, but to concentrate on following Jesus.

Christians down through the ages have been challenged by these instructions to the apostles. Those who commit themselves to Jesus Christ must be ready to feed the flock and follow the Master. This is the true life and the only way.

CONCLUDING NOTES

The Author and His Purpose

THE AUTHOR

The author of the fourth Gospel identifies himself, but only on one of two levels. This approach is similar to the pattern in the whole of the Gospel. Examples can be found of two levels: one of outward appearance and then further information given just below the surface. On the surface, the author does not name himself anywhere in the narrative; but just below the surface, he identifies himself in specific terms. This identification reaches its climax in John 21:20-24: "this is the disciple" who gives his testimony.

The author was present at the Last Supper; so we know he claims to be one of the twelve apostles. He refers to himself as "the disciple whom Jesus loved" and "the one who had leaned back against Jesus at the supper"; so he must be one of the disciples who were very close to Jesus. Peter, James, and John were an "inner circle" among the Twelve (Mark 5:37; 9:2; 14:33). In John 21:20-24 (see also 13:24), it is plain that the author was not Peter; so the one most likely indicated should be James or John. The added fact that James died very early (A.D. 44; Acts 12:2) helps decide the question. Surely the fourth Gospel was not written that early, and so the author indicated by the process of elimination would be John the apostle.

This conclusion is corroborated both by indications within the Gospel itself and by the word of early Christian writers. Though it has been disputed, we see no adequate reason to doubt that John was really the author of the Gospel known by his name.

DATE AND SETTING

Early notices have pictured the writing of this Gospel in Ephesus toward the close of the first century. Nothing in the narrative dates the work positively. For various reasons, some students argue for an earlier date and some for a later one. However, their reasoning seems too weak to overthrow the testimony of the early writers, who date the writing of John about A.D. 90, when John was living at Ephesus.

If this Gospel was written at the close of the first century from Ephesus, is there anything in the setting of that time and place that contributes to our understanding of the Gospel?

C. H. Dodd spends a large portion of his commentary on John in a study of Gnosticism. This Hellenistic philosophy infiltrated Christian circles and became a major problem to the church of the second century. It claimed to possess special, secret knowledge. All flesh is evil, the Gnostics maintained, and only the spirit is good. This world is a part of the material, evil existence created by evil agents. In such a conglomeration, the role of Jesus became distorted from that of the Christ proclaimed by the apostles. After treating the system at length, Dodd finally decides that actually, very little Gnosticism is reflected in John. This is as it should be. John is telling us of teaching and action in Palestine in A.D. 26-30. If his writing reflected much of Ephesus at the end of the century, one might question its faithfulness to the original setting.

PURPOSE AND PLAN

The purpose of this particular Gospel is explicitly stated. "But these are written that you may believe that Jesus is the Christ, the Son of God, and that by believing you may have life in his name" (John 20:31).

All must agree that his expressed purpose is supported by the presentation of the Gospel itself. The author lines up the testimony for Jesus page after page—who He was, what He taught, and what He did. Many suggestions are made as to more specific areas of purpose: (1) to supplement the Synoptics, giving other details and further spiritual significance, (2) to build a defense against attacks from the Jewish religious leaders, (3) to make absolutely clear that Jesus came in the flesh as a man, and (4) to provide discourses and narratives appropriate for the worship of the church.

One finds a contrast between the plan of the Synoptic Gospels and that of the Gospel of John. In the Synoptics, the ministry of Jesus before the final week is almost wholly confined to Galilee.

In John, a major part of Jesus' recorded work is centered in Jerusalem. Personal interviews are common in John. Claims to be the Messiah occur early in the fourth Gospel, but always to individuals, not to the crowds. The miracles recorded in John are not as numerous as those recorded in the Synoptics, but those that are included seem to be carefully chosen to serve as special signs, examples of the proof of Jesus' power, and testimony to the truth of His message. He was worthy of the faith put in Him.

John's interest is not so much in chronology or geography as in the presentation of Jesus, the Son of God. Many have claimed that some of the recorded events have become displaced from the order in which the author originally placed them. Moffatt, for example, is so sure of this that in his translation of the New Testament he changes the order of the chapters in John at five different places. No textual evidence from the manuscripts supports these changes. Until there is more evidence to the contrary, it is best to follow the order of the text as it has been preserved.

THE GOSPEL OF JOHN THROUGH THE AGES

This Gospel has occupied an important place in the history of the church. It was used early by Gnostic writers to claim wrongfully a support for their teaching, but it was used by orthodox fathers of the church to refute Gnostic heresies. Even so today, it has become a center of controversy. Is the portrait of Jesus true to history, or is it distorted by the beliefs of the author? The evidence indicates that it is independent, but true history. Those who deny the reality of the miraculous in the ministry of Jesus feel required to destroy the trustworthiness of John's record. Those who deny the deity of Jesus try desperately to discount the testimony of this author. This explains much of the objection to accepting the apostle John as the author. He was an eyewitness, a companion of Jesus. His testimony is true. The author himself makes claim to his close relationship to the Master.

In contrast to the attacks of the skeptics, the Gospel of John has always drawn the admiration and constant use both by those who have been recently introduced to the Lord Jesus and others who have come to know Jesus well, but want to know Him better. When the New International Version was being translated, the Gospel of John was used as the first book to be brought to completion so that it would serve as an example for the work on all the rest of the books of the Bible. The new convert is urged to read the Gospel of John. No other book presents more strongly the person of Jesus as the Son of God.

One should approach the reading of this Gospel with a confidence established at the outset in the work of God's inspired writers and confirmed through the ages by the lives moved to accept Jesus. He is the true life and the only way. This Gospel narrative was written to lead a person to Christ, and to challenge him to further depths of spiritual truth from the first step throughout his life in the Lord.

John tells of a spiritual life that transcends the worldly existence of the unbeliever. Jesus has the living water that renews our souls. He has the light that drives back the darkness of ignorance, sin, and guilt. He shows the way to life, the true life, life eternal. This is life beyond the restrictions of the mere physical; it penetrates the metaphysical. It is deeper than the surface sight; it grapples with the meaning and significance of it all. To know God is life eternal (John 17:3).

For all the depth in John's treatment of Jesus' life, he used simple language and vivid, real incidents. The surface is clear, but the depths are fathomless. It has been said that the Gospel of John is like a pool where a child may wade, and an elephant can swim at the same time.[30] The newest Christian can gain breathtaking truths from its words, while the most advanced Biblical scholar is drawn to further studies of its passages because he knows the treasures of the fourth Gospel have never been exhausted.

---

[30] Cited in Leon Morris, The Gospel According to John, (1971), p. 7.

VISIT THE PLACES

From the four Gospels, these places are named only in the Gospel of John:

1. Bethany beyond Jordan (John 1:28; Bethabara, KJV)
2. Cana in Galilee (John 2:1, 11; 4:46; 21:2)
3. Aenon near Salim (John 3:23)
4. Salim (John 3:23)
5. Sychar (John 4:5)
6. Jacob's well (John 4:6)
7. Pool of Bethesda (John 5:2)
8. Tiberias (John 6:23)
9. Solomon's Colonnade (John 10:23)
10. Ephraim (John 11:54)
11. Kidron Valley (John 18:1)
12. Gabbatha (John 19:13)

For Your Attention:

1. From antiquity, the Gospel of John has been known as the "Spiritual Gospel," and its emphasis on the eternal and that which is beyond our physical sight bears this Out.
2. Some today would have us believe that John reports his theological belief or the beliefs of the early church, and that the author of the fourth Gospel has no interest in historical details.
3. The list above and the following chart, however, show that John's interest in specific places is commensurate with the naming of specific places in the other Gospel narratives.
4. John does not simply specify the same places designated in the other Gospels, but he has more places named individually by one writer than any of the other Gospel accounts.
5. This supports the conclusion that John notes historical details, as well as spiritual significance and eternal consequences.

Places Designated

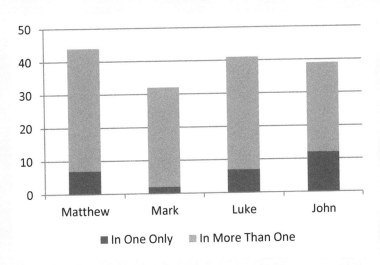

	Places Designated (Total)	In One Only	In More Than One
Matthew	44	7	37
Mark	32	2	30
Luke	41	7	34
John	39	12	27

INDEX

A

B

C

K

L

O

P

W

Z

SUGGESTED READING

Barret, C. K. The Gospel According to St. John. London: SPCK, 1955.

Bernard, J. H. The Gospel According to St. John. International Critical Commentary, 2 vols. Edinburgh: Scribner, 1928.

Brown, Raymond E. The Gospel According to John. Anchor Bible, 2 vols. Garden City, New York: Doubleday, 1966, 1970.

Dodd, C. H. Interpretation of the Fourth Gospel. Cambridge: University Press, 1953.

*Godet, Frederic. Commentary on the Gospel of John. 2 vols. New York: Funk, 1886.

*Hendrjksen, William. Exposition of the Gospel According to John. 2 vols. Grand Rapids: Baker, 1953-54.

Lindars, Barnabas. The Gospel of John. New Century Bible. London: Oliphants, 1972.

Marsh, John. The Gospel of St. John. Pelican New Testament Commentaries. Middlesex, England: Penguin, 1972.

*Morgan, G. Campbell. The Gospel of John. Old Tappan, N. J.: Revell, n. d.

*Morris, Leon. The Gospel According to St. John. New International Commentary. Grand Rapids: Eerdmans, 1971.

*Plummer, Alfred. The Gospel According to St. John. London: S. L. M. Press, 1890, Baker reprint, 1981.

Sanders, J. M. and B. A. Mastin. The Gospel According to St. John. Black's New Testament Commentary. London: Adam & Charles Black, 1968. Harper's New Testament Commentaries. New York: Harper & Row, 1968.

*Tenney, Merrill. John: Gospel of Belief. Grand Rapids: Eerdmans, 1948.

*_____ . The Gospel of John. The Expositor's Bible Commentary, vol. 9. Grand Rapids: Zondervan, 1981.

*Tasker, R. V. G. The Gospel According to St. John. Tyndale New Testament
    Commentaries. Grand Rapids: Eerdmans, 1960.

Turner, George and J. R. Mantey. The Gospel According to St. John. Evangelical
    Commentary. Grand Rapids: Eerdmans, 1964.

*Westcott, B. F. The Gospel According to St. John. London, 1881; reprint,
    London: John Murray, 1958.

Those titles designated with an asterisk are recommended conservative works.